MEANING IN *COMEDY*

Meaning in *Comedy*.

Studies in Elizabethan Romantic Comedy

by John Weld.

State University of New York Press, Albany, New York,
1975.

Published with assistance
from The University Awards Committee
of State University of New York

First published in 1975 by
State University of New York Press
99 Washington Avenue, Albany, New York 12210

Library of Congress Cataloging
in Publication Data

Weld, John, 1914–
Meaning in comedy.

Includes bibliographical references and index.
1. English drama (Comedy)—History and criticism.
2. English drama—Early modern and Elizabethan,
1500–1600—History and criticism.
3. English drama—
Medieval—To 1500—Historyand criticism. I. Title.

PR646.W4 822'.052 74-30168

ISBN 0–87395–278–2
ISBN 0–87395–279–0 microfiche

In Memoriam,
Alan Downer.

Contents.

Acknowledgements.

I wish to thank the Research Foundation of the State University of New York for its generous award of two summer research grants toward the completion of these studies. I also wish to thank Miss Janet Brown, Miss Caroline Jakeman, and the staffs of the libraries of The State University of New York at Binghamton, Harvard College, and Cornell University. They have served the needs of the scholar with efficiency, courtesy, and learning.

This book owes much to many people. I hope that most of my specific debts are acknowledged in the footnotes. Others, more general, are too numerous to list, but a few must be mentioned here. Of these, not the least is my debt to my students, who for many years have provided challenge and stimulation and often guided me toward wisdom. I have had the great joy of collaborative teaching with my colleagues Peter Gruber, Seymour Pitcher, Elias Schwartz, and Melvin Seiden; in classroom and corridor they have often corrected my follies, and they have always broadened my understanding of the drama. Saul Levin has tactfully guided my faltering Latinity. My wife has read much of the manuscript several times; she has battled with me on many points, stylistic and substantial. She has sometimes won; for her victories readers can be grateful. Any work of this nature must acknowledge its great indebtedness to the monumental historical foundations of Chambers and Bentley, without which all speculation would be folly. In addition, I must record my debt to Arthur Colby Sprague, who first wakened me to the importance to the text as staged, and to Alan Downer for many years my friend, fellow actor, director, critic, and best of companions.

My greatest debt is to Bernard Huppé. My approach to late medieval and early Elizabethan drama was largely inspired by his lectures on Chaucer and Old English and by the approach to Middle English literature which he and D. W. Robertson pioneered. The book was written under his kindly lash; his influence upon it has been deep and pervasive.

Introduction.

The main purpose of this book is to interpret a number of Elizabethan romantic comedies and related plays. "Romantic comedy"
is a loose term of late invention and dubious respectability, but it
has some value in grouping certain Elizabethan plays. Taken to
include, say, *Twelfth Night*, *A Midsummer Night's Dream*,
Greene's *Friar Bacon and Friar Bungay*, Dekker's *Shoemakers'
Holiday*, and the anonymous *Merry Devil of Edmonton*, it con-
notes the festive celebration of true love and merry hearts in a
love story, presented sympathetically but with amusement, leading to a happy ending. This description will be embroidered,
stretched, and shrunken later, but it will serve for the time being.
It suggests, since it fits equally three-fourths of the popular dramatic fluff of the last three centuries, the reason both for the popularity of the type and for the fact that critics often dismiss it.
Interpretation of such drama, save in sociological terms, seems
wasted effort.

Yet many Elizabethan comedies deserve and reward closer attention. Their "meaning" can be defined in various frames of ref-

erence. The concern of the present study can be defined as the sense a playwright of the time might reasonably have expected a significant part of the audience would make of his play. Such a concern is fairly restrictive, excluding many meanings frequently and legitimately sought; it should be examined.

First, in its insistence upon the playwright's contemporary audience, it excludes whatever *different* meanings the play may have had to later generations, such as Restoration audiences, the audiences that Garrick, Irving, and Gielgud have played to, or readers such as Coleridge, Bradley, or G. Wilson Knight. It also excludes the meanings which result from modern directors' deliberate attempts to relate the plays to new times and circumstances. The study of such meanings is a worthy pursuit; they are often valuable in themselves, and they are frequently relevant to the study here proposed; but they are not in themselves the object of the study.

Second, the book is not concerned with direct evidence of what the author intended (as distinguished from what he might reasonably have expected) to communicate to his audience. Such evidence has its place; it is often useful to many ends, including the one chosen here, but for the plays to be considered, it is scanty and doubtfully relevant. Direct evidence of the playwright's intention in another sense, however, that is, of the way he intended the lines to be read or the scene to be played, is often subject to intelligent speculation based on stage directions and indications in the text. Although overt speculation of this sort seldom appears in the following pages, it has constantly guided the interpretation of the plays. The study assumes, furthermore, that the dramatists intended their plays to make fairly coherent sense and to interest their audiences.

Third, the kind of meaning defined here excludes what Panofsky has named the "intrinsic meaning" of the work, its significance, that is, as a symptom of a basic attitude within the cultural context of its time. This too lies outside the scope of this study.

Finally, the study proposes to stick close to the most general and the most obvious; it is not exhaustive in intention; much is left untouched. In particular, two special categories of meaning have been systematically excluded: the topical allusion, overt or secret, and meanings available only to the lower levels of consciousness. Although this latter category resists precise definition, its boundaries can be roughly outlined. Meanings that might emerge in the tavern after the show are part of the study; more occulted guilts are not. The unconscious response of the audience to the projection in *Hamlet* of the primal, Oedipal sin will remain untouched.

The limitations and qualifications, it may be noted, accept the semantic truism that speech has no intrinsic or "autonomous" meaning; it means something only to someone, the speaker or an audience. As E. D. Hirsch remarks,

"Almost any word sequence can, under the conventions of language, legitimately represent more than one complex of meaning. A word sequence means nothing in particular until somebody either means something by it or understands something from it. There is no magic land of meanings outside human consciousness. Whenever meaning is connected to words, a person is making the connection, and the particular meanings he lends to them are never the only legitimate ones under the norms and conventions of his language." [1]

Meaning, in short, must be defined in relation to someone, and it remains for the interpreter to select the someone with whose understanding of the text he is going to concern himself. As Hirsch, again, says,

"Since it is very easy for a reader of any text to construe meanings that are different from the author's, there is nothing in the nature of the text itself which requires the reader to set up the author's meaning as his normative ideal. Any normative concept in interpretation implies a choice that is required not by the nature of written texts but rather by the goal that the interpreter sets himself." [2]

The goal set here has been chosen in part because it seems an obviously significant one and in part because it seems more clearly definable in operational terms than such attractive alternatives as "the author's intention." [3] One may argue of course that "the sense which a significant part of the audience might reasonably have been expected to make of the play" probably includes most of the author's intention. The argument seems plausible.

Three other features implied by meaning thus defined may be noted. The meaning is often multiple (or a complex of meanings); it, or any of its components, is merely probable, and it must often be expressed as a vague statistic. This is not to suggest that interpretive data can be quantified and fed into a computer. At least in dealing with Elizabethan drama, however, we must recognize our own vast ignorance of the Elizabethan scene; hence our conjectures can be no more than probable. Nor is it safe to assume a single homogeneous "Elizabethan" response; the responses of Elizabethan, as of modern, spectators may be expected to vary. Any response, furthermore, as described by a modern critic— at best a crude simplification—can only pretend to generalize for a significant percentage of the audience.

These assumptions are not novel; they are tacit in a great deal of criticism, and they are stated here merely for the sake of clarity and because another limiting consequence follows from them: that the meanings discussed can claim to be true only in relation to the audience proposed. Other meanings may be quite as true for other audiences, and any meaning advanced in good faith is presumably *the* meaning of the given work to the proposer. One meaning may be less or more interesting than others or less or more complex or make the work lesser or greater, or it may simply indicate a private unique association, but it is undeniably a meaning to the critic who claims it is. *The Comedy of Errors,* for instance, can be interpreted with fair consistency as a modern parable of social alienation, the search for identity, and the failure of communication. Such an interpretation is quite as "true" as that which will be proposed in this study, and it may well be more interesting or in some way superior today. The meaning proposed merely purports to be what a significant number of well-educated Elizabethan spectators might be expected to see in the play.

Such a relativist approach, it may be added, is of some help in clarifying issues and avoiding fruitless debate. For instance, the argument over whether *Tamburlaine I* is Christian or anti-Christian would probably dissolve or at least change its nature if antagonists defined the audiences they had in mind. Clearly *Tamburlaine* is a Christian play to some people and is not to others. We can dispute whether part or all of the original audiences would probably have seen in it a confirmation of their Christian teaching; whether Marlowe intended to shock the orthodox or reassure them; whether he himself was an atheist or a deist; whether one interpretation or the other suppresses potential subordinate meanings. All these questions are capable of reasonably clear definition, and probable answers to them can be given. The difficulty comes in arguing that in some absolute sense the work "is" Christian or not. The interpretations in the following pages, at any rate, do not pretend to that kind of authority.

ii.

The specific audience whose interpretation this book focusses upon I have defined as a "significant part" of the audience the playwright wrote for. The phrase recognizes the heterogeneity of the audience. We cannot, again, assume a monolithic group, trained by our favorite background reading, in, say, *The Book of Homilies*, Machiavelli, or Montaigne, and responding with well-defined "Elizabethan" reflexes. The *a priori* unlikelihood is reinforced by the remarks of contemporary prologues, writers of dedications, and social satirists who distinguish among the spectators on the grounds of native intelligence, taste, education, age, sex, slowness of wit, frivolity, love of bawdry, independence of judgment, and bloody-mindedness. Doubtless they were more like each other than the crowds at the Venice Bienniale or even a West-End or Broadway theater; still it would be absurd to expect them to agree as one upon the interpretation even of *The Merchant of Venice*. We shall do well if we can approximate what twenty-five percent, or even ten, might see in the play.

One tries, of course, for the "best" part: what an idiot might

5

understand is chiefly interesting to a psychologist. We can also disregard the meaning as understood by the Joseph Partridges of the audience. Our ideal spectators are intelligent, trained theatergoers, educated, and normally conversant with the customs and the gossip of the day. But such qualifications are so general as to be almost useless. If we wish to go beyond them and beyond, also, whatever wavering "constants" in human nature we still trust in, we must define the audience chiefly in terms of its knowledge, very little in terms of its beliefs and sympathies.

The difficulty with beliefs and sympathies is dual: evidence for them is scanty, and they are usually irrelevant to interpretation. There is, it is true, some good evidence, some of it from the plays themselves. During the 1580s and early 90s, for instance, playwrights apparently could not, at least did not, count on much anti-Puritan hostility in their audiences. They did play upon it, but not often and not with anything like the later virulence and frequency of Jonson and Middleton. One can make similar appraisals of other biases that playwrights seem at various times to take for granted: anti-Catholicism, chauvinism, the sentiment for or against duelling, and so on. When these are obvious and common, they are helpful. Eleanor Prosser's massive documentation of her thesis that playwrights did not, to say the least, take for granted "the sacred duty of revenge" certainly forces a reassessment of common assumptions about *Hamlet*.[4] Clearly Shakespeare must have had to count on a significant part of his audience as denying any such notion.

Evidence from outside the plays can also sometimes be found. We know enough about propaganda, for instance, to be able to predict that a saturation campaign, granted a reasonably receptive populace, will persuade a very significant portion of that populace. Billions of dollars are spent on advertising and public relations by men who have learned that this premise is sound. The two books of homilies which the Elizabethan government published to be read in churches were precisely such a saturation campaign, and it is a reasonable assumption that many of the people who heard them were persuaded by them. A playwright, then, would have to count on a significant part of his audience as believing in their teaching. But of course this is an oversimplification. The very fact that the homily writers felt it necessary to write on certain of the topics demonstrates the existence, at least at the time of writing, of opposition or ignorance. The long homily "against disobedience and wilful rebellion," which was first published separately in 1570, was a frank attempt to counter the kind of rebellious sentiment which had led to Northumberland's rising in 1569. The homily "against whoredom and uncleanness" proclaims the popularity of the opposing view: "This vice is growne into such an height, that in a manner among many, it is counted no sinne at all, but rather a pastime, a dalliance, and but a touch of youth: not rebuked, but winked at, not punished, but laughed at." [5] A sermon against sin implies that there were sinners, not that there were none. The playwright, then, would often have to count upon significant splits of opinion in his audience as well, of course, as upon individuals whose beliefs were divided or who were split between impulse and belief.

The spectators' beliefs, however, are less important than their knowledge in defining their understanding of the plays. In understanding *Richard II* one does not have to believe in the common interpretation of the biblical events alluded to (e.g., the fall of man, the killing of Abel, the crucifixion), or in the common teaching about the correspondence of order in the universe, nature, society, the family, and the soul, but knowledge of the teaching is helpful in fitting together the parts of the play to make a whole. I shall argue later that in *The Comedy of Errors* the law that condemns Aegeon unless he is ransomed is analogous to the law of Moses, as it was then commonly understood, by which all men are condemned until redeemed. Belief in that doctrine is irrelevant to understanding the analogy; knowledge of it is.

Questions such as Elizabethan acceptance of the doctrine of revenge, as it applies to *Hamlet*, might seem to be an exception. Clearly *Hamlet* becomes different as one does or does not see Hamlet as morally obligated to revenge his father's murder by killing his uncle. Clearly, too, if we postulate as audience members of a closed, tribal society who accept unquestioningly the doctrine of revenge, then in their eyes Hamlet should get on with the revenge. It is not clear, however, that an audience drawn from a more open society, aware of other values than its own, will judge action on the stage with such a machine-like response. Spectators who have been taught and believe that blood revenge is wicked are aware that not all men believe as they do and that belief in revenge may be a postulate necessary to make sense out of the play. Indeed, this seems to have been the case of most critics of the last two hundred years. Very few of them, after all, have themselves accepted the sacred duty of blood revenge. Most of them have accepted it as a postulate for the play, however, because it seemed necessary, and probably, because they assumed that Shakespeare and his audience accepted it. Their actual belief or disbelief was irrelevant to their understanding of the play; what mattered, what they made use of, was their knowledge that many people accept a code of revenge.

"Knowledge" in this context, however, implies a more sympathetic involvement than the kind of acquaintance gained from reading an article in an encyclopedia. One understands an action or motivation or hypothesis about human nature insofar as it "makes sense," insofar, that is, as one can verify it from one's own experience. The ordinary human frailties need little explaining of this sort; we all understand, all too well, how men can be motivated by revenge, as well as avarice, pride, lust, and so on. That is not always true, however, of sophisticated doctrines such as the divine right of kings, the wickedness of ambition, the depravity of human nature, or the untrustworthiness of anyone over thirty; people often reject these, not simply as untrue, but with violent emotion, as not making sense. They tend to reject, furthermore, any work the understanding of which depends upon such a nonsensical doctrine, as nonsense itself, or they reinterpret it in other ways. While belief in a doctrine may not in itself be important, therefore, evidence of belief, such as Eleanor Prosser has accumulated, is evidence that the audience has understood the teaching, and that is directly relevant to our present purpose.

The point may seem like scholastic whittling, but it has a pleasant consequence. It is much easier to describe the knowledge of the Elizabethan audience than its beliefs. It is still difficult; there will still be great differences among the spectators; but what men of the time were taught, what they read, and what they listened to can be ascertained, or at least what significant numbers of them were taught, read, and listened to. On this basis an audience can be postulated whose understanding of the plays should approximate the substance sought with distortions which will largely depend upon the relevance of the knowledge that is selected for consideration. Once that selection is made, the interpretation of a given play can be defined as "the sense that people who were cognizant of such and such beliefs and facts would probably have made of the play." Within this definition there is still room for dispute, but the issues may be clearer.

iii.

From the errors of irrelevance inevitable to selection, only wisdom and the kind of experience variously thought of as trial and error, successive approximation, or circular reasoning can deliver us. Fortunately, we are heirs to considerable critical experience. I have found two areas of knowledge especially pertinent: first, the moral-psychological lore of the time and its broadly philosophical, sometimes theological, underpinning; and second, the sheer knowledge of plays and the theater that Lyly or Greene or the young Shakespeare might reasonably have expected of many of their spectators. This latter area becomes relevant, of course, largely as skill, gained through experience of plays, in understanding what is going on while it is going on and in piecing the scenes together. Plays, no less than language, employ arbitrary conventions, and every generation, whispering its puzzlement in the distracted ear of its parents, must learn the conventions of its day and stage. The sophisticated playgoers of, say, 1587, had cut their dramatic teeth upon earlier stuff. Probably all had been trained in the popular repertory, largely moralities, and some also upon the more or less academic plays of school, university, inns of court, and private theaters. These plays had instructed them in how plays work.

They had also instructed them in what plays say—their subjects, their themes, and general courses of action: an intrigue of youth versus age with Jack getting his Jill; a satire unmasking the greediness of worldly choosers and the bloodiness of usurers; a moral of the courtship and marriage of Wit and Wisdom. This is what one learns to expect in the theater, and although one's expectations may be upset, the novelty is perforce seen as novelty, as a twist of expectation. The effect may be sharply contrastive, as in manifesto plays like *Tamburlaine* and *Hernani*, or it may be so minimal as to seem only a variation on a formula, as in the *commedia del arte* or the American Western, but it is important and inevitable. Many of our ancestors apparently found *Ghosts*, seen against the background of the plays they knew, excitingly obscene. Against the dramatic background of the 1970s (e.g. the Swedish film *I Am Curious (Yellow)* or Kenneth Tynan's *Oh, Calcutta!*) it is not. The history of the drama is important for the interpretation of plays, not because one play or playwright has influenced another, but because audiences are conditioned by their playgoing experience, and a play is what it is to an audience partly because of that conditioning. That Lyly probably influenced Shakespeare is significant to the biographer; that he influenced Shakespeare's audience is important to the interpretive critic.

iv.

Behind every interpretation in the following pages, there is a concern with the effects upon meaning caused by different ways of playing the play. To the ambiguities of relativism and the uncertainties of our ignorance, theatrical production adds another variable. Meanings vary as the words are spoken with different intonations and timing, with different facial expressions, gestures, and action, by actors whose appearance, costumes, and familiarity to the spectators may be quite different from production to production. We speak of the director's or the actors' "interpretation" of a play, or of the text as a musical score which is not itself music and can be played this way or that. The text alone gives only the general outlines of the play; it is a bear whelp that must be licked into shape, and can furthermore be licked into different shapes.[6]

These are truisms, but they are sometimes denied. Let us examine them briefly. Consider first the sometimes heard claim that to the eye of the really skilled director most well-written texts are not in fact ambiguous. Granted the stage and playing conditions for which it was written, the text will be found to define precisely the way in which it must be played. As the battle-boast of a program manifesto, this is understandable; as a statement intended to be taken literally, it seems highly dubious for any plays I can recall. However, granted that a director may mean it literally, it is not in conflict with the truisms listed above. The director who utters it, after all, however wise or foolish he may be about the unerring precision and completeness of the stage directions coded in the script, has taken seriously his job of staging it, in his mind or on the stage. He has licked the bear whelp into shape. Further, as long as he acknowledges the historical fact that the play has been played "successfully" in other ways, ways which he rejects (Petruchio should *not* carry a whip; Hamlet should *not* overhear the King and Polonius plotting) he grants the problem of ambiguity, or error, that confronts critics whose apprehension of the "one true way" of playing the play is less intuitively swift than his own. Any theologian, to cite a useful parallel, no matter how convinced of the sufficiency of the scriptures, admits, though sadly, that heretics have in fact misread them.

The argument of the determinedly literary critic, who denies that the theatrical production of the play should be borne in mind when interpreting it, must also be considered. This denial sometimes merely masks an assumption, often unconscious, of a certain way of playing the play. Such a tacit assumption, though one might urge a more catholic consideration of other possibilities, is again, not in conflict with the truisms we are considering. Like the director who is convinced that the text leads unequivocally to a single way of playing it, this critic has done the job of staging the play in his mind.

A continuation of the romantic attitude that runs from Lamb through Bradley, however, holds that at least Shakespeare's great plays—*Lear* is the chief example—reveal their full depth and richness only to the reader; staging them inevitably limits the reverberations of meaning and makes them shallower. This argument is not strictly relevant to the aims of this book. One might reply that if the meanings the Elizabethan spectators might be expected to understand were relatively shallow, *tant pis*. We may lament the Elizabethans' lot, but accept it as a fact and get on with the business of finding out what those meanings were. We can judge better of their shallowness after we view them.

This answer must ultimately serve, but in the meantime a brief consideration of the importance of the meanings conveyed in the theater may be useful. First, as I have already suggested, we need not limit ourselves to meanings caught on the wing during a single viewing of the play. As Granville-Barker, I believe, says somewhere, just as we expect to have to listen to a major symphony many times, each time deepening our understanding of it, so we should expect to see a great play many times. We should also expect it to be discussed informally, and such discussion to be freshened when possible by reference to printed texts. To insist that our meaning be quite theatrically pure and uncontaminated would be absurd.

But it is important to pay attention to that component of meaning that only theatrical production can convey. What the audience will see and hear is something that the playwright must constantly be aware of and anticipate the effects of.[7] It becomes, then, a major means of communication to the audience. In *Lear*—since *Lear* is a test case—the grotesque appearance of a near-naked and filthy Edgar and of Lear himself stripped to dirty under-garments, acts as a powerful, Swiftian statement of man's de-formity and weakness. The almost unbearable brutality of the blinding of Gloucester, as it is conveyed by the efficient, ruthless twisting and binding of the torturers, by Gloucester's screams of pain, by the bloody cut-and-thrust of Cornwall, his servant, and Regan, and by Gloucester's agonized rising with blood stream-ing from his eye sockets, is an obviously planned effect which contributes with crude and terrible force to the central vision of horror. It is well, for want of an actual production, to stage such things in the mind's eye, but we must bear in mind that the visual impact of the objective deed is a different experience. It is that which we must try to capture.

Lear is typical in its dramaturgy; examples of such important set pieces carrying a large burden of communication, are com-mon: the feasting scene in *Antony*, for instance, in which Caesar, Antony, Pompey, and Enobarbus join hands in a drunken dance; Bottom's transformation in *A Midsummer Night's Dream*; the fourth-act explosion of *The Alchemist*; the dance of madmen in *The Duchess of Malfi*; Simon Eyre's changes of clothing which mark his climb; or the grotesque and horrible kissing of the poisoned skull in *The Revenger's Tragedy*. Marlowe, as Jocelyn Powell demonstrated in an excellent article, makes constant use of such set pieces—or, as Powell calls them, emblems—"which continually develop one into another to create concrete dramatic images of the spiritual action they describe." Powell cites many examples. At their simplest they are illustrated by the drawn sword which Sigismund presents to the Turks to make visual their choice for peace or war, but they are occasionally elaborated with great complexity as when the tangled tackling from Aeneas's ships, strewn about Dido, becomes the visual symbol of the emo-tional net that has entangled her.[8]

This kind of visual symbolism, as Powell points out, is a direct continuation of the dramaturgy of the moralities, but while it runs like contrasting threads through the fabric of late Eliza-bethan and the Jacobean plays, in the drama of the preceding two hundred years it is the fabric itself. As Powell, once again, remarks,

"The morality was certainly a drama of spectacle—spectacle in its basic theatrical sense, where its function is communicative, not simply decorative. . . . The authors of the moralities used dramatic spectacle to attack the understanding of the audience through the eyes as well as through the ears. . . . The groups into which the actors were manipulated by the story, the costumes they wore, the properties they held, all communicated the author's message in visual terms." [9]

It will be argued later that the failure to "see" the moralities largely accounts both for a serious misunderstanding of the way they work and for the critical disregard of the morality as a genre ever since antiquarians began to reprint them. Briefly stated, the argument is that as long as we view the morality as a dialogue between abstractions, we tend to find it dramatically dull. Such a view mistakes the nature of the form. What the audience sees is not so many abstractions, but people—red-faced, tall, short, fat, greasy, grotesque, and sly; and they are not involved in inter-abstractional relationships; they hit each other, brawl, kiss, ring bells, and chase each other around the stage.

So much in defence of visualizing the play as theater. Theatrical performance, however, also shapes the meaning that the spectator perceives as the actors speak and act in this way or that. This is not to say, of course, that any play text is infinitely malleable or that all texts are equally so. No director or critic, to my knowledge, has tried to make *Macbeth* into a farce of intrigue and cuckoldry or argued for playing *The Winter's Tale* as a problem play *focussing* upon international relations. *Hamlet*, furthermore, can apparently be more variously interpreted than *Lear*, and *Lear* than *Romeo* (or *Hedda Gabler*). But it seems a safe surmise that almost all plays can be successfully played—interpreted—by different casts and directors in quite different ways.

It becomes doubly misleading then, because of both theatrical malleability and literary relativism, to argue that Hamlet "is" thirty years old or suffers, or does not suffer, from an Oedipus complex, or that *Measure for Measure* "is" a cynical satire. One can argue rationally that Shakespeare thought of Hamlet as fat, thirty, and ridden by an Oedipus complex, or that the Lord Chamberlain's men played him, and the audiences of 1603 understood him, in that way and that those of 1760, watching Garrick, did not. Or one can argue that the play is the better or worse if he is so played. But, again, one cannot reasonably argue that Hamlet "is" thus or so. That many acute and sane men have seemingly argued in precisely this way, however, is not merely testimony to the perverse human tendency to dispute unverifiable hypotheses, and the arguments are not always fruitless, since they usually conceal the assumption that we are concerned with the playwright's intention or with the effect on the original audiences, or with the best possible modern stage interpretation. The last concern, of course, is the director's, and his frequent manner of counsel—"Remember, Hamlet is an insolent egocentric," or "Volpone's praise of gold is simple and devout"—conceals as premise, "for the purposes of the production we are engaged in." He is trying for a best interpretation or one relevant to the times or a "best-under-the-circumstances."

For brevity's sake and to avoid tedious reminders, the discussions that follow sometimes use this directorial locution, but they keep in more explicit view than is usual both the possibility of theatrical variation and the varying effects resulting. To the best of my knowledge these considerations constantly check and guide the assertions which the demands of space and a decent regard for the boredom of mankind enforce. Within the limits defined by theatrical possibilities and by the training and background of the Elizabethan spectators, the interpretations have been guided by the same general considerations that govern most directors: the theatrical effectiveness of each scene, its consistency with other scenes, and its effectiveness in contributing to a whole which is a recognizable product of human consciousness.

Such an approach begs the question whether the play is in fact a coherent and consistent whole. This is a fair question, but it must be disregarded until desperation turns us to it. We *are* dealing with products of human minds, and it is a fair assumption that they made coherent sense to their authors and the audiences they were written for. The playwright must be presumed innocent of incoherence until proved guilty, and "proof" can only be the critic's despairing failure to find a pattern. But despair, as Satan discovered, is a rotten foundation. "Proofs" of this sort disproved by the next generation's broadened scholarship or change of critical *Zeitgeist* warn us to be humble.

One point more must be noticed. The interpretive critic who, quite properly, consciously stages the play in his mind, accepting one way of playing the scene and rejecting others, to a limited but significant extent shapes the play which he then proceeds to explain. His interpretation, it may be said, is self-confirming since he generates part of the data upon which it is based. That is true. It is another example of the self-confirming nature of interpretive hypotheses which Hirsch points out, and the usual checks must be observed.[10] But it is in any case impossible to escape the responsibility of deciding how to play the play. The interpreter who makes his decision unconsciously, who *assumes*, for instance, that Petruchio is a sadistic brute, has created data for his interpretation of the play quite as much as the director who supports the interpretation of his program note by giving the actor a whip.

V.

The organization of the book requires a word of explanation. Part I, the first three chapters, is concerned with the dramatic tradition in which the audiences of Lyly, Greene, and of Shakespeare's early plays had been trained. Part II, the rest of the book, interprets the comedies. Part I is selective; it is designed merely to guide the reader in the devious approaches of Part II. It is not a complete study of the whole comic tradition or even of the whole problem of meaning in earlier comedy. It focusses upon one means of dramatic communication, which I have called, following Downer, "dramatic metaphor," and upon the semantic complexity that resulted from its use by the pre-Marlovian dramatists.

So narrow a focus omits much that is useful in the understanding of later comedy, but that much has been often and well discussed; the emphasis here is upon an aspect of dramatic meaning that has received less attention and the discussion of which seemed helpful. Yet narrow as that focus is, it includes matter that is relevant to more than romantic comedy—to tragedy and history and especially to dramatic satire. This is inevitable. All the dramatic kinds used much the same techniques and were concerned with many of the same themes, especially in the century or so before Marlowe, when the kinds themselves were little differentiated, and what is said of one must apply in large measure to all. Part I, then, is prefatory, though not a preface, to a wider study than Part II; for Part II is limited to romantic comedy and its near relatives, partly because limits of some sort are necessary—and the virtues of depth seemed in this case to outweigh those of breadth—and partly because romantic comedy had from the beginning claimed my interest.

I have also, without trying to be inclusive, limited the study to comedies written before about 1597. The temptation to include later Shakespeare, especially *As You Like It, Much Ado*, and even *Measure for Measure*, was very great, and the application of the discussions that follow to these plays will, I think, be evident. The very obviousness of this application, however, weighed heavily in the decision not to consider them; enough is sometimes enough. On the other hand, to discuss these plays in the dramatic context of their time implies some discussion of the dramatic context of their time, and that is a new world. It includes the early comedies of Chapman, Jonson, Marston, Dekker, and Middleton, and the felt challenge of romantic comedy to comical satire. This is important territory, but it is another book.

PART

ONE

Dramatic
Tradition:

I.

Dramatic Exemplification and Metaphor.

When Shakespeare began writing plays in the late 1580s or early 90s, he wrote for an audience which, through earlier experience in the theater, expected plays to express ideas. His audience had been trained to expect other kinds of experience too, of course: entertainment of various sorts, the release of misrule or playing holiday, wonderment at spectacle and acrobatics, and simple narrative suspense and resolution. Yet to an extraordinary degree the drama of ideas, however new for the British avant-guard in the 1890s, was, for the Elizabethans, a tradition sanctified by the approval of bourgeois, artisan, peasant, parent and grandsire.

The morality play was the idea in action—not pure, not unmixed with matters of mirth or spectacle or even sometimes scandal—but with a structure that coheres in unity only as the expression of an idea, not of an action conceived as apart from or independent of that idea. Consider, for instance, the first part of *The Castle of Perseverance*, which presents Mankind's gradual corruption. The plot is simple: World, Flesh, and Devil introduce themselves; Mankind enters, newborn, flanked by his good and evil angels and torn between them. After deciding to go with the evil angel, he is joined by, or joins, successively, Lust-liking, Folly, the World, Covetous, Pride, Wrath, Envy, Gluttony, Lechery, and Sloth. Simple as the action is, it is long, and it could easily be cut by reducing the number of vices. Two or three—or one—would serve effectively to seduce Mankind; Avarice alone is sufficient in the latter part of the play. But here the action is shaped by the ideas that man is led to sin by lust-liking and folly, that there are seven main sins, and that they belong, variously, to the world, flesh, and Devil. If, to economize in casting the play, we eliminate two or three sins, though the action will still run smoothly, the idea of seven deadly sins will be mangled.

So with such Elizabethan plays as Thomas Lupton's *All for Money* (c. 1568) or Robert Wilson's *The Three Ladies of London* (c. 1581). The first has an almost revue-like structure. A prologue explains that it is about the abuse of money, and the following six scenes present different aspects of this theme: a dialogue of Theology, Science, and Art, lamenting that they are served only for money; a short farcical allegory of Money giving birth to Pleasure, Pleasure to Sin, and Sin to Damnation; a comic quarrel and a conspiracy of Satan, Sin, Pride, and Gluttony; a debate and discussion, in Heywood's manner, of Learning With Money, Learning Without Money, Money Without Learning, and Neither Learning Nor Money; a courtroom scene in which All For Money hears the petitions of various bribing rascals; and a lament by Judas and Dives that they have sold their souls. A final dialogue moralizes on the theme. Unity of action is almost non-existent here, but unity of theme is rigorously observed. The main action of *The Three Ladies of London* shows the harsh treatment and corruption of the ladies Love and Conscience in London. This action is supplemented, however, by several scenes in which an honest Jew is bilked by a Christian rascal before a Turkish judge. These scenes are mechanically quite unrelated to the main action; cut them and they leave no ragged edges. But they are bound to the rest of the play by their perfectly clear development of the theme.

The point is not that all scenes in all morality plays were tightly bound in thematic unity, but that whatever unity the plays possessed was thematic. The celebrated scenes of vulgar farce in *Mankind*, which are often cited as irrelevant and distracting, are so, if they are so, only as comic relief or entr'acte entertainment. Though one is free to feel that the heart of the playwright and audience is with them, they do not constitute an independent, unified action. The play makes what coherent sense it does (rather more than less, I should judge) only as Mankind's fall and redemption.

So strongly entrenched was the popular demand for thematic unity that even when, after the mid-sixteenth century, popular plays became common in which the surface action, understood as referring to "real people," did have some sort of unity, it was often interpreted explicitly as the illustration of an idea. Allegorical framing devices or allegorical figures mingling with the others, usually make the matter clear.

Thomas Garter's *Susanna* (c. 1568) and R. B.'s *Appius and Virginia* (c. 1567) as Madeleine Doran points out, have plots that very nearly satisfy Aristotelian requirements.[1] Yet morality figures mingling with the historical persons are used to draw the action to a clear thematic point. True Report, Ill Report, Voluptas and Sensualitas (the wicked judges) shape the story of Susanna to the moral that "God champions the innocent who trust in him." *Appius and Virginia* has a short but nicely formed tragic action, but by means of the Vice, Haphazard, a figure of Fortune in which blind worldlings place their trust, it makes the point that Justice, not Fortune, rules the world.

Serving the same sort of function, allegorical framing devices (induction, entr'acte shows, and epilogues) shadow forth the generalizations illustrated in the fairly coherent actions of such popular plays as *The Rare Triumphs of Love and Fortune* (c. 1582), *Locrine* (c. 1591), and *A Warning for Fair Women*

(c. 1599) as well as such academic Inns-of-Court plays as *Gorboduc* (1562), *Tancred and Gismund* (c. 1566), and *Caesar's Revenge* (1592–1606). They are used to unify quite unrelated actions, however, in Tarlton's *The Seven Deadly Sins* (1585), and Yarington's *Two Lamentable Tragedies* (1594–1601), and to unify episodic satire in *Histriomastix* (Marston's version, 1599).

All this is to touch only on the explicit use of thematic indicators. The implicit thematic unity, of, say, the history play as it developed during the sixteenth century and flourished in the 1590s, brilliantly argued by Tillyard and Ribner, could also be brought in evidence. Indeed the recognition of thematic unity in Tudor drama has been a main contribution of twentieth-century scholarship and criticism. What the implicit theme of a particular play is, how seriously intended, how successful in yoking together the play's parts, still serve as subjects of debate (to which later chapters of this book will contribute). But that the audiences for which Shakespeare and his contemporaries wrote had been trained to expect a unifying theme seems fairly clear. Not always to expect, perhaps, and of course to expect much else; but this among other riches was in the normal course of playgoing in 1600.

To convey the idea, Elizabethan playwrights had at command, and their audiences had been trained to grasp, a number of conventions including the straight didactic lecture. For the purposes of rough analysis, however, the specifically dramatic conventions, those, that is, relying upon action, music, *mise en scène*, and character, may be conveniently reduced to two: the example and the dramatic metaphor.

On the one hand is the exemplum, the particular instance of the general truth, clear because it is a cliché, or because it is emphasized and clarified by caricature, by type names, by parallel or contrasting instances, or by the bare-faced explanation of a presenter. The trembling wretch in *Everyman*, scared by Death, represents every man, as sample does its class, and his name makes the point clear. On the other hand is metaphor, the comparison between things of different sorts: the feeble woman to whom he turns is *like* (not an example of) the impotent good deeds of the unshriven. Her name, again, and didactic speeches clarify the fact. This distinction is crude; it will not always work; it lacks the sanction of Elizabethan critics of the drama; but within limits it is useful.

However complex the dramatic example may be in practice, its basic principle is fairly simple and calls for little discussion here. It is familiar from the Middle Ages. In the twelfth century Tegernsee *Antichristus*, for instance, Rex Teutonicorum, who rejects the bribes and defeats the armies of Antichrist, exemplifies Germanic incorruptibility and martial prowess, and these splendid qualities are contrasted by example with the corruption and feebleness of Rex Francorum and Rex Grecorum. Or in the miracle plays Cain is characterized to exemplify, in contrast to Abel, faithless avarice. Thus he speaks in the *Ludus Coventriae*:

> Amonges alle ffolys that gon on grownd,
>   I hold that thou be one of the most
> To tythe the best that is not sownd,
>   And kepe the werst that is nere lost.
> But I more wysly xal werke this stownde,
>   To tythe the werst. . . .[2]
> (3.92–97)

At its simplest and most dismal, especially when combined with contrasting parallelism, the exemplary technique results in the straightforward banalities of such plays as *The Nice Wanton* (contrasting a godly little prig named Barnabas with his brother and sister who tread the primrose path to ruin), *The London Merchant*, and more recent essays in Socialist Realism. But it also leads to the contrast of Hal and Hotspur, to the first-act parallel of Voltore, Corvino, and Corbaccio in *Volpone;* Ibsen found it useful, and Gorky, and Shaw, and at times, Chekhov. It is, again, the exemplary method that we assume when we seek to classify Hamlet as a melancholic or manic depressive, or when we see in *Twelfth Night* the conflict between hospitable old

Merry England of the manorial past and the new, efficient, Puritanical commercialism.

The example seems to have been the chief didactic technique—aside from wise and witty sayings that could be culled from context—recognized by Elizabethan critics, both apologists and opponents of the drama. That it could, and sometimes did, teach by example was agreed. This Philip Stubbes admits,

"And whereas you say there are good Examples to be learned in [plays and interludes], truly so there are: if you will learn cosenage; if you will learn to deceive; if you will learn to play the hypocrite, to cogge, lie, and falsify . . . to play the vice, to swear, tear and blaspheme both Heaven and Earth . . . to murder, slay, kill, pick, steal, rob and rove . . . to rebel against Princes, to commit treasons . . . to play the whoremaster, the glutton, drunkard, or incestuous person . . . and to commit all kind of sin and mischief, you need to go to no other school, for all these good examples may you see painted before your eyes in interludes and plays." [3]

It was largely on the ground of their moral examples, also, that the teaching of Plautus and Terence was defended by the humanists: comedies, as Sir Thomas Elyot declared, "wherein iuell is nat taught but discouered; to the intent that men . . . beinge therof warned may prepare them selfe to resist or preuente occasion." [4] The schoolboys of the better schools must have had a very thorough training—how much of it stuck is beyond conjecture—in the generalized moral reading of Latin comedy.

But the basic clarity of the exemplary principle is muddied by the frequent mixture of example with dramatic metaphor, which is in itself more complex. Contemporary criticism is silent upon the principles that dramatic metaphor involves, and playwrights occasionally use the word "example" loosely to refer to the metaphors of their allegorical drama. Still the distinction is there for the critic's eye, and of course it is recognized in non-dramatic literature by contemporary rhetoricians and logicians.

Taken in analytical isolation, the metaphors cause no difficulty. I have already instanced the feeble woman, Good Deeds, of

Everyman, and the variety and extent of the device can be indicated from earlier and later drama. The five pathetic young women of the eleventh-century Limoges *Sponsus*, trying in vain to borrow or buy oil for their empty lamps, are presented as like the hapless unregenerate at the last judgment. In the fifteenth century *Castle of Perseverance* and *Ludus Coventriae* the conflicting claims of truth, mercy, justice, and peace are presented as a friendly debate between four sisters, the daughters of God. In the sixteenth century *Wit and Wisdom—Wit and Science* plays, the intellect's struggle with tediousness or irksomeness is presented as a young man's fight with a monster. Dekker in *Old Fortunatus* presents man's yielding to vice and consequent moral deformity as the eating of a fair-seeming apple and subsequent sprouting of horns. Jonson in *Cynthia's Revels* presents the absurdity of self-love as a sort of magic drunkenness from drinking at a fountain (labelled "the fountain of Narcissus, or self-love").

These all certainly seem clear enough. The trouble comes when we notice that the vehicle of the metaphor (in medieval terms, the "literal" level, the "surface," or the "sense" as distinguished from "sentence") frequently receives a development and elaboration which is independent of, and occasionally seems to conflict with, the tenor (the "sentence," or, in the most general sense of the term, the "allegorical meaning"). Thus in *The Trial of Treasure* (c. 1567) Just wrestles with Lust in an early scene, is defeated once, but rises to overthrow him. The action clearly is a metaphor of Just's wrestling with his lust, and Lust is a personification of that quality. Later in the play, however, Lust assumes the role of the lustful *man*; he is led astray by the Vice Inclination, momentarily frightened by God's visitation, and is consoled by Lady Treasure with the promise,

> . . . there is no physician but we shall have with us;
> To the ease of your body they will you bring,
> And therefore I pray you despair in no thing.[5]

When Time at length summons him to his doom, he cries out like an Everyman, "Let treasure remain still with me," and he leaves the stage with the anguished question, "Whither go I now, to misery or bliss?" Yet he goes, not to the Hell that Everyman feared, but very much as in Marvel's poem, to be turned into dust. A moment after he leaves, Time reappears "with a similitude of dust," remarking, "Behold here, how Lust is converted into dust; This is his image, his wealth and prosperity." [6] He is simultaneously the wicked and his concupiscence, man and desire. The effect is that of double exposure in which the two pictures alternately come into focus, slightly puzzling, dazzling as one becomes conscious of it. Indeed nothing in his life of exemplary wickedness becomes him quite like his allegorical leaving of it.

A cruder and more radical division of functions is shown by the Vice Idleness in Merbury's *Marriage of Wit and Wisdom* (1579). In the first part of the play he performs his traditional role of misleading young Wit, but in the last half he becomes, as Professor Spivack has pointed out, a fairly concrete rogue who is robbed and beaten by other rogues and who demonstrates a comic mastery of disguise that is completely irrelevant to his "meaning" as the inclination to laziness.[7]

Still more radical relationships of vehicle and metaphor, arranged with very conscious art, are illustrated in Dekker's *Old Fortunatus* (1599, probably a revision of two earlier plays). For instance, toward the end of the play the scrapegrace Andelocia, newly reformed (he has just wooed Virtue and eaten her bitter apple), induces Lords Montrose and Longaville to eat the apples of Vice so that horns sprout on their heads. In a scheme to regain his magic purse and hat, Andelocia now shifts into the disguise of a French doctor and cures the two by feeding them the apples of Virtue. The miraculously cured sinners are quite unrepentant, and it is later explained to them

> . . . you were forgiven
> By Virtue's general pardon; her broad seal
> Gave you your lives, when she took off your horns.
> (5.2.228–30) [8]

But granted this general allegory, nothing in the management of the scene, with its suspense (will Andelocia regain the magic purse and hat?), its bustle of intrigue, and comic stage-French dialect, remotely suggests the religious-moral burden that it is made to bear.

These kinds of far-fetched dramatic metaphors are often seen as faults and often as a product of the Elizabethan transition from the earlier morality to a more realistic drama. There is indeed, at least when viewed from a later stance in time, a disturbing illogicality in them. Clearly they violate Dr. Johnson's dictum:

"Fame tells a tale and Victory hovers over a general, or perches on a standard; but Fame and Victory can do no more. To give them any real employment, or ascribe to them any material agency is to make them allegorical no longer, but to shock the mind by ascribing effects to non-entity." [9]

It is precisely this real employment given to characters bearing the names of abstractions that is the stock in trade of the moralities, shocking as it may be. More recently even Bernard Spivack, who examines the moralities with great sympathy and understanding, defines the personification as dramatic character in terms that leave little room for personality or action:

"A personification, no matter how persuasive its human similitude and vital energy in play or story, is subject to none of the multiplicity which defines the moral condition of human life. It is an elemental force, constrained to its single activity by what C. S. Lewis calls its "esse." What it does is what it has to do by virtue of what it explicitly and indivisibly is. Personifying is one of the irreducible modes of life's complex substance, its behavior and motivation are inherent in its name." [10]

This concept of personification has critical consequences when he turns to those Elizabethan plays in which personifications mingle with "real" people and the Vice is "clothed with the traits of human life and given a local habitation and a biography."

"Since the traditional aggression is thus bereft of its metaphorical, or subjective, *raison*, the practical motives of human life flow in to fill up the vacuum. . . . Unfortunately, the role, in its essential nature, is not amenable to such exterior transformation. At its heart, giving it the shape and dynamic that made it so popular and long-lived, are characteristics that belong to its origin in metaphor—its amoral temper, its homiletic dimension, and its self-sufficiency as a demonstration. To such a role human motives are superfluous, and they do not adhere no matter how energetically they are daubed on. They do not adhere to Common Conditions; and his successors, depending on how much of the old Vice remains in them, suffer in varying degree from the same cleavage and the same lack of verisimilitude." [11]

A still more serious criticism of disparity between tenor and vehicle, reflecting perhaps the modern demand that tenor "grow out of" vehicle, is well phrased by Robert Ornstein while discussing allegorical interpretations of the Duke in *Measure for Measure* as a representation of God:

"The symbolic vision which allegory embodies in art cannot dictate our response to the immediate realities of life or to the image of life presented on a stage; it can only build upon that response, illuminating the shared qualities of "thing" and idea—the analogical relationships between character and concept—which allow the mind to move freely between the realistic and symbolic levels of action. When the mind of the audience cannot move freely in this way because the analogical relationships are obscurely, ingeniously, or casuistically contrived, then the allegory is decadent. When the symbolic vision seeks to identify the devious and the Divine, then the allegory is immoral." [12]

I shall not quarrel with the esthetic and moral principles upon which these judgments are based. But the frequent radical independence of dramatic vehicle and tenor, however illogical, esthetically unsatisfactory, decadent, or immoral, was a theatrical convention in the plays on which Shakespeare's audience was trained. To understand plays as the Elizabethans understood them we must accept it as a fact, make it make sense as presumably it made sense to them, and discover if we can the pleasure that it gave them.

It was common moreover in the drama of the preceding two

centuries. This fact is important because it suggests that the device was not the uneasy and unsatisfying hybrid of an interim age between one dead, one struggling to be born, but a dramatic norm. It was enjoyed and taken for granted by many generations, a mode of theatrical experience which they found as "natural" as we find musical comedy or naturalism, and one which may offer great satisfactions.

We sometimes, it is true, speak loosely, perhaps recalling the savor of *Everyman*, of a "pure" morality type in which the abstractions are presumably so little personified that we perceive them in full Platonic sunlight. Of this (rather chilly) purity, plays like *The Three Ladies of London* or *The Marriage of Wit and Wisdom*, with their bustling action, apparently irrelevant farce, and only semi-abstract characters, seem inevitably a corruption. But such a purity is hard to seek on the English stage, and even the earliest extant morality plays do not show it. Although the metaphors run smoothly enough on the printed page, a little flat perhaps and a little dull (even as Fame telling a tale or Victory hovering over a general), performance forces upon the vehicle literal life. And crowding in with this literal life come the attendant irrelevant complications of gesture, voice, personality, and human action. It is a pretty conceit in *The Castle of Perseverance* that makes Covetise the World's treasurer and Backbiter the World's messenger. Translated into the personification-by-capitalization of neo-classical verse, the half-realized metaphors would probably cause no inconsistencies and would rouse no critic from his slumbers. Not so with Covetise: his personification is complete. He appears, not as an abstraction but—above all—visibly, a man, dressed perhaps in a furred gown and wearing a golden chain, carrying keys and welcoming his guest with patronizing bonhomie:

> Ow, Mankynde! blyssyd mote thou be!
>   I haue louyd thee derworthly many a day,
> & so I wot wel that thou dost me;
>   cum up & see my ryche a-ray!

> it were a gret poynte of pyte
> but Coueytyse were to thi pay.
> Sit up ryth here in this se;
>
> (830–36) [13]

This is lively theater; it has the jingling appeal of patter-song, and, since we know the malice behind it, it provides the thrill of dramatic irony; it also begins to build the fascinating personality of unctuous, rotten jocularity. But it is only the loosest of metaphors, and it is not at all a speaking abstraction. The *esse* of avarice is to be avaricious; avarice operates on a man to make *him* avaricious, and while a commonplace metonymy will yield "avarice tempts man" (more precisely, money tempts man) or "avaarice deceives man" or "promises him comforts and fine clothing," it is hard to see how avarice can be thought of as professing love for him. Vehicle, the theatrical impression of the false friend or even the diabolic friend, has become dominant here; tenor follows at a distance if indeed it does not slip momentarily from the spectators' consciousness.

So with Backbiter (Detraccio in the speech headings), the World's messenger. His quality is to cause dissension by bearing malicious reports:

> all thingis I crye a-gayn the pes
> to knyt and knaue; this is my kende,
>
> (651–52)

But the metaphor that makes him a messenger sends him on errands, any errands—leading Mankind from the World's stage to Avarice's, for instance, and recommending Mankind to Avarice's good graces—so that the primary metaphor, the personification of backbiting, is pretty well lost sight of in the whole first half of the play. And although it is emphasized in the second part, a new logical difficulty arises. Mankind has reformed and is installed in the Castle of Perseverance, guarded by the seven Virtues. Malus Angelus orders Backbiter to report this disaster to the World, Flesh, and Devil, and he obeys with great gusto, urging them to punish their subordinate sins:

> Lo, syr Werld, ye moun a-gryse
> That ye be seruyd on this wyse!
> Go pley you with syr Coueytyse
>   Tyl his crowne crake!
>
> (1850–53)

World, Flesh, and Devil respond heartily, beating the sins in fury, and Backbiter is delighted:

> Ya! for God, this was well goo
>   thus to werke with Bakbytynge!
> I werke bothe wrake and woo,
>   & make Iche man, other to dynge.
>
> (1779–82)

This is good theater and Backbiter is at last acting according to kind. But as a consequence the seven deadly sins and their masters have assumed a dramatic life irrelevant to their meaning. The three primary *temptations* are not angry with their associated sins; three diabolic princes are angry with their diabolic subjects. For the time being, in the minds of playwright and audience, the stage characters have assumed a life that obscures the allegory.

A disclaimer may be wise at this point: the foregoing analysis has been deliberately forced. The logical difficulties raised exist only for the painful scrutinizer of the printed page. They do not exist for the spectator, who, without a thought of the logical consistency, follows the double line of vehicle and tenor untroubled. He does, that is, if he has been trained in the convention, or not too rigorously trained in a different one, like an Ibsen devotee at his first musical comedy. The purpose of the hair-splitting is solely to suggest that there was a dramatic convention, ancient and honorable, that did in fact require the spectator to follow the play on the double track of tenor and vehicle; further, to suggest that this experience was not difficult, that it lies well within the imaginative range of most modern play-goers, and indeed that to become aware of its logical difficulties requires a literary examination, painstaking, scholastic, and untheatrical. This is not

33

to argue for the ultimate esthetic or moral validity of the convention, only to point to its existence.

Instances are common in the early morality plays. Consider for instance, the late fifteenth-century *Mary Magdelene*, the first part of which stages Mary's corruption in morality fashion. A flattering bawd entices her from the castle of Maudelyn and leads her to a tavern where they are joined by a fashionable gallant. He and Mary flirt, declare their love, and leave. When she next appears she is gloating over her lovers. The action is perfectly clear on the level of exemplum. Mary has yielded to lust.

But the allegory, although it makes the same point, makes it in a different way and makes others as well. It is the bawd, not the gallant, who is Lechery. The gallant is Curiosity (an alias of Pride). Thus Mary's offstage fornication was metaphorically not an act of lust, but a yielding to Pride (and perhaps other sins too). She had yielded to Lust already, and Lust had led her to the tavern (the World/Gluttony?) and Pride. Lust, furthermore, in greeting her, had appealed, not to her lust, but to her vanity; it is Curiosity who makes the direct, gay, audacious appeal to her "love."

The result is the tantalizing near-parallelism of fugal counterpoint. The two themes of pride and lust are introduced simultaneously on different levels, change places in the next scene, and are resolved only in the third.

The convention, it is true, can be used in less artful ways. One suspects that the highly generalized role of virtue played by Mercy in *Mankind* has been necessitated by the limitations of a small touring company. Mercy is the only Virtue character in the play and has to act them all. Consequently, one sometimes feels, for instance, when she scolds the Vices,

> Thys ydyll language ye xall repent!
> Out of this place I wolde ye went,
>
> (142–43) [14]

that the quality of Mercy has been strained.

Somewhat different theatrical considerations may have slightly strained even the metaphors of *Everyman*, which generally hews to a highly consistent metaphorical line. Perhaps it is not entirely inappropriate that enfeebled Good Deeds should offer counsel to Everyman, but counselling is certainly not her *esse*, and dramatic economy dictates that as the only faithful friend on stage, she do her bit. Again, when Five Wits joins Knowledge in a lecture on the sacraments, one suspects the operation of the well-tested principle of splitting speech into dialogue—"always make two men carry the trunk."

However, in both cases the dramatic vehicle has sufficient life in itself to carry the play forward regardless of any metaphorical inconsistency. Mercy, as critics have often noticed, is clearly characterized as a trifle ridiculous—rather dull, pompous, given to aureate terms which Mischief mocks—and the consequent conflict of the slightly crabbed parson and the young scape-grace vices (also ridiculous in their way) is viable drama. In the same way, in *Everyman*, the dramatic vehicle is the anguished search of a man to find his true friends, who will go with him on his dark journey. And this action gives life and function to the friends as friends, though their "meanings" flicker for a moment.

Medwall's two-part interlude *Nature* may serve as a final example from the early drama. It is more typically English than *Everyman* and has a less restricted cast than *Mankind*; it is also somewhat politer, written presumably for Morton's court. It demonstrates nicely the near-inevitability of the constant play of tenor against vehicle.

The action is simple: in each part Man is corrupted and then restored. In the first part he is seduced from the guidance of Reason by Sensuality, Mundus, Worldly Affection, and Pride. He returns with the help of Shamefastness. This is all staged in the mode of formal allegory. A certain Margery is mentioned, but she never appears on the stage, and no Tom Tosspots, Dick Dicers, or other type characters clutter the personae. Yet the action tends constantly toward an almost Jonsonian social comedy.

This effect is produced, as in *The Castle of Perseverance*, largely by the dialogue and action between the "abstractions."

Reason and Sensuality (the Aristotelian sensitive soul), for instance, meet and dispute as allegory demands. Reason commands the allegiance of Sensuality, and Sensuality rebels, "So mote I the!" (262).[15] Sound doctrine: we have been taught that Sensuality will do this. But at the same time the visible image of a soberly dressed nobleman and a young fop is claiming our attention, and even the dialogue reinforces this impression. Reason tries in vain to calm Sensuality:

> Sekur thy selfe man/ I aduyse the hardely
> Be not so passyonate/ ne yt so furyouse
> thou turmentyst thy selfe/ and wotyst not why
> No well aduysed body/ will demean hym thus
> Be sure thy mynde/ is all erronyous
> thou takyst a selfe well [sic]/ and wrong opynon
> Whyche shalbe thyn and others confusyon.
>
> (246–52)

The general metaphor holds well enough, but Sensuality has also become a man who can be advised to control himself, who torments himself, who has an erroneous mind, a self-will, and a wrong opinion that will bring him to confusion.

So with the other characters. Pride is appropriately proud, a young rake-hell, extravagantly dressed; he sports a dagger, and enters boasting of his parentage. He must also function to make Man proud, and he explains how he will do so:

> I wyll byd hym/ thynk how he ys create
> To be a worthy potestate
> And eke that he ys predestynate
> to be a prynces pere
> (867–70)

and so on. The dramatic focus shifts constantly between these two roles: the scornful young gallant and the temptation in Man's mind. As gallant, he can be, or pretend to be, angry with his naive young friend:

> Alas alas man ye be mad
> I se well ye be but a very lad
> On my fayth I was very glad
> Of your fyrst aquayntaunce
> And now I forthynk yt vtterly
> That euer I knew you fy fy fy.
> (987–92)

And when the alarmed young Man (who mistakes him for Worship), pleads with him, "Wurshyp for goddys sake greue ye not," he replies,

> I wys ye ar but an ydeot
> I pray you syr make not me a sot
> I am no tryfler.
> (1003–6)

He explains his scorn and offers his own good advice in a scene that becomes increasingly Jonsonian:

> ye alow the counsell of a karle borne
> Byfore myne I haue yt in scorne
> It ys a thyng I can not bere
> *Man.* Whom meane ye Reason
> *Pride.* Ye that same daw
> *Man.* What ys he a wyse man
> *Pride.* He ys a straw
>   Bycause he kepys you vnder aw
>   ye be therein blynd
> *Man.* And so doth he wythout faynyng
>   For hyderto I myght do nothyng
>   But after hys wyll and byddyng
>   And that groged my mynde
> *Pride.* Grouge quod a yt ys no maruell hardely
>   It shall greue me certaynly
>   As longe as I am in your cumpany
>   To se you demeaned in that wyse
>   ye be now in good way

but in fayth I lyke not your aray
It ys not the fasyon that goth now a day
For now there ys a new guyse
It is now .ii. dayes a gon
Syth that men bygan thys fassyon
And euery knaue had yt anon.

(1008–29)

The young dolt, of course, joins him in instant condemnation of his own apparel; he will have the new fashion.

I think it is a falsification of the play-going experience to say that this is Jonson in morality guise; the speech headings that loom so large in the italics of print are non-existent on the stage. What we see is the comedy of young master Stephen or Asotus or Sogliardo being mocked and molded by Bobadill or Amorphus or Shift. The abstract names occur, it is true, from time to time in the dialogue. They insure that we will not forget the tenor of the metaphor, even as Jonson will also keep us aware of his meaning, but the vehicle of social comedy is fleshed out in fully human terms and enjoyable in its own right.

Indeed, Medwall is quite willing to let it take over the stage from time to time. Sensuality enters to Pride and Worldly Affection a little later, and announces that he has introduced Man to the offstage Margery at a tavern. That is, of course, his "office." But Pride, it appears, has also slept with Margery, and Sensuality recalls unkindly Pride's recent misadventure with her:

She that bygyled you parde so prately
and bare away your shyrt the last mornyng
Stede of her smok whyle ye lay slepyng.

(1117–19)

He also warns Pride and Worldly Affection,

Medyll ye no more wyth margery
For by cokkys precyouse body
If our mayster may yt espy
Or haue an vnderstandyng

That ye vse her company
I tell you he wyll be angry
(1172–78)

Clearly they are servants here, *not* Man's Pride and Worldly Affection. And yet, when Pride takes his leave, Sensuality goes with him, explaining "It ys accordynge for Sensualyte/ Wyth Pryde for to go." (1269–72)

These devices are not the ineptitudes of the unpracticed playwright. Nor are they the careful awkwardness of the cloistered literary man. This is not Medwall's only or first play, and the standards of entertainment at Morton's court, if we can believe accounts, were high. It would tolerate some fairly heavy lecturing (like Nature's opening speech explaining some of her arrangements and referring the inquisitive to Aristotle for more information), and it would tolerate witty impromptus of the skillful amateur, but not laboured clumsiness. The devices, moreover, are typical of the period, and the play, read with an eye toward staging, reveals itself as potentially a fairly successful comedy. They would seem then rather to show the experienced craftsman working with the grain, taking advantage of the conventions the stage offered him and then turning them to good dramatic account.

ii.

It is one thing, however, to point to a dramatic convention as a loose but convenient dramatic device which would trouble only the scrutiny of the determined classicist; it is another to see it as somehow making sense in a way which the severest critic might respect even though he finally rejects it. The task may be made easier if we consider first, as sympathetically as possible, the various reasons for it and the rationalizations that may have helped justify it in medieval and Renaissance eyes.

In the first place the inconsistent or fitful metaphor is nearly inevitable in dramatic allegory. Even in narrative allegory, as Dr. Johnson's warning makes clear, it is hard to avoid. The momentary symbolic action, the personification established in one phrase and dropped from sight in the next, run no risk of inconsistency. But once the metaphor is continued through an extended action, its vehicle begins to gather irrelevant or even contradictory connotations and implications. This is especially true when the narrative vehicle itself is prescribed, as in myth or scripture. Samson, it has been noted, served the medieval painter or sculptor nicely when he is depicted carrying off the gates of Gaza. The action is a type or figure of Christ bearing away the gates of Hell. But to place the action in narrative context, showing Samson rising from the harlot's bed, demands, if the allegory is to be maintained, ingenuity and iron faith. Because church fathers had both, they solved the problem easily, but a poem or play on the subject is more taxing. (It was one episode Milton did *not* list as the possible subject of a Samson tragedy.) Similarly, granted that Hermaphroditus can serve as a symbol of Christ's dual nature, it might require some temerity for a modern Christian poet to carry through an *allegorical* poem describing the nymph Salmacis and her mad dash into the water to merge with the hapless lad in a lustful embrace. The medieval Ovidians, however, met the challenge cheerfully.

To the complexities of continued metaphor, drama adds others stemming from the inescapable implications of personality in the characters, from the often quite irrelevant delights of song, fireworks, and fine footwork, and—sometimes, especially when the actors are familiar—from the actor himself, showing through his role. Even in the simplest and most abstract actions, like the debate of the four daughters of God—Truth, Justice, Mercy, and Peace—the play of personalities glitters across the tenor of the metaphor. Mercy in *The Castle of Perseverance* begs her father to comfort *her;* Justice begs a boon; Peace solemnly warns the others "loke our joyes be parfyth." In the *Ludus Coventriae* they are delicate and high-born ladies and show just a hint of the strain of temper and vanity upon their breeding:

Justicia. Mercy, me mervelyth what yow movyth,
   ye know wel I am your syster Rightwysnes . . . .
Misericordia. Syster Ryghtwysnes, ye are to vengeabyl . . .
Pax. [recalling them to their functions]
   To spare your speches, systeres, it syt,
   It is not onest in vertuys to ben dyscencion.

(89–114)

Yet beneath the play of personality the basic metaphor continues and gives the scene its coherence and meaning in the play.

iii.

Inevitability aside, however, medieval allegorical theory justified a very great disparity between tenor and vehicle. To seize the issue at its thorniest, we may recall that the allegorical interpretation of scripture was often used precisely to turn unedifying examples into edifying allegories. Here is Augustine on the subject: "whatever appears in the divine Word that does not literally pertain to virtuous behavior or to the truth of faith you must take to be figurative," [16] and in the *Confessions* Augustine explains how Ambrose's allegorical explanation of many apparently immoral passages of the Old Testament led him to accept its truth. The implication of a wide disparity of meanings is obvious, and indeed if we follow Augustine precisely, the two levels of scriptural meaning must always be not merely different, but opposed. "In the consideration of figurative expressions a rule such as this will serve, that what is read should be subjected to diligent scrutiny until an interpretation contributing to the reign of charity is produced. *If this result appears literally in the text, the expression being considered is not figurative*" [17] (The italics are mine).

Since, then, expressions are figurative only if the literal meaning is opposed to charity, and since the figurative meaning is always that of charity, literal and figurative meanings are always opposed. In practice, however, passages like Abraham's sacrifice

41

which inculcated charity on the literal level were frequently given an allegorical meaning as well. The two meanings might be different but they were not necessarily opposed as good and evil. Yet they could be and often were.

What has been said of Augustine applies in full or part to the pagan allegorists of Homer, to Philo Judaeus, to most of the Western Church Fathers, to Bede, Alcuin, Scotus Erigena, Dante, Petrarch, Boccaccio, Salutati, Chaucer, Gower, Hawes, Erasmus, Spenser, Francis Bacon, Jonson, Donne, and Chapman, to name a few. The theory became standard in the aesthetic of the Middle Ages and Renaissance. The surface of poetic fiction is a veil, a rind, a husk, beneath which one must try to discover truth, the kernel. The reader's difficulty is admitted:

"You must read, you must persevere, you must sit up nights, you must inquire, and exert the utmost power of your mind. If one way does not lead to the desired meaning, take another; if obstacles arise, then still another; until, if your strength holds out, you will find that clear which at first looked dark." [18]

But difficult as interpretation is, and shocking as so radical a theory of metaphor may be to neo-classic or romantic eyes, it can lead, as Bernard Huppé has shown, to a literature of highly intellectual appeal.[19] It offers, in Marrou's phrase, the pleasures and benefits of "le gymnastique intellectuelle." [20] It is an appeal which Augustine felt and which he was puzzled to explain. He preferred, for instance, the figurative language of the Song of Songs to the plain statement which he saw it veiling. He is not sure why —"Quare suavius videam . . . difficile est dicere"—yet no one, he asserts, "doubts that everything is learned with more pleasure when learned through similitudes and when, having been sought with difficulty it is discovered with pain." It is akin to the pleasure of problem-solving, or of puzzling out *Finnegan's Wake*. But other benefits were also commonly claimed for veiling the truth: it helped to abate pride; it protected the pearl of truth from the profane swine; it coated with sweetness the sometimes bitter pill of truth; it stimulated the discussion and airing of many opinions, and, in the splendid Platonic phrase of Scotus Erigena, it trained the mind "to rise from the external, corporal senses, to the perfected understanding of intelligible things, as if from an imperfect puerile understanding to a maturity of the inner man." [21]

It is impossible to generalize about the use of allegorical obscurity in the drama, even the English drama. There is, of course, the more or less veiled topical allegory of the sort found, perhaps in the fifteenth-century *Mind, Will and Understanding*, and almost certainly in such plays as Skelton's *Magnificence*, the Marian *Respublica*, Lyly's *Midas*, some of the court masques, and Middleton's *Game at Chess*. And this shades into the non-allegorical portrait and allusion, flattering or satirical, which required a quick mind or inside information to recognize: the fair vestal throned by the west, the Elfin counsellors of Dekker's *Whore of Babylon*, or the caricatures and counter-caricatures of the war of the theaters. This sort of thing is largely irrelevant to the present discussion, but it suggests that the delights of *gymnastique intellectuelle* mixed with the smug consciousness of recondite information were recognized, if occasional, theatrical fare.

Obscurity in dramatic allegory that points to the general, the abstract, or the Providential plan of history, is more difficult to judge. Consider, as an early example, the Limoges *Sponsus*, a dramatization, part French, part Latin in the extant version, of the parable of the five wise and five foolish virgins. It begins with two songs which announce the coming of the Bridegroom. Then the foolish virgins approach the wise virgins and beg oil of them. The wise virgins reject and send them to the merchants. These also reject them; they lament; the Bridegroom appears and apparently lets the wise virgins silently pass through a door. The foolish virgins beg Him to open the door for them also, but He rejects them, and demons carry them off to Hell.

While the general sense of the parable is clear enough (the foolish are the damned and the wise are the saved), understanding the details requires a considerable knowledge of biblical exegesis and has embroiled modern critics in extensive controversy. The action and sung dialogue are concerned with the frantic attempt of the foolish virgins to obtain oil. Each four-line stanza of the dialogue, however, is followed by the refrain of the foolish virgins, "Dolentas, chaitivas, trop i avem dormit!" [22] And this refrain is inexplicable by reference to the action. Even if we suppose, with some editors, that the foolish virgins have been shown sleeping at the beginning of the play (a conjecture that the latest editor considers *aventureux*) the lament itself is unrelated to their attempt to obtain oil, and their empty lamps are unrelated to their sleeping. The puzzle is clarified only by exegesis, in which the foolish virgins are nominal Christians who have wasted their oil, that is their love, either by their failure to do good works or by doing good works for the sake of human praise. They have failed, in other words, to love God (the Bridegroom). Hence, *by another metaphor*, they have slept (since sleep is a metaphor of spiritual sloth), and hence, in turn, their doleful refrain. [23] On the level of exemplary action the play is incoherent; it becomes coherent only if we understand the two parallel metaphors.

The simple action and vernacular portions of the text provide a clear enough plot line and suggest that the audience included laity. Also, clearly enough, the audience is given plenty of opportunity to enjoy whatever of the recherché pleasures of intellectual gymnastics it is capable.

Obvious puzzles of this type are rare. In contrast is the comforting illusion of comprehension offered by the English Corpus Christi plays. Their surface action has seemed to most critics to be without difficulties and to afford pleasures no deeper than the bumbling charm of a peasant dance. Granted, the muse of their monkish authors was not unlettered and their rhymes were not uncouth, they were nevertheless shaped artlessly to the naïve vision of the rude artisans (Bottom, Quince, and Snug, doubtless) who overacted them and the simple rustics who clumped in from the fields to view them. Although a few plays like the Wakefield *Secunda Pastorum* exhibited welcome flashes of boisterous realism, most of them, considered as art or as dramatization of God's ways to man, could only implore the passing tribute of a sigh. [24]

This view has been modified in the past twenty years, both by performances which revealed an unexpected power in the plays, and by scholarship which demonstrated that their apparent art-lessness conceals a considerable complexity of thought and structure. Of special interest for our present purposes is the dramatists' use of typology, which had gone unnoticed by critics of the nineteenth and early twentieth centuries. Rosemary Woolf argued the case for the Abraham and Isaac plays in 1957, and in 1966 V. A. Kolve demonstrated that it was very largely typology which gave the Corpus Christi cycle unity and focussed it upon Christ's redemption of mankind.[25] The cycles, Kolve pointed out, did not dramatize a random selection of events. The Old Testament episodes were selected because they were traditional types and figures foreshadowing the redemption. For instance, Cain's murder of Abel is a figure of the crucifixion; Abraham's sacrifice is a figure of Christ's; the Ark is a figure of the Church, and Noah is a type of Christ. It was these analogies, established by Pauline and patristic exegesis, that, when understood, gave to the cycle its coherence, binding its parts together as the drama of man's fall and redemption. The early plays, or pageants, of the cycle operated as large dramatic metaphors of the later ones.

Obviously the clerical playwrights were aware of the typological principles which they made use of. The percentage of the audience that was also aware of them can only be guessed at. As Kolve remarks, "a lowest-common-denominator approach to the medieval audience has characterized too much of the scholarly attention this drama has received." Turning, then, from the simple, red-necked, rude forefathers beloved of nineteenth-century scholarship, to the same part of the audience we have postulated for the interpretation of Elizabethan drama, the part, in Kolve's words, "equipped to respond to the plays most fully—intelligent and attentive laymen, whether lettered or not, as well as priests and clerks," [26] we can reasonably assume a significant part of the audience that would be aware of these typological significances. As Rosemary Woolf and Rosemund Tuve have shown, there is evidence, especially in England, of a widespread knowledge of common typology: its appearance in the liturgy, in collections of homilies like Mirk's *Festial*, in church art, in carols, and in the *Biblia Pauperum*. There is also, as Miss Woolf remarks, "a possibility that the audience may have been reminded of the typological meaning by some device in the production. Isaac, for instance, may have carried his wood in the form of a cross, as he so often does in visual art." [27]

So much for the commonplaces of typology. For those spectators who savored them, more recondite meanings were often made available. "Characters with names like *Expositor, Poeta, Profeta, Prologue,* and *Doctor,*" as Kolve points out, "exist chiefly to facilitate a more advanced understanding." [28]

The prefiguration of Christ by the Lamb which Abel sacrifices in the *Ludus Coventriae* might escape notice did not Abel himself draw attention to it. Although in the Chester plays one might well grasp the point that, when Abraham offers a tenth of his battle spoils to the priest Melchisadech, he is exemplifying tithe-giving, and that when Melchisadech in turn gives Abraham bread and wine, and Lot gives Melchisadech bread and wine, the host is prefigured, without the presenter one might fail to see that, whereas Abraham's gift signifies the Old Law, Lot's signifies the New Testament, and that Abraham the tithe-giver simultaneously represents God:

> By Abraham vnderstand I may
> the father of heaven in good faye,
> Melchisadech a priest to his paye
> to minister that sacrament
> that Christ ordayned on Sherethursday
> in bread and wyne, to honur him aye;
>
> (137–42) [29]

Furthermore, to increase the pleasant complexity, although Abraham symbolizes God the father, the next speaker is Deus himself, speaking to Abraham, promising him offspring.

The sacrifice of Isaac follows, and this too has its double meaning. On the level of exemplary action Abraham is emphasized throughout as the obedient servant of God. He replies to the

stern command without hesitation, "My lord, to thee is my en-
tent/ ever to be obedyent" (217–18); his constantly repeated
anguish testifies to the strength of his resolution:

> O my sonne, I am sorry
> to doe to thie this great anye:
> Gods Comaundment do must I.
>
> (293–95)

> Lord, I wold fayne worke thy will.
> this younge Inocent that lyes so still
> full loth were me him to kill.
>
> (397–99)

And the dramatic climax comes when the angel, seizing the tip
of the descending sword and commanding Abraham to stop, explains,

> for thou dreades God, well se I
> that of thy sonne has no mercy
> to fulfill his byddinge.
>
> (426–28)

Yet while Abraham is the obedient servant of God, and the action is a test of his will to obey God, he is simultaneously God
himself:

> By Abraham I may vnderstand
> the father of heaven that can fand
> with his sonnes blood to break that band
> the Devil had brought vs too.
>
> (469–72)

Isaac is, of course, "Ihesu that was obedyent aye."

That this kind of discrepancy between vehicle and tenor, is
neither extreme nor the late, degenerate product of an exhausted
tradition is suggested by the example of the twelfth-century
Latin *Isaac and Rebecca*. Young Esau is presented with great
sympathy. When Isaac sends for him he replies in song,

47

Letus ad patrem ambulo
eius me fouet visio
et mutua colloquia
sic res pelletur anxia.

(45–48) [30]

It is a song of happy filial devotion, and when Isaac asks for veni-
son, Esau responds dutifully and carefully removes his precious
robes before taking to the field. But the *allegoria* sung by a chorus
of boys explains that he represents the faithless synagogue; when
he removes his clothes he is abandoning the decalogue, and so on.
It is Jacob the deceiver who represents the true Church, the
adopted children of Abraham.

This is indeed shocking by most modern standards, and Miss
Woolf comments on "the disastrous literary effect" that if the
allegory "does not ruin the play completely, it is an unhelpful en-
cumbrance." [31] One may sympathize, yet the allegory was quite
conventional; it was, in medieval eyes, the truth veiled by the
deceptive appearance. And one could even argue that the opposition of rind and core has a positive value in so far as it shocks us
into an awareness of the tremendous distance between the "external, corporal senses" and the "perfected understanding of
things."

However that may be, it should be clear that nothing in the
development of the surface action and dialogue, including a clear
exemplary theme, precludes a quite different tenor. The veil,
after all, that conceals the truth ceases to veil if it is too transpar-
ent, and the fun is lost. On the other hand, if it is too thick, the
husk too concealing, the audience may either feel frustration or,
in Augustine's words, like the Prodigal Son, ignorantly feed upon
the husks. To avoid the dangers both of a too obvious clarity
and an impenetrable obscurity is often impossible, especially if
the audience is heterogeneous. How a poet or playwright meets
the problem will depend upon his temperament as well as his
estimate of the audience. For latent in the concept of the veiling
fiction is the temptation to dismiss rather large numbers as tram-

pling swine and to guard the pearl of truth over-zealously. Perhaps Petrarch in his invectives, perhaps even Boccaccio, reveals a touch of this arrogance. Chapman certainly, to come closer home, shows it in the prefaces to his allegorical poetry, warning off the "prophane multitude" and inviting only those "searching spirits whom learning hath made noble and nobility sacred." The dramatist, one would think, could less afford to be selective, yet even for so completely popular a show as the pageants welcoming James I to London. Jonson displays similar contempt for the unlearned. "The Symbols used," he explains in his printed description,

". . . are not, neither ought to be, simply *Hieroglyphics, Emblems* or *Impreses*, but a mixed character, partaking somewhat of all, and peculiarly adapted to these more magnificent Inventions: wherein, the garments and ensigns deliver the nature of the person, and the word the present office. Neither was it becoming, or could it stand with the dignitie of these shows (after the most miserable and desperate shift of the Puppits) to require a Truch-man, or (with the ignorant Painter) one to write, *This is a dog;* or, *This is a hare:* but so to be presented, as upon the view, they might, without cloud or obscuritie, declare themselves to the sharpe and learned: And for the multitude, no doubt but their grounded judgements did gaze, said it was fine, and were satisfied." [32]

This tone is familiar in Jonson as well as other Jacobean playwrights, but it is used here specifically to defend the symbolic veil which obviously some grounded judgments found too concealing. (It should be noted, however, that even here where narrative interest is absent, Jonson has, or thinks he has, provided a vehicle which would in itself provide some measure of satisfaction.) His note to the masque of *Hymenaei* also suggests that the more select audiences of the court occasionally complained of obscurity:

"And, for the *Allegorie,* though here it be very cleare, and such as might well escape a candle, yet because there are some, must complaine of darknesse that have but thicke eyes, I am contented to hold them this Light." [33]

The explanation follows. So in the *Masque of Queens* he has presented twelve famous queens, ranging from Penthesilea to Anne of Denmark, seated in the House of Good Fame, and he undertakes to answer the "possible objection": "How *I can bring Persons, of so different ages, to appeare properly, together?*" He answers from the allegory, "Nothing is more proper; Nothing more naturall: For these all live; and together, in theyr *Fame*; and so I present them." This is in the holograph copy that he gave to Prince Henry, but in the printed quarto he adds, "For other objections, let the lookes and noses of judges hover thick; so they bring the braines: or if they do not, I care not." [34]

The early masques, indeed, are full of such explanations, usually given with less asperity. They indicate roughly the extent of the courtiers' knowledge of iconology, and they reveal the irritated pedant and literary swashbuckler, but behind that they reveal also Jonson's faith in the ancient poetic game of appealing to the intellectual curiosity of the audience, inviting it to pierce the beguiling veil of spectacle and music. "The things subjected to the understanding" are "impressing and lasting." Those "objected to the sense" are "but momentarie, and merely taking."

"This it is hath made the most royall *Princes* and greatest *persons* . . . not onely studious of riches, and magnificence in the outward celebration, or shew; (which rightly becomes them) but curious after the most high and heartie inventions, to furnish the inward parts: (and those grounded upon antiquitie and solide *learnings*) which, though their *voyce* be taught to sound to present occasions, their *sense*, or doth, or should alwayes lay hold on more remov'd mysteries." [35]

This is prefatory to a masque, designed for only one performance, momentary as air; yet to those who "squeamishly crie out, that all endeavour of *learning*, and *sharpnesse* in these transitorie *devices* especially where it steps beyond their little, or (let me not wrong 'hem) no braine at all, is superfluous," Jonson replies with contempt and sends them home to enjoy their empty trenchers, "fittest for such ayrie tastes." [36]

The theory, deriving from allegorical interpretations of my-

thology and scripture, that the poetic fiction is a veil or husk concealing the "more removed mysteries" clearly helps to explain the frequent disparity, so shocking to modern sensibilities, between tenor and vehicle. It explains how intelligent and learned men could accept, indeed be fascinated by, a mode of allegory in which the vision of conceptual reality does not build upon our response to the immediate realities of life, in which in fact the two clash in a shock that marks the sudden rise from a puerile understanding to the maturity of the inner man. The theory offers a justification for such clashes where, in letters or drama, they occur. It suggests, too, one reason why men of the middle ages and Renaissance were readier than we to accept a very loose-fitting metaphor even where, as in most morality plays, there was no veil to pierce. Acute and learned men had been trained to expect a disparity between tenor and vehicle that we have been trained not to accept.

iv.

But to explain why the loose-fitting metaphors of morality plays could be accepted by such men as Morton, Medwall, More or Rastell still leaves unexplained the positive enjoyment that these plays may have given them, or how they followed them mentally. I have already suggested that the difficulty is only apparent; it is largely a product of over-analytical criticism, divorced from the theatrical experience. The enjoyment of loosely parallel meanings is akin, as I have suggested, to that of polyphony or counterpoint.

In more theatrical terms, the experience may be defined as that which the late S. M. Bethel described so brilliantly and named rather less happily, "multi-consciousness." The term points to the fact that "a popular audience, uncontaminated by abstract and tendentious dramatic theory, will attend to several diverse aspects of a situation, simultaneously yet without confusion." Bethel illustrates his remark with a now famous example, a Harold Lloyd film in which

". . . the comedian performed a series of hair-raising evolutions on the front and very near the top of a formidable skyscraper. The audience must have had several concurrent reactions: (a) they would admire the performance of a brilliant 'equilibrist;' (b) they would be amused at his (recognisedly feigned) clumsiness; and (c) they would be concerned for the hero's safety, in sympathy with the heroine watching anxiously from below." [37]

This kind of experience is familiar. Furthermore, as the example implies, it can be fun, a satisfaction in itself. It is, or can be, a quite simple, unreflective experience (hence "consciousness" is misleading), and at this level it is a world away intellectually from Augustine's—or Jonson's—conscious search for meaning and the peculiar joy of breaking through into understanding.

Bethel himself has listed a large number of Shakespearian scenes which seem to call for this kind of multi-consciousness and has, indeed, suggested its relevance to allegorical or symbolic meanings in the plays. There would be little point in duplicating his list or adding to it. My object here is merely to emphasize that the experience is a quite positive theatrical pleasure, comparable to irony or suspense, pity, fear, or laughter, and that again as Bethel also suggests, it is a traditional pleasure which the audience had been trained to expect.

After what has already been said about pre-Elizabethan drama, the last point should need no arguing. Obviously the simultaneous—or rapidly alternating—impact of tenor and vehicle offers a constant opportunity for exploiting this source of pleasure. Metaphor apart, however, the medieval stage constantly relies upon the simultaneous exploitation of different levels of theatrical reality and upon the audience's reaction to them. One brief example, by no means the most complex, may serve as illustration: the fight between Noah and his wife in the Wakefield *Noah*. It is, of course, possible to stage this on only one plane of reality. One can imagine a poor production in which the image of the embarrassed and awkward carpenter would blot out all consciousness of the full theatrical effectiveness of Noah's role

as he struggles with his wife, the servant of God striving with Eve, *das ewige weiblich*, and as he simultaneously engages in the comic marital combat of current jest and common life. Noah, indeed, makes the immediate application for the audience:

> Yee men that has wifis, whyls they ar yong,
> If ye luf youre lifis, chastice thare tong.
> Me thynk my hert ryfis, both levyr and long,
> To se sich stryfis wedmen emong.
>   Bot I
> As haue I blys,
> Shall chastyse this!
>   (397–403) [38]

Beyond this there is the skill to admire—of both word and action. There are the trivial miracles of rhyme, alliteration, and patterned lines:

> *Uxor.* Yit may ye mys,
>   Nicholl Nedy!
> *Noe.* I shall make the still as stone,
>   begynnar of blunder!
>   I shall bete the, bak and bone,
>   and breke all in sonder.
> (They fight.)
>   (404–7)

There is the artful, feigned boxing, the comic miss, the comic dodging, the final locked grappling, now husband on top, now wife, and the rhymes caught up from before the fight:

> *Uxor.* Out, alas, I am gone!
>   Oute apon the, mans wonder!
> *Noe.* Se how she can grone
>   and I lig vnder!
>   (408–9)

Cutting across the admiration there is, of course, suspense, and there is laughter at the sexual suggestion. For at least some mem-

bers of the local audience there is the sight of their familiar fellow-townsmen, Rafe and Thomas of yesterday; and the hairy-legged masculinity of Uxor. And for some there may be, even in this scene, a flickering awareness of the commonplace typological meaning in which Noah prefigures Christ and the ark, the church. A moment later, at any rate, Noah has seized the helm; his wife by his side, he is steering the ship through the wild waves and cries out to his divine counterpart,

> Help, God in this nede!
> As thou art stere-man good,
> and best, as I rede,
>   Of all,
> Thou rewle vs in this rase,
> As thou me behete hase.

(426–30)

We are accustomed to pointing out as typically medieval these mixtures of farce and solemnity, of apparent irreverence and reverence. But such mixtures are merely an aspect of the general radical disparity between levels of meaning and of the mental habit that could accept them simultaneously. Noah is simultaneously a ridiculous human being and a similitude of Christ, even as Samson is a wicked human being and a similitude of Christ, as Griselda's cruel husband is a similitude of Providence, as the obedient and pathetic Abraham is a similitude of the Lord he is obedient to, or as the faithful Esau is of the faithless Synagogue. Beside such disparities, those of the morality plays seem pale—the temperamental confidence man who is a similitude of Pride, the fool and scapegrace who is a similitude of Idleness, the besotted worldling who is a similitude of man's Lust, or Dekker's clever-foolish rogue disguised as a comic French doctor, whose self-seeking trickery is a similitude of the divine pardon extended freely to all sinners.

Such disparities, however decadent we may think them, find, as we have seen, justifications of various sorts: in pleasures both intellectual and unreflective, and in the philosophical training

they offer the mind in rising from "the external, corporal senses, to the perfected understanding of intelligible things." But they may also be justified as reflections of the actual state of affairs, in which the appearance of things is usually at odds with the reality that it masks. This radical opposition of appearance and reality is the common assumption of Renaissance moralists and satirists and was frequently dramatized by the metaphor of disguising—vices masked as virtues—discussed below.[39] It is memorably stated by Erasmus's Folly in the imagery of the Sileni of Alcibiades:

"All humaine thynges lyke the *Silenes or duble images of Alcibiades* have two faces muche unlike and dissemblable, that what outwardly seemed death, yet lokyng within ye shulde fynde it lyfe: and on the other side what seemed life, to be death: what fayre, to be foule: what riche, beggerly: what cunnyng, rude: what stronge, feable: what noble, vile: what gladsome, sadde: what happie, unlucky: what friendly, unfriendly: what healthsome, noysome. Briefely the Silene ones beyng undone and disclosed, ye shall fynde all thynges tourned into a new semblance."[40]

Given a world of this sort, the vehicle of a dramatic metaphor—the veil—might well conceal a reality of a quite different and surprising sort.

II.

Dramatic Metaphor in Moralities and Other Entertainment.

The training in the theater of metaphor that we might reasonably suppose late Elizabethan audiences to have received can be gauged in only the roughest fashion. The morality play, it should be noted, was not the sole vehicle of this training. It was the most important, however, at least for popular audiences in the first half of Elizabeth's reign, and its record may be discussed first.

This record is irritatingly vague. One cannot be much more precise than to say that the morality flourished through the seventies and eighties and that by the early nineties, at least in London, it was dead but well-remembered. The evidence can be briefly reviewed. In his revision of *Annals of English Drama* Mr. Schoenbaum classifies as probable moralities about twenty to twenty-five percent of the new plays throughout the sixties, seventies, and early eighties, but the proportion drops to less than ten percent after 1583, and it dwindles to almost nothing (three out of nearly two hundred) in the nineties.[1] Most of the plays listed, however, are necessarily classified on the basis of their titles alone, since texts survive for only about a quarter of those of which there are records. The play titles, to judge from extant plays, indicate thoroughgoing moralities, including the so-called "intermediate" moralities, fairly reliably, but they do not indicate "hybrids," that is plays like *Cambises* which have a romantic or historical main action in which personifications mingle with the "real" characters. It was during the sixties and seventies that they became popular, and Mr. Bevington, distinguishing the popular repertory (plays offered for acting or produced by men's companies) from academic and private theater plays, concludes that almost all pre-Marlovian plays in the popular repertory were either moralities or hybrids.[2] This seems to be true, certainly, of the extant plays (the few exceptions and doubtful cases are minor), and it seems plausible in general if we do not take "pre-Marlovian" with literal exactness. The fact means, of course, that until the middle and late eighties, personifications and explicit metaphorical action would have been part of every playgoer's experience unless he selected most carefully among productions by the Inns of Court, the schools, or the boys' companies.

Other evidence gives this conclusion a little support. Gosson in 1582 refers to a recent production by Leicester's men at The Theatre of two of his plays written some five or six years before. One was a comedy, "a cast of Italian devices," and the other a morality.[3] There is no indication in his report that he considers the first play avant-garde or the second old-fashioned. He also refers to a defense of plays in the form of morality, *The Play of Plays and Pastimes*, of about the same date.[4] Whetstone in 1584 refers to clerical attacks on "Stageplays (unproperly called, tragedies, comedies, and morals);"[5] William Rankins, in attacking the stage in 1587 confidently puts his satire in the form of a narrative description of a morality.[6] So does the anonymous anti-Martinist pamphleteer (perhaps Nashe) of 1589, who is probably describing an actual satirical morality, the performance of which had been blocked.[7] The traditional morality buffoonery of Vice and Devil in Greene's *Friar Bacon* (1589–92) is without explicit metaphorical significance, and so is that of *Faustus,* but at least the playwrights felt free to use this old fashioned kind of clownage, and these plays continued to be played through the nineties. The point is worth observing because it was precisely Vice and Devil and the kind of moral interlude with which they were associated that some allusions of the nineties look back upon with amusement and contempt. In 1592, for instance, Nashe defends plays as discouraging the avaricious, who "know when they are dead they shall not be brought upon the stage for any goodness, but in a merriment of the Usurer and the Devil." [8] This is almost certainly an allusion to a popular moral interlude (perhaps a version of a play of the forties by John Radcliffe), and Nashe speaks of it as the sort of thing one might still see. He is contrasting it, however, with the "noble obsequies of histories drawn from the chronicles" and "true tragedies" of "emperors, kings, and princes" —the new histories like Shakespeare's Henry VI plays—and he is obviously contemptuous of the older form as well as of its avaricious protagonists. Greene, writing in the same year, is even clearer. The protagonist of his *Groatsworth of Wit* meets a player who has made his reputation in a repertory which is both old fashioned and apparently provincial. It includes "Delphrigius and the King of the Fairies," "The Twelve Labors of Hercules," and "three scenes of the devil in the highway to heaven." He asserts, too, that he "was a country author, passing at a moral;" he wrote "the moral of man's wit" and the "Dialogue of Dives." But now, he adds "my almanack is out of date":

> The people make no estimation,
> Of morals teaching education.[9]

As a consequence, he enlists the protagonist, a university man, as playwright. Clearly, a new drama is supplanting the old. A reference to moralities in *Sir Thomas More* (c. 1590–93) also looks back to a drama of the last age, telescoping play titles (*The Dialogue of Dives, The Marriage of Wit and Wisdom, Hit Nail o' the Head, Impatient Poverty*) which seem to come from the fifty years that span the mid-century, into a repertory of More's day.[10] The telescoping itself, of course, indicates a felt distance from the plays, which are beginning to look alike. In *Histriomastix* (1599) the effect is even more pronounced. A list of titles probably to be understood as moralities and hybrid moralities (*The Devil and Dives, A Knot of Knaves, Lady Nature, The Lascivious Knight, The Prodigal Child, A Proud Heart and a Beggar's Purse, A Russet Coat and a Knave's Cap, The Widow's Apron Strings*) and purporting to be the repertory of a poor travelling company of the time, is heavily satirized as crude and ridiculously old fashioned, but also as the sort of repertory still used by inferior travelling companies.[11] For Shakespeare's Feste, about the same time, the Vice is "the old Vice," a skipping vaudeville figure of remembered fun. For Jonson a few years later, in the 1607 preface to *Volpone*, Vice and Devil belong to a remote and uncivilized past. He discusses the wish of those men who "desire . . . to see fools and devils, and those antique relics of barbarism retrieved, with all other ridiculous and exploded follies." [12] In 1616 he revives the Vice and the Devil as obvious and amusing archaisms.

The tone of amused contempt in the remarks of Nashe, Greene, and Marston does not, of course, imply the existence of a universally felt, automatic reaction to Vice and Devil merriment. Nashe and Greene were propagandizing for the new drama; Marston was flattering the carriage trade audiences at the newly reopened Paul's, assuring them that they were *not* like certain popular audiences. Even in 1607 Jonson was pointedly addressing the universities, and his remarks acknowledge the existence of an educated opinion which would revive the ridiculous entertainment of the past. Obviously during the nineties there was a significant number of theatergoers who still relished the merriment of their youth or the provinces, and certainly everyone could be expected to recognize allusions to it. Richard III, Prince Hal, Feste, and Hamlet all speak of the Vice quite casually; Shakespeare obviously expected his audiences to respond to the allusions.

The morality was not all the buffoonery of Vice and Devil, however, and more serious morality plays as well as scattered morality scenes in other plays continue, though with diminished frequency, through the nineties. Robert Wilson's *The Three Lords and Three Ladies of London* (c. 1588–90) is a thorough-going morality. His *Cobbler's Prophecy* (1589–93) is a hybrid, mingling characters such as Lust and Contempt with representative social types. Marlowe's *Faustus* uses, besides the devil, the parade of the seven deadly sins, and it projects Faustus's psychomachia as the counsel of good and evil angels. The anonymous *Knack to Know a Knave* of 1592 is in part closely modelled upon the old social morality which exposes corruption, and the standard role of castigator of abuses is given to Old Honesty. *A Knack to Know an Honest Man* of 1594 has a wildly romantic plot in which, however, two of the main characters take the names and corresponding roles of Charity and Penitent Experience. Yarrington's *Two Lamentable Tragedies* (1594) and the anonymous *Warning for Fair Women* (1599) both use elaborate entr'acte morality scenes which comment on the main action. Marston's *Histriomastix* (1599), despite its mockery of interludes like *The Devil and Dives*, is a hybrid morality in which an elaborate allegorical action, involving such characters as Peace, Plenty, Pride, Envy, War, and Poverty present a cyclical theory of history which is exemplified by the "realistic" characters. Dekker's *Old Fortunatus* (1599) is also a hybrid. Fortune, Vice, and Virtue have significant roles, and the trees and fruit of Vice and Virtue figure in a long and conceited metaphorical action. Jonson's *Cynthia's Revels* (1601) is almost a pure morality save that its characters bear Greek instead of Latin or English names. In addition there are the two plays, *The Seven Days of The Week*, I and II, productions of which are noted in Henslowe's diary for 1595 and 1596 [13] and which were probably moralities; several plays such as *2 Henry IV*, *Mucedorus*, and *Poetaster*, in which a personification speaks the prologue; there are the allegorical characters of Summer, Autumn, Winter, and Spring in Nashe's *Summer's Last Will and Testament* (1592); there is the apparent production, noted by Henslowe, of Ulpian Fulwell's morality of the sixties, *Like Will to Like*, by Pembroke's men at the Rose in 1600; most surprising of all, there is the court production in 1601 of *Liberality and Prodigality*, a lively moral interlude in the style of the sixties or seventies. Even in the seventeenth century there were a few moralities, although these were usually written for the academic stage.[14] Jonson's *Staple of News*, a hybrid, was produced by the King's Men as late as 1626.

The list, in any case, is not long. Clearly the morality was not viewed as a get-penny during the nineties, but equally clearly the audiences could be expected to be familiar with it, to recognize allusions to it, and to be sufficiently comfortable with its devices to respond to them.

The morality, however, was by no means the only dramatic, or quasi-dramatic, form that used explicit metaphors, and any discussion of Elizabethan training in the understanding of dramatic metaphors must consider the other forms too. The most obvious of these is the show or pageant, such as the Lord Mayor's, or pageants welcoming royalty. These range widely from almost fully developed drama to static *tableaux*. At one end of the spectrum is the disguising or masking which finally developed into the Jacobean court masque. At the other are the arches of triumph studded with emblems and allegorical figures, sometimes commented upon by a presenter, and these, in turn, shade off into similar allegories and emblems upon the facades of public buildings and thence into printed emblems. Between these extremes there are a mass of devices, allegorical battles, savage men and nymphs greeting royal visitors, debates resolved by the royal presence, mermaids on dolphins' backs and triumphal chariots of Fortune or Time. Not all the shows made use of visible metaphors, but these were common and occasionally, as examples to be cited later demonstrate, were developed with great ingenuity. As might be expected, these shows make increasing use of classical mythology during the sixteenth century, and in the very long run they become increasingly elaborate, culminating in Jonson's court masques and in the highly wrought civic pageants of Munday and Middleton and Dekker.

The somewhat similar little shows which were used as inductions and entr'acte commentary in the last part of the century will also be noticed later. They were usually allegorical, employing personifications and emblematic devices, and often vaguely "classical" in that deities such as Venus, Fortune, Mars, and Discord appeared. Classical myth or legend also provides the basis for the main plot in a number of English and Latin plays from early in the sixteenth century. To judge from the few extant plays, the plot itself was often treated in a straightforward historical way and any personifications were confined, in the fashion of hybrid moralities, to the secondary characters who surround the principals. Such are *Appius and Virginia*, *Damon and Pythias*, and *Horestes*, all of the sixties. But titles or designations like *Beauty and Venus* (an interlude of 1513), *The Story of Orpheus* (possibly a play, possibly a masque of 1547), *Cupid, Venus, and Mars* (probably a comedy, also lost, of 1557), *Narcissus*, *Perseus and Andromeda*, and *Alcmaeon* (of the seventies), all performed at court and all lost, suggest that a tradition of dramatic mythological fantasy, related to the masque and entertainment, may have developed during the early years of the century. Such titles further suggest that, like the masque, and like Lyly's plays (which then form part of the development), its plays were sometimes highly allegorical.[15] Peele's *Arraignment of Paris* employs a conceit in which there is a clear though very pallid metaphor, but Lyly's seven mythological plays employ many metaphors and, as I shall argue later, these greatly extend the dramatic vocabulary available to both audiences and playwrights.

The vocabulary of dramatic metaphors inherited from the moralities, however, was both extensive and flexible; its nature and scope deserve review. It was not, it must be stressed, by any means limited to personification, although personifications provide the readiest means of identifying moralities, and we sometimes talk as if they contained nothing else. Even personifications, furthermore, as the last chapter has suggested, often imply more action and feeling than our common use of the term allows.

To illustrate, while the playwright, to indicate that a man is led by avarice, may use the device of a personified Avarice who leads him (as in *The Castle of Perseverance* or *Enough Is as Good as a Feast*), an alternative device personifies Wealth, whom the man serves, sues for, or courts (as in *The Three Ladies of London, Liberality and Prodigality*, and *Cynthia's Revels*). This latter device involves a more complex action than the former and can be developed in more elaborate detail. Indeed, in *The Staple of News*, where young Penniboy courts Lady Pecunia, it gives Jonson half his plot.

The point is worth making only to emphasize that action is metaphor, and it may be noticed that this is true of all the morality plays, the earliest as well as the latest. The main action of the second half of *The Castle of Perseverance* is the assault on the Castle of Perseverance; in the *Pride of Life* it is the battle between the kings of Life and Death; in *Everyman*, the preparation for the journey of death. Young Penniboy's courtship of Lady Pecunia differs from these in its subject and its elaboration of realistic, topical detail, but its use of action as metaphor is the same.

Besides these large metaphorical actions, moreover, there are a number of smaller, emblematic pieces of business, some of which through repetition become clichés. Thomas Craik has called attention to several of these and discussed their continued use in later plays.[16] The vices put virtue in the stocks, for instance, in *Hickscorner, Youth, The Thrie Estaitis* (and, of course, in *Lear*), and they threaten to in several other plays (the incident is pictured by Flettner and Dürer). Formal entrances, like the triumphal entry of Fortune, are sometimes arranged in emblematic metaphors. In *Old Fortunatus* she enters leading four kings. In *Liberality and Prodigality* she enters in a chariot drawn by kings, very much as in the illustrations of Petrarch's *Triumphi*, and the scene is probably echoed by the entrance of Tamburlaine, who has usurped the place of Fortune. The entrances of the vices are also sometimes staged as metaphors, as in *King John*, where Dissimulation pointedly brings in Private Wealth, who in turn brings in Usurped Power, and all three rascals then regroup to bear in Sedition on their shoulders. In *All For Money* Money gives birth on the stage to Pleasure, who gives birth to Sin, who in turn gives birth to Damnation. In the *Trial of Treasure*, Just, as noted above, wrestles with Lust, and Inclination is literally bridled and shackled. The exile of a virtue or vice and the execution, or attempted execution, of a vice are common. Greediness dies in *The Tide Tarrieth No Man*, but the symbolism is countered by the Vice's happy cynicism:

> Why fool, Greediness will never die,
> So long as covetous people do live.[17]

In *The Three Ladies of London*, Usury kills Hospitality, Lucre offers Sincerity the parsonage of St. Nihil, and Sir Nicholas Nemo fades off the stage while inviting Sincerity to dinner. This sort of manneristic trickiness reaches its peak in Wilson's *Three Lords and Three Ladies of London* (c. 1589) and in *Nobody and Somebody* (c. 1605). The former is a light-hearted tour-de-force of such conceits as preciosity keeps in play: Lord Desire, who comes a-courting Lady Lucre, is awarded the cold comfort of a stone labelled *Care* (care accompanies avarice); Lord Devotion, courting Lady Conscience, is awarded *Remorse* (devotion to conscience is sorrow for sin, i.e., remorse). *Nobody and Somebody* builds a main plot on the double pun of making the wicked Somebody (who waddles on stage all body and no legs) responsible for the realm's corruption while the innocent Nobody (all legs and arms, no body) bears the blame. The quarrel of the Vices, as a standard scene which often begins a morality, is responsible for a good deal of the liveliest action, vulgar, vigorous, and amusing. As meaning, it is the psychological and social discord inevitable when law and reason fail to rule. In the words of Erasmus,

"The affections or appetites of the body strive to go before reason, and reason is in a manner compelled to incline and follow the judgment of the body. Thou mayst compare therefore a man properly to a commonalty, where is debate and part taking among themselves. Which commonalty for as much as it is made of sundry kinds of men gathered together, which be of diverse and contrary appetites; it cannot be avoided but that much strife shall arise therein, and parts taken often times, unless the chief rule and authority be in one." [18]

This is the dual strife, outer and inner, denoted by Jonson's metaphors of dance and "contentious musique" in the first part of *Hymenaei* and more directly by the beatings and fisticuffs, arguments and jeering matches of unruly passions and vices with each other in a long list of plays extending into the seventeenth century. Commonly the quarrel takes place when the vices are greeting each other during the exposition. Sometimes it springs from a casual, good-humored insult taken the wrong way, as when Imagination in *Hickscorner* objects—astonishingly—to Free-will's hint that his mother was a whore. Sometimes it is a contention for precedence or authority or the largest share of the loot, as in *Respublica, The Tide Tarrieth No Man,* and *Enough is as Good as a Feast.*

Occasionally it arises as a metaphor of the nature of one of the vices. Backbiter causes dissension in *The Castle of Perseverance,* Envy in *Nature;* Wrath almost does in *The Longer thou Livest.* The subject and the outcome of the quarrel are also occasionally metaphorical, like the argument between Idleness and Incontinence in *The Longer thou Livest* about the former's claim to be the parent of all vice, or the frequent emergence of Avarice as boss of the other vices, or the victory of Courage (unrestrained appetite) over three other vices in *The Tide Tarrieth,* which he predicts and explains in the lines,

> What can three do against one,
> I having courage, and they having none.[19]

Always after the fight the vices make peace and agree to cooperate in their ruinous enterprise, for therein lies the main plot. Rarely (only in *Liberality and Prodigality,* I think, and the two late University plays, *Lingua* and *Pathomachia*) does their dissension provide the main plot.

Frequently, however, the fragility of their truce is implied by a continued exchange of taunts and threats; in a few plays (*The Castle of Perseverance, Nature, Magnificence, Good Order,*

Respublica, Wealth and Health) they betray or seek to betray each other; and always the half-vice, half-worldly man, like Lust in *The Trial of Treasure* is betrayed to his ruin by another, guiding vice.

The immediate theatrical picture created by the gathering rogues is of casual insolence and threatening foolery; we see dangerous men joking with tough humor and leaping to the rough and tumble fight: "Cock's precious soul, let us conquer the knave." [20] But this, the metaphor insists, is the turbulent meeting of lust, sturdiness, and inclination in the soul, or the treacherous combination of avarice, oppression, insolence, and adulation that ruined Respublica. In *Respublica*, it is Avarice who stills the quarrel with the whip of his sneer and is leader of this gang; the scene as a whole is the speech of Shakespeare's Ulysses made visible: everything includes itself in appetite.

Transposed into topical realism the traditional quarrel scene is the brawl between Face and Subtle that opens *The Alchemist*, Dol interfering finally to subdue the combatants by force. The tenor of the metaphor here, as in *Magnificence, Wealth and Health*, and *Respublica*, is political. Dol Common, as she tells the others, is "your republique" in which all things—with a glance at the common jest about Plato's women guardians—are "in common," and her state is threatened with ruin by their "ciuill warre." Face is "Generall," Subtle "soueraigne," and Dol forces him to swear "to leave your faction . . . and labor, kindly, in the common work." [21] For the trained audience the quarrel includes not only the three rogues in a house in Black-friars but the larger forces of political dissension, united in appetite with the body politic, Respublica, a common whore.

A more general theatrical symbol is the change of costume to signify either a moral disguise or a change of status or aim. Both conventions arrive early and stay late. Disguise itself, indeed, antedates the morality play, in the very early disguise of Christ as the gardener, meeting Mary Magdelene, for instance, or, probably, in the appearance of the hypocrites ("sub silentio et specie humilitatis inclinantes"), in the Tegernsee *Antichristus*. Even characterizing costumes, like those of Mundus and Avarice (dressed as a king and his treasurer) in *The Castle of Perseverance*, though they identify and characterize the characters, also disguise their real nature from intended victims, here from the stupid Mankind, who is deceived by their show of good. But the business of actually shifting into a moral disguise occurs first in the English drama in *Wisdom*, where Lucifer changes to a goodly gallant in order to seduce, without frightening, his victims. The metaphor was implied verbally, though perhaps not realized by costume changes, in Skelton's *Magnificence*, where all the vices assumed the names of virtues. Bale, in *The Temptation of Our Lord*, has Satan disguise himself as a hermit, and the author of *Respublica* specifies elaborate onstage comic business as his vices don disguising costumes and, at the end, are stripped of them. This becomes a common Elizabethan convention, used with variations by Lewis Wager in *Mary Magdalene*, by W. Wager in *Enough is as Good as a Feast*, by Wilson in *The Three Ladies of London* and *The Three Lords and Three Ladies of London*, and by Jonson in *Cynthia's Revels*.

Change of clothing as a metaphor of a moral or material change probably first enters the theater in the scene showing Adam and Eve's expulsion from the garden. In the Chester *Creation*, for instance, God gives the common gloss on His action in clothing the guilty pair with dead beasts' skins:

> For deadlie bothe now bene yee,
> and death no way may you flee;
>
> (365–68)

and in the Norwich grocers' pageant the Holy Ghost dresses them in the Pauline armor of righteousness. In *Wisdom* both Anima and her three powers change costumes when they are corrupted and again when they are redeemed. In *Mankind* the hero's gown is cut down to a frivolous jacket by the vices. Everyman dons the garment of contrition. The convention continues, through *Nature*, *Hickscorner*, *Youth*, *Impatient Poverty*, and the late Henrican fragment *The Four Cardinal Virtues*, as far

67

as the morality itself. It gathers additional meanings, however, and becomes more complicated in presentation. Magnificence, in Skelton's play, undergoes economic as well as spiritual vicissitudes. He is given rags by Poverty and later, after he repents, a new "abylyment" that implies both his moral reform and return to solvency. The same sort of double meaning is conveyed by the new robe of Respublica near the end of Udall's play after the reform of her realm has begun, and by Poverty-Prosperity's costume changes in *Impatient Poverty*. The new coat of the hitherto threadbare People in *Respublica* seems, as Craik points out, to symbolize a purely material improvement, and the simple decline into poverty is marked by the beggarly costumes put on by the rogues in *Like Will to Like* and the prodigal in *The Disobedient Child*. The appearance of the wanton Dalila, reduced to beggary and disease in *The Nice Wanton* seems, on a literal reading, to signify a similar unequivocal material disaster, but the insistence on her sin (led to whoredom, gambling, and cheating by Iniquity) is so powerful that her appearance serves inevitably as an emblem of the moral condition that she confesses:

> The worm of my conscience, that shall never die,
> Accuseth me daily more and more:
> So oft have I sinned wilfully,
> That I fear to be damned evermore.[22]

The change of clothes, to a fool's coat, marks young Wit's decline into folly in both Redford's *Wit and Science* and the later anonymous adaptation, *The Marriage of Wit and Science*. In Wager's *The Longer Thou Livest the More Fool Thou Art* it marks both the end of the little brief authority that Moros has been dressed in and his recognition of his lifelong folly. Finally, it is the symbolism of gorgeous clothes, the furred robes of avarice and the gay clothes of pride and prodigality, that commonly signal man's corruption by these qualities, from Pride's command to Mankind in *The Castle of Perseverance*, "Jagge thi Clothis in euery cost," to the scene of young Penniboy and his clothiers that opens *The Staple of News*.

There are various other standard pieces of business, like the scene in which the young man is lulled to sleep in the lap of the wanton lady. Variations on this occur at least nine times in the sixteenth century, in the hybrid morality *Old Fortunatus*, in *A Midsummer Night's Dream* and *1 Henry IV*, and in six moralities: Redford's *Wit and Science*, the anonymous *Marriage of Wit and Science* (1569), Merbury's *A Marriage between Wit and Wisdom* (1579), the lost *Cradle of Security* (c. 1570), the lost *Play of Plays and Pastimes* (c. 1582), and Robert Wilson's *The Cobbler's Prophecy* (1594). The lady tries to carry out the action in Greene's *Looking Glass for London and England*, but the man stands her off. Allusions to it are common in the drama, and of course it is a celebrated subject in both painting and non-dramatic poetry. In *The Play of Plays and Pastimes*, the lady was apparently named Honest Recreation, and the young man rose refreshed from her lap. In the other five it carries the meaning, besides the obvious one of the young man's surrender to lust, of his moral blindness and his folly. To these meanings Dekker's play adds the meaning of pride, and three of the plays emphasize idleness.

To glance ahead, one may speculate briefly upon the effect which the memory of the standard scene would have on an Elizabethan spectator's understanding of the two similar scenes in Shakespeare. In Bottom's slumber in Titania's lap, it seems to me, the effect would be negligible, perhaps a slight reinforcement of the already obvious folly of Titania's love in idleness. The scene is not really a seduction scene of the traditional sort, and the ass's head has already been put on Bottom. But the standard scene remembered adds moral commentary to the charming scene in which young Mortimer surrenders to his wife's entreaties. It diagnoses his weakness not, or not simply, as Glendower does ("You are as slow/As Hot Lord Percy is on fire to go"), but as a moral blindness caused by his infatuation. For spectators alive to the larger moral issues of the rebellion, furthermore, Mortimer's surrender to the flesh is counterpart to Hotspur's vaulting ambition for worldly honor and Glendower's constant association with the devil. They are, after all, even now dividing the kingdom among them and laying plans for the furious close of civil butchery. The great hope expressed by Henry IV in the opening scene of the play for mutual well-beseeming ranks marching all one way, toward Jerusalem, has been betrayed, in part, as the play is usually played, by Henry himself, but also, obviously, by the rebels. This brief, delightful emblematic scene explains Mortimer's betrayal of this hope; though both his personality and motivation are sketched in with great sympathy, he is shown as seduced by his passion and blinded to the overriding moral issue of the peace and unity of the realm.

It may be noticed that behind most of these standard metaphors stands the ubiquitous concept of moral deception. This is the commonest of all motifs in the morality plays and it appears in countless forms: the disguises, the false names, the sophistical arguments of Avarice and Pride, the glitter of false women (Lady Treasure, Luxuria, Fortune), the concealing cloaks, double visors, betrayals, maskings, and characters whose names themselves imply it (Perjury, Counterfeit Countenance, Dissimulation, Feigned Love, Ignorance, Folly, Fancy, Fraud, Ambidexter, Perverse Doctrine, Mendacio, and their opposites, Verity, Truth, True Report, and Old Honesty). The morality play is preeminently the drama of deception, focusing on both deceiver and deceived. Erasmus's remark about the deceiving nature of the Sileni, quoted above to characterize the educative effect of the radically disjunctive metaphor, may be cited with even sharper relevance to describe the experience of the characters within the plays. They live in a world where the contrast between appearance and reality is not only the common rule but the premise of the action. Like the audience, they too move toward enlightenment, the anagnorisis: "enter Lady Verity." Old Honesty steps forward; young Wit sees himself in the mirror of Reason; Lady Love is confounded by the witness of Conscience; the unmasked wantons at the court of Cynthia perceive their follies. When the recognition comes too late, of course, the end is tragedy, and it is specifically the tragedy of human blindness. When Worldly Man, in *Enough is as Good as a Feast*, dies unrepentant and damned, he is attended by his chaplain Ignorance.

We therefore do wrong, I think, to see even such a Vice as Ambidexter in *Cambises* as a purely theatrical vestige, without ideological function. *Cambises*, it is true, is in many ways a ridiculous play and it is radically dishonest, exploiting the crudest sensationalism throughout and smirking virtuously at the end. Furthermore, Ambidexter himself is only inconsistently shown as influencing the decisions of the tyrant whom he claims to be tricking. His name, as Bernard Spivack has noted, is not a moral designation like Pride, Envy, or Avarice. But he is sufficiently characterized by his name and actions, teaching deception and deceiving several other people besides Cambises, to allow us, or the audiences of 1560, to understand his nature. He is the similitude of deceit or deceitful flattery, and the thematic unity which he provides is the tragic—and farcically comic—consequence of delusion. Tyranny is the result of being deceived, just as Plato said; so are the comic squabbles of rustics. The psychology of this point is not explored, but the assertion is vigorous and lively, and the metaphor of deceit is amusing: a low comic rogue, rather winning in his clever knavery, by turns a whisperer at court, a *miles gloriosus*, and an arrogant, bribe-taking informer. He is one of a long line of similar rogues of whom Autolycus is only the most charming and most famous. In the metaphor of this play he is what Deceit is like.

Finally, it should be noticed that in the morality plays deception leads to a mistaking of wrong for right. It is moral error, not the mere mistaking of identities, a long lost son for a stranger, familiar from Roman and Italian comedy. The Roman device often has moral implications of course, and it can, as I shall argue later, be fashioned to a moral metaphor, but it is not explicitly moral. The English deceptions are. The deceived may remain the pattern of suffering virtue, like Udall's Respublica, or—apparently—the Conscience of *Impatient Poverty*; more often the metaphor includes the deceived as morally erring; in any case the mistake itself is of bad for good: Avarice for Policy and Envy for Charity.

71

This is true, I think, even for the Wit and Science plays, in which the tenor of the metaphor may seem purely psychological, a morally neutral analysis of the operation of Wit, Study, Will, Idleness, Tediousness, and the like. The characters and actions of the vehicle, however, are strongly though humorously, colored as morally good or bad. Idleness is a deceiving drab or a rogue; Tediousness is a cave-dwelling monster, and so on; the metaphors as they are staged leave no doubt about the moral coloring of the tenor.

So much, by way of survey, for the kind of metaphor used by the traditional morality. Besides these, however, there were the clever conceits, often based on classical mythology, formally distinguished from realistic action, and highly elaborated in the Renaissance manner, which became fashionable in the latter part of the century and which provided a distinctive feature of the very late moralities, such as *Cynthia's Revels*, noticed above. These metaphors are not, it is true, completely novel in their kind. "Formal" is a relative term here, and certainly the debate of the four daughters of God as it appears in, say, the *Ludus Coventriae* is quite as formal an allegory as anything in these later moralities. Yet the novelty of the late Renaissance formality is obvious, and one can clearly distinguish between say, an allegorical dumbshow or an emblematic set-piece of bickering goddesses and the more naturalistic and more integrated metaphors which run through *The Three Ladies of London* or which result when one sees Falstaff as Riot or Iago as Othello's vice.

The avant-guard *Gorboduc*, produced at the Inner Temple and at Court in 1561–62, marks the new departure. Each of the five acts is preceded by a dumb show which summarizes the following action and its generalized significance. The first is representative:

"First the music of violins began to play, during which came in upon the stage six wild men clothed in leaves; of whom the first bare in his neck a fagot of small sticks, which they all, both severally and together, assayed with all their strengths to break; but it could not be broken by them. At the length, one of them plucked out one of the sticks and brake it; and the rest plucking out all the other sticks one after another did easily break them, the same being severed, which, being conjoined, they had before attempted in vain. After they had this done, they departed the stage, and the music ceased. Hereby was signified that a state knit in unity doth continue strong against all force, but being divided is easily destroyed; as befell upon Duke Gorboduc dividing his land to his two sons." [23]

This is allegory of a fashion new at least to the drama. Possibly influenced by the Italian *intermedii*, it also shows relationships to the tableaux of civic pageants and royal entries, princely entertainments, and emblem books. Its display of, and appeal to, pride in classical learning is obvious, but still more striking is its teasing, slightly enigmatic quality. Presumably the audience would recognize the point of the fable easily enough, but it is left waiting to apply it to the play that follows. This quality is even more emphatic in the second dumb show, which presents a king who, after rejecting drink from a glass, drinks from a golden goblet and falls dead. The printed page explains that "as glass by nature holdeth no poison, but is clear and may easily be seen through, ne boweth by any art, so a faithful counsellor holdeth no treason . . . but giveth wholesome counsel, which the ill-advised prince refuseth." [24] The "delightful gold filled with poison," on the other hand, betokens flattery. The point is exemplified throughout the play.

Elaborate such allegories and they become *précieux*, a danger that playwrights and pageant writers faced courageously. Again, the danger is not entirely new. One recalls that in *The Castle of Perseverance* Charity and Patience bombarded their foes with roses, and Chastity drenched Lechery. But such conceits are only the starting point of the similar allegorical siege, called *The Fortress of Perfect Beauty*, presented before the Queen and the French ambassadors in 1581. It consisted of a two day attack by the four Foster Children of Desire (who included Sidney and Greville) on the Fortress of Perfect Beauty, the gallery at the end of the tilt-yard where the Queen sat. The conceits included roses as ammunition of course, also sweet water and sweet powder shot from guns, and music for the sound of guns. The speeches were part Euphuism, part Arcadian, part unclassified Renaissance Ornate. On the first day the besiegers entered in a rolling trench of canvas, "the mount," mounted on wheels and painted to look like earth. The speech of their herald indicates the nature of the conceits (marginal notes are bracketed):

"View with what unresistable determination themselves approach, and how not only the heavens send their invisible instrument to aid them [Meaning the music within the mount.]: but also the very earth, the dullest of all the elements, which with natural heaviness still strives to the sleepy center: yet for advancing his enterprise, is content actively [as you shall see] to move itself upon itself, to rise up in height, that it may the better command the high and high minded fortress [Wherewith the Mount moved and rose up in height]." 25

It is an astonishing achievement, precisely translating the Sidneian figures into theater.

Much the same kind of effect, with a smaller financial outlay, is often Lyly's aim. In *Gallathea*, for instance, Diana captures Cupid and sets him to untying love knots, a pretty conceit in itself, but only the foundation for the verbal conceits that follow as Cupid explains each knot in turn. Of the first, for instance, which remains tied, he explains, "it is the true love knot of a woman's heart, therefore cannot be undone." Of the next, which falls apart: "It was made of a man's thought, which will never hang together," and of two others which untie easily: "It was because I never tied them; the one was knit by Pluto, not Cupid, by money, not love; the other by force, not faith, by appointment, not affection." 26 And so on. This sort of thing is easily surpassed, however, by some of the conceits in Wilson's *Three Lords and Three Ladies of London*, already glanced at, and in his *The Cobbler's Prophecy* (published 1594). The latter stages the traditional business of the swain beguiled upon his leman's lap, but the old scene is new-painted with mythology, spectacle, and ingenuity. The swain is Mars, the lady Venus. She sings, and her attendants provide dancing and instrumental music. Later her child, begotten by Contempt, is displayed by her handmaidens, Ru and Ina. The child is named *Ruine*.

Such things call attention to themselves, asking to be admired because they are spectacular or witty. They would seem to have had particular appeal to the taste of the Court, the Inns of Court, and the private theater audiences, and their full development depended on the purse strings of the Revels office. Even plays produced in the public theaters may have had special shows of this sort written in for court productions. It is Fredson Bowers's reasonable speculation that Dekker wrote some of the elaborate shows in *Old Fortunatus* specially for the court production, since Henslowe records a payment to him "for the eande of Fortewnatus for the corte," and other plays may have had similar adornments.[27]

But the difference between private and public theater plays or even public theater productions in this matter should not be exaggerated, especially in discussing plays before the Blackfriar's re-opening of 1599. Plays for the public theater repertory were thought fit fare for the Court and Inns of Court, and some members, at least, of the audiences of the early private theaters attended the public theaters. From *Cambises* on, there is a discernible though intermittent stream of emblematic set pieces in plays which seem clearly from the public repertory. Certainly such figures as Venus, Cupid, Mars, Fortune, and Vulcan, as well as ingeniously conceited dumbshows were, if not the daily fare of the public theater, a familiar spice. Furthermore it would be difficult to show that this sort of thing on the public stage involved a less recherché mythological allegorizing than any but the more extreme examples of Lyly or Jonson.

III.

Semantic Complexity: Macrocosm and Microcosm.

The preceding chapters have so heavily stressed the dramatic use of metaphors, especially far-fetched metaphors, that a caution may be wise at this point. It should be clear in the first place that although a considerable disparity between vehicle and tenor was allowed, it was not enforced. Tenor and vehicle were not always at odds; they often coalesced in both earlier and later drama. Mercy in *Mankind* is merciful as well as stern and irascible. Idleness, in *The Marriage of Wit and Wisdom* is Wit's temptation as well as a clever fool in his own right. Dekker's Fortune is capricious; Jonson's Philautia is full of self-love, metaphor becomes example.

In the second place, although for obvious reasons metaphor requires a great deal of discussion, exemplification was an extremely important, perhaps the most important, means of conveying meaning, especially in the latter half of the century. The distinction between the two methods is not sharp, but it can often be made. It is obvious, for instance, that the main plot of *Cambises* relies chiefly upon exemplification to show the course of tyranny and, as the discussion below makes clear, Wapull's *The Tide Tarrieth No Man* exemplifies commercial chicanery, though both plays also reach beyond these surface meanings with the help of metaphor.

It is the extension of meaning to different levels that makes the metaphors important. They comprise a rich and extensive vocabulary which almost forced the dramatist, however simple or shallow his aim, into polysemantic depth and complexity. Not always happily or very far, but farther and deeper than any other third-rate English dramatists (one thinks of Mrs. Behn, Boucicault or Coward) have ever ventured or been pushed.

This is evident in many ways, but perhaps most easily so in the dramatic use of the common analogies between the social macrocosm and the moral-psychological microcosm. Between these the individual—his actions and personality developed with greater or less relevance—stands mediate, simultaneously or in alternation a metaphor of concepts on both levels. Falstaff stands as Falstaff—"unimitated, unimitable Falstaff, how shall I describe thee?" But at the same time he is, as Dover Wilson and M. M. Reese have made clear, that reverend Vice, that grey Iniquity; and that vice, in turn, is both inner and outer, both the Prince's temptation and Riot in the commonwealth.[1]

Taken seriously the dramatic device assumes as premise that the analogies are real, that man's moral-psychological conflicts and harmonies are writ large in the social unit—the family, court, or kingdom—indeed, in a Providential order. If this premise is accepted, the device is potentially a very powerful means of exposing, behind and beyond the common disguises of appearance, personality, and local circumstance, the ultimate significance of human action in the social and moral order that gives it meaning.

These analogies are familiar in expository prose, in non-dramatic poetry, and in highly developed, theatrically sophisticated form, in such plays as *Lear*, where the correspondences of disorder in the heavens, the kingdom, the family, and Lear's own mind, have often been noticed. But their theatrical use is not a development of the late Elizabethan drama nor the mark of a single dramatist. It is a convention, part of the working syntax of the stage, learned as such by audiences, used in a fairly simple way by early Tudor dramatists and only elaborated into sophisticated Shakespearian patterns late in the century.

In their simplest, proto-dramatic form they may be seen in the pageantry surrounding royal entries and coronations. Here the visual symbolism is based upon the theory that the monarch, as man, rules himself as he rules his kingdom. The dual function of the pageantry to flatter the monarch and, with something like sympathetic magic, to engender success through mimesis, implies that both man and commonwealth will be well run. Thus, greeting Henry VI in 1432, a pageant at the conduit presented the throne of Justice on which sat a king surrounded by Truth, Mercy, and Clemency, with two judges and eight lawyers. Most obviously it is a hopeful prophecy of the happy kingdom under Henry, but it is simultaneously a flattering picture of the young king facing it, moved by his own love of truth, mercy, and clemency, and counselled and aided by his magistrates and lawyers.

The corresponding pageant which greeted Elizabeth at the Cornhill in 1559 is similarly ambiguous. It showed "The Seat of Worthy Governance." A child queen appeared on a throne supported by personifications of Pure Religion, Love of Subjects, Wisdom, and Justice, each treading on opposing vices. Latin verses displayed on a table and English verses spoken by a presenter make clear that the virtues belong to the subjects:

> While that religion true shall ignorance suppresse,
> And with her weightie foote, breake superstitions head,
> Whyle love of subjects, shall Rebellion distresse,
> And with zeale to the Prince, insolency downe treade . . .
> So long shall government not swarve from hir right race. . . .[2]

Yet the anonymous chronicler quoted by Holinshed stresses the equally obvious interpretation in which the virtues are the queen's:

"The ground of this Pageante was, that lyke as by vertues (which doe aboundantly appeare in her grace) the Queens Majestie was established in the seate of governement: so shoulde shee sitte fast in the same, so long as shee embrased Vertue, and helde vice under foot." [3]

Even this commentary, however, may be interpreted in still a third way, as a warning that the queen should further virtue in her subjects and magistrates. Indeed, that seems to be the interpretation which the queen herself placed on the pageant, for when she had heard the presenter she "most graciously promised hir good endeavour for the maintenance of the saide vertues, and suppression of vices." [4]

One of Dekker's arches erected for James's coronation emphasizes a similar ambiguity. Astraea sits aloft; below her are Fortune, a turning globe filled with all estates of the land, personifications of the four cardinal virtues; and Zeal of Subjects, the presenter. The whole pictures the happy land under James's rule. Yet the presenter's verses (written by Middleton) make clear to James that "These foure maine virtues [are] figurde all in you" and that Astraea is "lockt . . . in your rightfull brest." [5]

Examples of this sort suggest the casual, taken-for-granted nature of the double reference for such symbolic *visibilia*. Since man is a microcosm of the state, the sculptured vice or virtue points indeterminately to the quality within and its political counterpart. Most often in the royal pageant the virtue is specifically the monarch's, his clemency, his wisdom, and the realm's, for it is he who is preeminently a microcosm of the happy land which he so wisely, so mercifully and so justly rules.

The power of the analogy to relate layers of meaning is clearly illustrated by the Jacobean court masque. The masque uses the same formal symbolism as the welcoming pageants, but the tableaux break into action that allows greater complexity to both symbol and meaning. Jonson's *Hymenaei* illustrates the power well; it also suggests the limits of the form as a medium of communication, since his notes reveal complaints about the obscurity of his allegory.

The action is simple; Hymen leads a bride and bridegroom to sacrifice at the anagramatic altar of Iuno-Unio; the ceremonies are interrupted by a sort of antimasque of the four humours and four affections, but Reason reduces them to order, and clouds open to reveal Juno aloft and Jupiter, still higher, ruling the universe. The now obedient humours and affections join in a masque with the eight powers of Juno; an epithalamium (cut short in performance), prays for the perfection of the marriage in children.

Even a summary makes evident that the action is a metaphor of fruitful marriage and the control of passion by reason, meanings linked and paralleled by the fact that marriage is a rational director of the passions to the end of fruitfulness. Less evident from the summary, but clear enough to the spectators, is the theme of social and political order, the rationally ordered harmony and union of men within the state. The link of this theme to the others is presented verbally in the speeches of Reason and Hymen, and it is presented visually by the machine of a "Microcosm, or Globe (figuring Man)" out of which the humours and affections issued. It was this symbol that gave trouble to some of the spectators. Jonson explains it in a footnote:

"First, as in *naturall bodies*, so likewise in *minds*, there is no disease, or distemperature, but is caused either by some abounding *humor*, or perverse *affection;* after the same manner, in *politick bodies* (where *Order, Ceremony, State, Reverence, Devotion,* are parts of the *Mind*) by the difference, or praedominant will of what we (*metaphorically*) call *Humors* and *Affections*, all things are troubled and confused." [6]

Simultaneously, then, the action shows the establishment of rational order within the mind, between man and woman, and in the state.

Beyond these meanings, reinforced by the presence of the King and the political context of January 1606, and made sufficiently clear to the spectators by the speeches of Hymen and Reason, is the marriage union of Scotland and England under the newly proclaimed King of Great Britain.

And beyond this is the universal marriage union in love, which binds

> The fighting *seedes* of things,
>   Wins *natures, sexes, minds,*
> And ev'rie discord in true musique brings.
>
> (100–102)

It is harmonious union which is ordered by God, symbolized here by the revealed Jupiter above the sphere of fire, by His deputy Reason, "seated in the top of the globe (as in the brain, or highest part of Man)" and by His earthly counterpart and deputy, more literally presiding over the ceremonies, and keenly conscious of his role in the divine analogy.

The universal harmony is also symbolized by the music and the dancing. Thus the Humours and Affections dancing with the Powers of Juno form symbolic letters and end "in manner of a chain, linking hands." Reason comments

> Such was the *Golden Chaine* let down from *Heaven;*
>   And not those linkes more even,
> Then these: so sweetly temper'd, so combin'd
>   By UNION, and refin'd.
> Here no *contention, envy, griefe,* deceit,
>   Feare, jealousie have weight;
> But all is *peace,* and *love,* and *faith,* and blisse:
>   What *harmony* like this?
>
> (320–27)

For his readers, Jonson identifies the golden chain as Homer's, and he adds that he himself is "specially affected in my allusion" to the interpretation of Macrobius:

"Since mind emanates from the highest God, and soul from mind, and since soul both forms and fills with life all that follows, and since one glory illuminates all things and is seen in all (as one face is seen in many mirrors placed in a row)—since all things follow each other in continuous succession, leading down step by step to the lowest depths, it will be found by careful considera-

81

tion that from the highest God to the very dregs of things there is one bond binding every link without a break." [7]

It is easy to cavil at the symbolism. Granted that the dance and the music serve well to symbolize harmonious order or even harmonious order controlled by reason, this specific chain, of the personified Humours, Affections, and Powers of Juno, is not the great chain of being which declines by ordered degrees from the highest God to the depths. This meaning is not realized theatrically; one must work it out, puzzle fashion, or turn to Jonson's note. More generally, D. J. Gordon remarks that the masque as a whole fails

". . . in the relationship it states between the classical forms and the political event, between past and present. The effect of failure is produced by the very cleverness with which Jonson has worked out the relationship. He did it . . . through the figure of Juno, whose name could be read, anagrammatically, as Unio. This was very clever. Too clever indeed, for his Juno is a cryptogram and never a potent symbol. The relationship between Juno and her rites and the king's Union is an intricate riddle—no more than this." [8]

So too one may remark of the spectacular effect when Reason appears to quell the discordant masquers: "the lights were so placed, as no one was seen; but seemed, as if only Reason, with the splendor of her crown, illumined the whole Grot." We may translate: by the light of Reason, society is instructed and the passions are ordered. We may even recall from Macrobius, "one glory illuminates all things and is seen in all." But the bridge between spendor of sight and idea is again ingenious, enigmatic, a puzzle for the intellect.

And there lies its justification, again, within that aesthetic which prizes the *gymnastique intellectuelle* and which assumes, or allows, a radical disparity between tenor and vehicle. Within that aesthetic the achievement is impressive. And it was fair to see, if we can believe Jonson:

"Such was the exquisit performance, as (beside the *pompe*, *splendor*, or what we may call apparelling of such Presentments)

that alone (had all else beene absent) was of power to surprize with delight, and steale away the *spectators* from themselves. Nor was there wanting whatsoever might give to the *furniture,* or *complement;* eyther in *riches,* or strangenesse of the habites, delicacie of daunces, magnificence of the *scene* or divine rapture of *musique.*" (568–76)

The beauty, of course, is directly relevant to the theme of harmonious union in a way familiar to later critical theory, but the fragile symbolism, the visual conceits, the anagram, the figured dancing, and the music, now contentious, now harmonious, work together to make a statement of a quite complex sort. They present a kind of riddle which is analogous to the riddle of the universe itself, but they also offer the clues to its solution, showing how, through a rationally directed love, the parts are related to each other and to the whole—"as one face is seen in many mirrors placed in a row."

So conscious and delicately adjusted a harmony of metaphoric meanings is of course rare in the legitimate drama, which has to reckon with greater complexities of character and with realism in action. The purpose of introducing the social macrocosm into legitimate drama, furthermore, was usually satiric, to expose abuses. Hence, although its concepts were similar and were blended in much the same way, the total effect is different.

The social theme, aside from occasional allusions in Corpus Christi plays, was apparently first introduced into English drama in *Mind, Will, and Understanding,* a morality of the late fifteenth century. This is a three-part play showing the soul in innocence, corruption and regeneration. Quite unexpectedly, however, after the first part has established Anima with her three "powers" (of Mind, Will and Understanding) as the collective protagonist, the second part introduces the corrupted powers not merely as psychic entities (corrupted to Pride, Lechery, and Perjury respectively) but also as corrupt social institutions: Maintenance, Gallantry and the Holburn Quest. The transformation is vivid. Each enters and leads a dance, the first of liveried halberdiers, the second of gallants and their doxies, the third of jurors wearing

83

doublefaced vizors. In the third part, when the soul is cured, the social theme is dropped; Mind, Will and Understanding appear in their original dress and nature.

In later plays the social theme is usually kept in view throughout the entire action, but the three part pattern of innocence, corruption and restoration remains much the same. Indeed, with minor variations it provides the basic plot structure for most dramatic satire throughout the next century and well into Jacobean times. Thus in Skelton's *Magnificence* (c. 1516) the first part introduces Magnificence, his counsellors and the rogues— Fancy, Folly, Counterfeit Countenance, Courtly Abusion, Cloked Collusion and Crafty Conveyence—who will bring him down. In the second the rogues reduce him to poverty and desperation; in a very short third part he is saved and set upon the way to recovery. The meanings oscillate across at least three bands. Visible upon the stage is the naive prince and his treacherous advisors who are engaged in a slightly caricatured back-stairs palace conspiracy. But the personifications and their action analyze the difficulties of Magnificence both in psychological terms (such as Fancy, Folly, and Liberty) and in social terms (such as Cloked Collusion and Courtly Abusion). Magnificence himself is not only a prince, but also fortitude, greatness of state, or probably, for some spectators, the state itself.[9] The brilliant Marean satire *Respublica* (c. 1553) possibly by Udall, and the less distinguished *Wealth and Health* of the same period (slightly revised to serve anti-Marean ends in the extant edition) also use the same basic plot structure. In *Wealth and Health* the corrupting rogues are Ill Will and Shrewd Wit, and they are both corrupting forces in the soul and charlatans who beggar the Health, Wealth, and Liberty of the country. The visible stage action of *Respublica* is bitter comedy; a set of clever, fast-talking rogues led by Avarice disguised as Policy deceive the well-intentioned great lady Respublica, take over her affairs, plunder the country, and reduce People (an honest old countryman) to ruin; they are finally unmasked by Lady Verity, who arrives with her sisters Peace, Justice and Mercy, and are judged by the goddess Nemesis. Much of the

84

play's effectiveness comes from the comic tension between the cynical, cheerful brutality of the rogues and the piously bland respectability they assume when Respublica is on stage. Their gowns, which hide the symbols of their identity (e.g. Avarice's money bags) constantly threaten to pop open; the blunders of Adulation, who stupidly names his companions correctly, must be covered up; they switch with dazzling virtuosity from open gloating to unctuous hypocrisy, and they pounce ferociously upon abject People when Respublica exits. The metaphors, however, point beyond this kind of gangster comedy, probably to specific counsellors of Edward VI, but also to the drives like Avarice and the political disorders like Insolence (masked as Reformation) that were ruining the land. In addition the metaphors of the denouement, in which the four daughters of God rescue the country, place these disasters of the social macrocosm within the still larger framework of the eternal Providential plan. The oddly sorted figure of the goddess Nemesis is explained by the prologue as represented by Queen Mary.

W. Wager's *The Longer Thou Livest the More Fool Thou Art*, a more complex and more tightly knit play of the next decade, uses a tragic variant of the same plot line. The protagonist, Moros, is a fool brought up wickedly and is already on the road to corruption when the play opens. He also rejects the chance to reform at the end, and he is carried off to Hell.

The action falls easily into four movements. In the first the three virtue characters, Exercitation, Discipline, and Piety lecture the insolent young Moros, who twists their words into comic nonsense but finally promises to stay with Piety. In the second movement the vices gather, just as in *Magnificence* or *Respublica*, and plot his ruin. Moros enters and joins them in a scene of fine comic foolishness, ending as he struts about with the sword and dagger Wrath has given him. Discipline enters to call his bluff, and the trembling fool is finally led off by the laughing vices. In the third movement Fortune exalts him in honor and riches, and the Vices, in new disguises, again plot his fall. Moros joins them in another scene of comic foolishness and orders them off stage to root out all followers of Discipline and Piety. There is more comic business; Discipline enters; Moros blusters, tries in vain to draw his sword, and finally leaves. Discipline laments the wicked fool in authority, and People, a figure from the social moralities, complains of the state of the country.

In the fourth movement, God's Judgment enters "with a terrible visor" and strikes down the now greying Moros while he is ranting and waving his sword, but Moros does not heed his warning, "If thou hast grace, for mercy now call." Then Confusion enters "with an ill favored visor and all things beside ill favored"[10] ("The portion of fools is confusion") and, at the command of God's Judgment, he strips Moros of his finery and reinvests him in his fool's coat. The bewildered Moros speculates,

> Am I asleep, in a dream or in a trance,
> Ever me think that I should be waking.

But after Confusion orders him to come along to his shameful end, he concludes (in lines 1823–44),

> *Sancti*, Amen, where is my goodly gear,
> I see well that I was asleep indeed.
> What, am I fain a fool's coat to wear? . . .
> Other I was a gentleman and had servants,
> Or else I dreamed I was a gentleman.
> *Confusion:* But thou art now a peasant of all peasants,
> A derision and mock to man and woman.

They leave, Moros not especially downcast, to go to the Devil.

The play, it may be noted, is not polished craftsmanship although the individual scenes are potentially effective as comedy, and are touched at the end with terror and wonder. It is an adequate play, theatrically viable, but not outstanding. It is, however, semantically complex.

A moral, the evil consequences of rearing children in wickedness and idleness, is stated at the beginning and illustrated throughout. All efforts of Exercitation, Discipline and Piety are lost; this twig has been bent, this soul lost. The theme is stated in a

Bildungsdrama in which Moros moves from catechism and school-room to manhood, political power, old age, and death. In the first movement, Discipline quizzes him, lectures him, threatens him, and finally (offstage) beats him. Moros clings to his childishness (his mother has cockled him in it), deliberately twists his lessons into comic nonsense, and pretends ignorance for a laugh: he is a caricature of the clever, insolent schoolboy. In the second movement he escapes to more congenial companions who at the end lead him off to taste "women's flesh." In the third movement he wears a foolish beard, in the fourth a gray beard. This is a variant of the development of such plays as *Mundus et Infans*, in which the hero shifts through five carefully labelled ages, or *The Nice Wanton*, in which the spoiled truant is led on a rake's progress, and memory of such plays would strengthen its emphasis. But we are not witnessing one half of *The London Merchant*; the development is the vehicle of a metaphor the tenor of which is the folly of the worldling. Exercitation, Discipline, and Piety, as David Bevington has pointed out, represent respectively the three laws of Nature, Moses and Christ which, in a common division of history, mankind has been successively placed under.[11] Moros the fool, will be ruled by none of them, and he is of all ages. He is caricatured in turn as the deliberately stupid schoolboy, the gull led on by cheats, the ruler counselled by evil counsellors, the "mad man with a sword in his hand," and throughout as the fool. On this level the apparent movement in time is fiction and a device for turning the pages of the *Narrenschiff*, each a different aspect of the same reality. The schoolboy mocking his teachers is a metaphor of the clever, worldly man mocking the virtues, and the young gull being taken in by his treacherous companions is a metaphor of the same worldling being deceived by seeming pleasure, pastime, and manhood. The figure in the foreground becomes a ridiculous king in his maturity; he chases a feather placed in his hat by his sychophantic counsellor; he rants, boasts, wounds the air with his sword, and is stricken by death. His actions are the vehicles of a metaphor of which the tenor is the foolish worldling's dream of greatness;

the worldling chases after the vanity of earthly power and pleasure, fights a shadow battle of his imagination, and then, finally, awakes from dreaming to glimpse the reality of his folly. The schoolboy who has become king enacts the story of Macbeth, made funny, but it is an acting out of the metaphors, the fool lighted to dusty death, the walking shadow, the sound and fury, the tale signifying nothing.

The dream is of greatness. The reality is folly and tyranny. But the third movement adds a social dimension. Moros's counsellors here, like the figure in the royal pageants, are ambiguous. Crudelitie (alias Policy), Ignorance (alias Antiquity, probably costumed as a Roman priest), and Impiety, (alias Philosophy) are all psychological (within Moros), and social (at work in the realm). Ignorance boasts that he drowns many papists in Hell; Crudelity and Impiety vow to root out all followers of Piety and Discipline. Both Discipline and People complain of the wretched state of the country.

The fourth movement, then, within the half-farcical mode of morality, is an early version of the great tragic ending of the Jacobeans, a triple mirror of madness, immorality and social chaos, overseen and controlled, however, by the guiding hand of Providence. People concludes his complaint in the third movement with the sound Tudor moral that God is punishing the country, and the country's cause must be referred to God. There follows immediately the comic horror of the gray-bearded, ranting Moros, waving his sword; the terrible figure of God's Judgment; and the sinister-comic figure of Confusion, "with an ill fauoured visure, and all things beside ill fauoured." The figure of Confusion is a final restatement of the theme sounded on Moros's entrance in the first movement, "singing the foote of many Songes, as fooles were wont"; repeated musically in the jumbled song of the second movement (which, as Wrath comments, "hangeth together like feathers in the winde"); and restated dramatically throughout the play in the incoherent nonsense of Moros's foolish replies. Its significance is revealed here as the confusion of Breughel's apocalyptic paintings, an ultimate comic nightmare.

88

Moros and his nightmare rule collapse together; he departs for Hell.

The effect of tragedy, despite high farce throughout, is achieved in part by the foreground emphasis upon the victim-villain about whom the social and moral metaphors are clustered. By contrast, a play like Wapull's *The Tide Tarrieth No Man* (published 1576) achieves the effect of satiric comedy by emphasizing the social metaphors. All but one of its main characters are firmly sketched social types, a wealthy merchant, a crooked broker, a young wastrel, and so on, engaged in intrigues that bring the rogues to affluence and the gulls to ruin.

The maneuvering is conducted with considerable realistic detail, meetings of servants and brokers, arrangements for bonds, rentals, and arrests, and is itself convincingly commonplace. A landlord evicts a poor tenant to obtain a higher rent; go-betweens take a quarter of a courtier's loan; a creditor arrests a debtor at a Paul's Cross sermon; a spendthrift couple is reduced to beggary. This action is set within and laced through by a metaphorical structure which adds another dimension to the play and provides a dynamic for it. The play does not merely illustrate abuses of the time; it also makes metaphorical statements about their psychological root in the unbridled will, about the masking of vice as virtue, the corruption of Christianity, and the need for governmental reform.

The main vice of the play, *The Vice*, in theatrical terminology, is Courage, a concept which, as he himself plays with the word, ranges from the modern sense of *valor* or *bravery* through *heart* or *spirit, encouragement*, and the *unregenerate, passionate will*. He is also, on the theological level, diabolic, or an agent of the Devil. He opens the play by introducing himself in lively Skeltonics and by summoning the audience to the Barge of Sin, now about to depart for Hell. The tide tarrieth no man. As he explains, his property is to encourage men to evil, but he sometimes.

> To color my guile
> Do give courage to good.[12]

More even than Iago he is the dramatic *regisseur*, marshalling the subordinate vices, arranging appointments, and throughout encouraging wavering mortals to take heart and follow the course that will ruin them. Although his dress and status are not specified, he is clearly the Elizabethan sharper and ruffler, fast-talking, knowing, quick-tempered ("out quickly with his dagger" reads one stage direction) on terms of easy familiarity with the Hell-bent of all classes. This is what courage, the headlong will, is like. And moving as he does, not simply individuals of all classes, but generic social types and forces, Greediness, No-good-neighborhood, Wilful Wantonness, and so on, he is a term not only in the psychological metaphor but in the social metaphor as well. At the end, indeed, he is not bridled by Reason or reformed by Faith or God's Word or Grace, but apprehended by Authority, who orders Correction to hang him. He dies, in short, ambiguously as social vice and man, but *not* as a faculty within the psyche of any of the characters.

The three subordinate vices, Hurting Help, Feigned Furtherance, and Painted Profit function as go-betweens in the various plots, the former as the cheating broker, the two latter as cheating servants. As such, again, they exemplify the truism that brokers and servants are often deceiving, and by the simple metaphor of their names they emphasize the point. But they are also vices, subordinate demi-devils moving in the pattern set by dramatic tradition for their kind: the infiltration and corruption of society under the direction of the diabolic master Vice. Like countless of their dramatic ancestors they meet and greet him early in the play, quarrel, submit, receive their orders, pause for a song, and then set about their business.

Courage, undisciplined and unregenerate, summoning all men to the barge for Hell, is the most evil, but he seduces men through a false show of good. This point is made in two ways: in the action of the primary metaphor, as Courage directly encourages them to seek money, honor, and wanton liberty; and in a secondary metaphor as he works indirectly upon them through his subordinates, false Furtherance, Help, and Profit. These, like the worldly aims they lure their victims with, are a promise of bliss that brings bale. They are metaphors of their aims, even as the treacherous Goods in *Everyman* or Lady Treasure in *The Trial of Treasure*. Though they ruin some of their victims financially, and though this financial ruin is emphasized with the zeal of a socialist tract, it is shown as incidental to their ultimate purpose of spiritual ruin. Greediness, whom they have actually helped to gain money, is finally reported dead and bound for Hell, and the spendthrift young husband, tempted to suicide, is rescued by the figure of Faithful Few, and then repents his sins. The spiritual fate of the society itself is presented by the vicissitudes of personified Christianity, who first enters sorrowing, bearing the shield of riches and the sword of policy. Faithful Few vainly tries to change these arms to Faith and God's Word; he is frustrated by pervasive Greediness. But at the end, with the help of Authority, he succeeds.

It is important to notice the dramatic emphasis upon spiritual values and disvalues because the coherence of the play depends upon it and because expectations based on easy generalizations about the Protestant Ethic are likely to obscure it. This is not a play about the prime virtue of sober thrift in a man's calling or the prime evil of free spending. Like Dante, the author balances greediness against prodigality as two forms of the misuse of money. But his more comprehensive theme, as the title indicates, is the radical opposition of spiritual and worldly values. The ambiguous title is interpreted in both senses. The vices urge it in the worldly sense of *carpe diem*, and Faithful Few in the spiritual sense:

> Amend thy life whilst here thou has space . . .
> So shalt thou enjoy the tide of [God's] grace.

The strategy of the vices is to insist upon the first meaning and to blind men to the second, and the fault of their victims—greed, prodigality, thirst for honor, or wanton liberty—is to be deceived. Their deception by the promise of worldly profit, not their financial ruin—or success—is the metaphor of their corruption.

The emphasis of the ending falls on the reform of Christianity (not the arrest of Courage) and the comfortable assurance that, with Authority's strong backing, all will be well. Since the play alludes frequently and favorably to preaching, an audience might easily see Authority's advent as a reference to the recent installation of Archbishop Grindal, who was trying to encourage preaching, or perhaps as a hope, vain of course in proof, that Elizabeth would henceforth encourage preaching. At any rate, there is hope of reform.[13]

Such hope is explicitly denied in Robert Wilson's *The Three Ladies of London* (c. 1581), a popular play produced by one of the professional companies.[14] The result of the denial is, on the one hand, unrelieved medieval satire of a world certain to go on to good men malignant, to bad men benign, an early example in the tradition that leads to the great virulence of *Volpone*. But though he exposes the foul body of the infected world, Wilson simultaneously manages to suggest a genuinely comic solution to the problem of living in it which looks forward to the comedies of Shakespeare.

The social macrocosm is chiefly the city of London, and its corruption is exemplified with documentary realism. Four rogues travel to the city, take service with a wealthy prostitute, and proceed to make their fortunes by rack-renting, simony, fraud, and usury. An honest but penniless university graduate seeks in vain for a benefice. A lawyer takes a crooked case. A ruffian murders a kindly old knight. A foreign merchant imports baubles and exports valuable commodities; he bilks an honest and forgiving Jew (in two scenes laid in Turkey). An honest artisan is forced to turn to fraud. A beadle whips an innocent man while a wealthy crook escapes punishment. Two poor women suffer rack-renting, are forced to pawn their gowns, and are finally evicted. One of them sells brooms for a living but finally enters service with the prostitute. The other marries one of the rogues. The prostitute and the two other women are finally brought to trial and condemned, but the judge who condemns them is carefully established as No Man, Judge Nemo.

But most of this exemplary documentation is metaphor as well.

Like *Piers Plowman,* the play puts its action in the general interpretive framework of all for money. The name of the powerful prostitute is Lady Lucre, whom many spectators would probably recognize as Lady Meed or the Whore of Babylon. The four rogues are Fraud, Simony, Dissimulation, and Usury. The two wretched ladies who are evicted and corrupted are Love and Conscience. Conscience becomes the bawd of Lucre; her face is spotted from a box of ointment—"the box of all abominations." Love marries Dissimulation; she has become Lust and wears a two-faced visor. The honest student is Sincerity, and Lucre, acting through Simony, mockingly bestows on him the parish of St. Nihil. Even the honest Jew Gerontus is, for those with a smattering of Greek, the Old Man or unregenerate human nature, which rejects with horror the chicanery of the nominal Christian. The wedding serves to introduce, again in the manner of *Piers Plowman* or *The Bouge of Court,* a long list of the wedding guests: Master Forgery, Master Flattery, Master Cruelty, Master Pickery, Mistress Fornication, Frisset False-measure, and so on. Doctor Hypocrisy—apparently a gibe at Romish prelates —performs the ceremony. Sir Nicholas Nemo invites Sincerity to dinner and fades off stage in the midst of his invitation. The old knight murdered in the streets is Hospitality, killed by the ruffian Usury.

It should be noticed that most of the actions are true metaphors whose tenors differ from the exemplifying vehicle. Thus Conscience's becoming the bawd of Lucre exemplifies a poor woman's enlistment by the bawdy house but metaphorically represents the corruption of society's conscience by avarice. The murder of the old knight is both the common crime of violence and an economic analysis of the decline of hospitality. The marriage of Dissimulation is made to exemplify the buying of the fair maid by the wealthy, repulsive rascal and to symbolize the hedging of political opportunism "if the world should change." But this sort of distinction is not observed with doctrinaire fidelity. Gerontus merely exemplifies the superior virtues of the Jew (or unregenerate nature), and the lawyer who begs to plead for Lucre is simultaneously example and metaphor of the same point. In this respect the technique of the play does not differ from that of preceding moralities.

I think it may fairly be claimed, however, that some of the metaphors are more ingenious and that the familiar interweaving of metaphor and example results in a more complex texture than has been common in the popular drama. The ending, the trial before Judge Nemo, is noteworthy. The guiding conceit, that no man condemns the corruptions of Lucre, Love and Conscience, is intellectually clear and satirically powerful. But it is paradoxically reinforced by the judgment and condemnation that the audience actually sees and hears, the judge in his robes surrounded by the officers of the court, the three women before him, the inquiry and the sentences. And in this visible action the meanings interweave eschatology, psychology, and political morality. Lucre is an insolent, jeering whore, overthrown finally by the witness of her wretched servant woman who is also (her) conscience; she is condemned to Hell as an unrepentant sinner:

Thou shalt pass to the place of darkness, where thou shalt hear
    fearful cries;
Weeping, wailing, gnashing of teeth, and torment without end;
Burning in the lake of fire and brimstone, because thou canst not
    amend.
Wherefore, Diligence, convey her hence: throw her down to the
    lowest hell,
Where the infernal sprites and damned ghosts do dwell.

(p. 368)

She is also, of course, Money, the root of all evil, the grand corrupter of the realm. Conscience, too, though the conscience of both Love and Lucre as they are women, is a woman in her own right to whom the judge can appeal to consider:

O Conscience, what a small time thou has on earth to live:
Why doest thou not, then, to God all honour give?
Considering the time is everlasting that thou shalt live in bliss,

94

If by thy life thou rise from death to judgment, mercy, and forgiveness. (p. 369)

She is furthermore, as she is condemned to prison to await "the
day of the general session," man's conscience, corrupted, suffering,
awaiting final judgment. Love, by contrast, though also a woman,
is as Love condemned to suffer "like pains with [Lucre]," which
are explained as the moral-psychological torments of conscience.
Her judgment thus becomes a myth explaining the pains that accompany deceitful love:

Care shall be thy comfort, and sorrow thy life sustain;
Thou shalt be dying, yet never dead, but pining still in endless
pain (p. 370)

Again and finally, the scene as a whole, which functions as an
assertion of absolute moral standards, condemns not only man's
corrupted love, conscience, and love of money, but by contrasting parallel, the corrupt administration of justice. The same
point is made with some slight inconsistency by the fact that
Fraud, Simony, Dissimulation, and Usury evade the law and
escape the judgment of the court.

The bitterness of the satire, however, is placed in comic per-
spective by the character of the clown Simplicity, a role which,
Collier plausibly suggested, Wilson may have written for himself.
Certainly it was written for a brilliant clown; it is painfully dull
to read, and dullness on the page is in these matters the surest possible indication of a brilliant slapstick comedian. Its function obviously includes that of comic relief. It also serves, it is true, some
function within the satire. Simplicity is in part choral commentator helping to expose the vices, in part the innocent sufferer, the
servant of Lady Love and the cousin to Sincerity, who is
whipped by the rascal beadle while the guilty Fraud, in robes and
furred gowns, stands by smirking. But he is mainly funny as a
fool, a natural or near-natural country antic who can think only
of feeding his belly, who mistakes words and mugs and clowns,
and as the familiar, favorite actor clowning *in* the role, sometimes
jesting with the audience.

Finally, he is Simplicity, the honest countryman, descendant of Commonalty and People. Neither vice nor virtue, he is that ridiculous frank simplicity of *l'homme moyen sensuel* which mirrors the bewilderment of the honest spectator in these deceiving times and invites the laughter of both sympathy and scorn. Because he draws sympathy and because he clowns and jests with the audience, mocking himself even while submitting to the unjust lashing, he invites an attitude toward his kind and his quality within us which resolves in comedy the problem of living in an unjust world.

This resolution is clearly not the only one in the play, and this problem is dramatically subservient to that of avarice. But the humility of this laughter, sympathetically mocking our own frailties and bewilderment, takes its place beside the near-desperation of *saeva indignatio*. We are not saints, for all our suffering. "The best of us all," as Judge Nemo remarks, "may amend." Furthermore, we are funny. Gulliver laughs at his own folly.

The dramatic reconciliation of the two attitudes is not, I think, perfect in this play, or at least not made perfectly clear. Simplicity, furthermore, is rather narrowly conceived to serve as the play's sole representative of folly, and at times he becomes merely the country gull, like Jonson's Master Stephen. Nevertheless, by whatever combination of design and happenstance, Wilson has discovered and made available one of the important devices for guiding the point of view toward that balanced Erasmian attitude which distinguishes Shakespeare's comedies or even *Bartholomew Fair* from such unmitigated satires as *Volpone* or *A Chaste Maid in Cheapside*. Not only is Simplicity usually presented with Shakespearian sympathy; as the companion of the virtue characters he becomes from time to time their attribute. For although both as persons and qualities they are his superiors and though they often instruct him and correct his misapprehensions, they are simple themselves in contrast to the devious vices; and they often trust in him and employ him to deliver letters, further their appeals, and pawn their clothes, as they refuse, or are reluctant, to employ the vices. He is their simplicity and, from the worldly point of view, their folly.

The achievement is a high order of semantic complexity within a searching and funny analysis of society and the plight of its members. By moving his characters and actions in dance-like exchange as subjects and attributes, Wilson shows the significance of the foreground, journalistically reported crimes and chicanery, and also of the general social dissolution to which they serve as metaphorical vehicle. The significance of the foreground action is economic, moral, and theological. The realm is ruled by money; poverty causes vice; the love and conscience of society are corrupted, and, together with its justice and its rule, are damned. The significance of the general social dissolution is that society has become a vast whorehouse, run for profit. Almost everyone is in its employ. Yet for the individual there remains not only the possibility of stubbornly resisting the general corruption but also the implied injunction to recognize the humor of his predicament as a simpleton among the shrewd.

One further point may be made. In certain respects the play resembles some of the plays of mid-twentieth century dramatists like Ionesco or Beckett; for instance in its employment of a fantastic metaphor as a premise for its action, in its highly theatricalist variations upon this basic metaphor, in its concern with a rotting society, in its refusal to give any easy answers to the problems it raises, in the central role it gives to the little man (*der kleine mensch*), its use of a clownish simpleton to represent him, and in its reliance upon the spectators' recognition of the traditional theatricalism and the conventions which enable it to speak with meaning. Although the parallel cannot be pressed far, it is worth noting if only to dispel any lingering notion that we are dealing with a naive drama or a naive audience. Such a play requires a sophisticated audience, both in the sense that it must be highly trained and in the sense that it is willing to think critically. That such a play was extremely popular is excellent evidence, the Sidneys and Gossons notwithstanding, for the existence of such an audience well before the university wits began to write for the public theaters.

97

PART
TWO.
The Plays:

IV.

Romantic Comedy: John Lyly.

By the early eighties satiric comedy, unlike romantic comedy, had already found its way; the stripping of abuses had been customary dramatic sport since the fifteenth-century *Wisdom*, and a fabulous centenarian who had seen, say, Medwall's *Nature*, Skeleton's *Magnificence*, *Respublica*, *Impatient Poverty*, *All for Money*, *The Tide Tarrieth No Man* and *The Three Ladies of London*, though he might have been puzzled by some of the features of *Cynthia's Revels* or *Volpone*, would have found their themes, their attitudes, and even their structure familiar. They expose avarice, pride, flattery, lust, vanity, and folly, and condemn them. They move, in the familiar three-part structure, from an expository convocation of the vices, through a demonstration of their quality in full career, to the final unmasking and judgment scenes.

The satiric comedies, early and late, are calls to reform; at least that is their professed aim. This does not mean that they present their case with evangelical one-siddedness or humorless zeal or that they fail to give the devil his due. Not only are the reformed sinner and the penitent vice forgiven, but the clever vice is allowed to draw admiring laughter, though all men of good will are summoned to root him out. Richard III, Falstaff, Volpone, and Mosca are in this respect too, traditional. Even details, like the last desperate cleverness of the comic rogue just before he is brought to judgment, are part of the established satiric tradition. Thus Avarice in *Respublica* greets the four daughters of God by suggesting to his fellow rogues, "Take eche manne a ladie sirs/ and leate us goo daunce," (line 1664) [1] and when Lady Verity reveals herself, he outbraves her with the cheerful bluster of Falstaff greeting the Chief Justice:

> I know my maister/ *your* father well afyne.
> welcome faire Ladye, swete ladye, litle ladye,
> plaine ladye, smoothe ladye, sometyme spittle ladye,
> Ladie longtong, ladye tell all, ladye make bate,
>
> (1700–1703)

Similarly Courage in *The Tide Tarrieth No Man* greets Authority and Faithful Few, who are searching for him, with affable insolence, claims to know the rogue they are seeking, and starts to run off stage to fetch him. (They stop him.) The vices often win empathy and admiration at this point, yet of course they are condemned.

The point is worth making because as this particular kind of double-consciousness appears in late Elizabethan or Jacobean comedy it has attracted considerable attention and because it needs to be distinguished from a similar attitude evoked by romantic comedy. But most romantic comedies of the time have little to do with exposing vice or with the exhibition of a villainy whose ingenuity evokes admiration: their social satire is marginal. Most of their laughter is unscornful—a gentle mockery directed, not so much at the vices of society or the sins of the man, as at the comic weakness and instability of human nature. Consequently their comic attitude is determined by the need, not for reform (as in Jonson's theory), but for some *modus vivendi* with the absurd flesh.

There are of course philosophical and religious answers to this problem, and they are often germane to romantic comedy. That the flesh is weak and that man must somehow come to terms with this weakness, not only remaining vigilant against it, but humbly aware that even the just man falls daily and must seek forgiveness —these are commonplaces. It is also a commonplace that the total view of man's life shows that life is something to rejoice in and that it ends happily. This was the pattern of man's life as Dante saw it, and it was also the pattern of comedy, which "begins with adverse conditions, but ends happily." Comedy, in the splendid phrase of Nevill Coghill, was "the shape of ultimate reality." [2]

Stage comedy defined in this way makes its appearance in the vast comprehensive plays of the late middle ages, such as the English Corpus Christi plays, the French *mystères*, and those religious moralities and *moralités* whose protagonist is mankind. These plays sought to include the great whole of man's history and of his spiritual journey to his final happiness, and in several ways they adumbrate romantic comedy, as well as Shakespearean romance, very closely. They emphasize man's weakness, sometimes though not always in humorous fashion, and his tendency to make mistakes, the literal usually symbolizing the moral error. They also emphasize forgiveness as a major structural device that ushers in the hero's final happiness; man does not earn his reward —he is given it (for the asking). And of course they emphasize the happiness itself. This is sometimes presented as the reality of final bliss, as in *The Castle of Perseverence*, where Deus welcomes Mankind to sit at His right hand; sometimes as a limited earthly state foreshadowing a larger felicity. This is more usual in sixteenth-century moralities such as *Magnificence*, *Youth*, and *The Trial of Treasure*, and in the marriages of romantic comedy itself.

The mysteries and religious moralities, moreover, like the romantic comedies and romances, define the values of their ultimate felicity in contrast to those of characters who oppose them or are alien to them and must be rejected, such as the damned of the concluding Judgment Day play, or Malvolio. It may be noted that when such characters and their rejection are emphasized strongly in the realistic mode, the play tends toward melodrama, as in *A New Way to Pay Old Debts* or toward satire, as in *A Trick to Catch the Old One*. When the rejection is moved back to "Act Four," as in *The Merchant of Venice*, or *The Trial of Treasure*, or when the blocking characters are converted, as in *As You Like It*, the play can close with full harmony.

Though the mysteries and religious moralities foreshadow romantic comedy in many ways, however, and very probably played their part in shaping it and in shaping audience reaction to it, they are obviously not romantic comedies. Their moral distinctions are much sharper; they do not use love as a subject, and, although they include many comic episodes, their tone, as they turn to the need for humility or even final joy, is uncomfortably solemn for comedy. *The Castle of Perseverance*, for example, presents Mankind's weakness in terms of his distressed perplexity when faced with his good and evil angels:

> Coryows Criste, to you I calle!
> As a grysly gost I grucche and grone,
> I wene, ryth ful of thowth.
> A! Lord Jhesu! wedyr may I goo?
> A crysyme I have, and no moo.
> Alas! men may be wondyr woo
> Wanne they be fyrst forth browth! . . .
> Whom to folwe, wetyn I ne may!
> I stonde in stodye, and gynne to rave.
> I wolde be ryche in gret a-ray,
> And fayn I wolde my sowle save!
> As wynde in watyr I wave.
> (320–80) [3]

The tone is closer to *Faustus* than to *Twelfth Night*. *Mankind*, indeed, moves a little closer to comedy in dealing with these matters. The scene in which Mankind, at the whispered urging of

Titivillus, interrupts his prayers to run off stage and answer the call of nature exploits clearly, though briefly, the farcical potential of human weakness. But most of the fun in the play arises from the comedy of the vices, and when Mankind, repentant, finally returns to Mercy, he is almost in despair, wearing a halter. The scene and the "happy ending" are both highly solemn.

Several other secular comedies and moralities share some of the characteristics of romantic comedy, but there are very few before the 1580s which most critics would consider as such. Medwall's *Fulgens and Lucrece*, the earliest of all secular comedies (1497), focusses upon the nature of true nobility, not love. It is a contest for the hand of a maiden waged as a debate between two young men representing rival concepts of gentilesse, as conferred by ancestry and as earned by virtuous behavior. The latter wins. In the parallel subplot the servants of the suitors contest, by singing and farcical combat, for the hand of the lady's maid.

The play has several common features of romantic comedy: the wooing, the parodic parallel of master and servant, and the comic courtship of the servants. But the emphasis is quite different. The text only hints at a potentially romantic plot. The poor-but-honest successful suitor is given a slight romantic edge over his aristocratic rival, but the actors must build up any love interest with minimal help from the dialogue. The debate is a real debate, and the lucky suitor wins by listing his accomplishments in civil and military life. When the girl announces her decision, she does so with both suitors absent, and we never see the happy couple together. Their "love," finally (the term seems oddly applied), is never remotely shadowed with humor.

John Heywood's *Play of Love* approaches very closely the interests and attitudes of romantic comedies, but it is not a play in the sense that they are. Rather it is a series of witty debates which are interrupted only once by action—literally fireworks— and its structure anticipates the Shaw of *Too True to be Good* rather than the Shakespeare of *Twelfth Night*. Like romantic comedy, however, it exploits love for the sake of laughter, and it comes to terms with this inescapable human weakness in much the same way and with the same wry gaiety. The four main characters (Lover Not Loved, Neither Loved Nor Loving, Both Lover and Loved, and Neither Loved Nor Loving) debate their relative bliss or misery in comic fashion, and gentle satire mocks the inevitable imperfections of the flesh thus revealed. They conclude by professions of unenvious contentment, recommending it as the best—though imperfect—earthly balm for the human condition. The real answer to the problem, however, as Lover not Loved explains, lies in seeking

> . . . the love of that lovyng lord
> who to suffer passion for love was content
> wherby his lovers that love for love assent
> Shall have in fyne above contentacyon
> The felyng pleasure of eternal salvacyon.[4]

The earthly passion with its satisfactions and limitations is thus set against God's love for man and man's for God, and the similarity and contrast of the two loves are emphasized by the conceited, courtly, almost *précieux* phrasing.

The human condition is thus gently ridiculed as a limited and imperfect and therefore funny version of the perfect state of being. But it is not merely ridiculed; it is also rejoiced in. Lover Not Loved continues,

> which lorde of lordes whose joyfull and blessed byrth
> Is now remembred by tyme presentyng
> This accustomyd tyme of honest myrth.
>
> [Sig. E iv]

The play is a Christmas play; it is festive, celebrating the occasion that makes possible a greater happiness than mere contentation. As the play presents it, therefore, life is joyful as well as funny. So is the play.

Heywood's play, however, though it shares many of the concerns of romantic comedies, lacks a fully developed plot. The three plays about Wit and Science or Wit and Wisdom, the earliest of which, Redford's *Wit and Science*, is probably fifteen to twenty years later than Heywood's play, are plays in a sense that *The Play of Love* is not, and they approach romantic comedy very closely. They have a well-defined and appropriate plot line (boy overcomes obstacles to win girl) and they focus upon human weaknesses rather than the vices to which weak man succumbs. On the level of the tenor (the plays are moralities) the weaknesses are the ignorance of untrained wit, its tendency to tire (represented by a battle with the monster Tediousness), its desperate need of recreation, and its tendency to confuse recreation with wanton idleness. The vehicle gets similar fun out of the parallel of the brash but appealing youth hot-spurring to successive pratfalls, finally victorious after he learns to take advice from his staid elders.[5]

Inherited technique and structural pattern, however, still keep the meaning admonitory, though jocularly so. Wit's stumbling journey to gain the hand of Science is modelled on the career of Mankind to gain salvation. As Mankind begins in innocence, falls into sin, recovers, perhaps falls again, and is again rescued, so Wit begins fresh and untried, is beaten by Tediousness, is recovered by Honest Recreation, succumbs again to Idleness or Wantonness, is recovered again, and finally gains the lady. The weaknesses, in short, take the place of the vices in the older moralities, and they are treated as vices, as things to be avoided, or overcome, or to be rescued from, not as the inescapable limitations of human nature that one must learn to live with, be humble about, and laugh at. This is especially true, I think, of the last of the three plays, *The Marriage of Wit and Wisdom* (1570-79), which was written for public performance and is in some respects more old-fashioned than the two earlier, private theater, plays. In this play Idleness is a dominating farcical Vice, "the purveyor here in earth for the Devil," possessing social as well as psychological meaning, a vice and rogue whom all good men will unite to root out although he is an extraordinarily funny fellow.

Nevertheless, it should be evident that these three plays are very close in subject, themes, and attitudes to the romantic comedies. They have the requisite love story; they laugh gently at the natural frailties of the young lover, and they end in mirth and joy.

Ralph Roister Doister and *Gammer Gurton's Needle* also resemble romantic comedies sufficiently to demand attention. The former, it is true, focusses upon the unsuccessful suitor rather than a love story, and most of the fun comes from the display of his humors—love, melancholy, braggadocio, and sudden blazes of egotistic euphoria—as these are manipulated by the sportive parasite Matthew Merrygreeke. Yet the last act turns to the true-love story, and the joy of the conclusion takes even the ridiculous Ralph to its bosom. Love is mocked in Ralph only. The true love of Christian Custance and Gawain Goodluck is clearly to be played straight. But unless I quite misread the text, the role of Christian herself invites the boy actor to play it for alternating pathos and a show of womanly impatience that is comic. Christian, who has been understandably exasperated by Ralph's outrageous behavior, must be persuaded to simmer down before she can help to form the forgiving and forgetting festivities which include Ralph. There is, furthermore, in this play as in the otherwise quite unromantic *Gammer Gurton's Needle*, a marked sense of life as potentially play, *ludus* in its widest sense. Merrygreeke is not merely a parasite out for a meal; he is out primarily for the pleasure of the human comedy:

> But such sport have I with [Ralph] as I would not lese,
> Though I should be bound to live with bread and cheese.
>
> (1.1.53–54) [6]

And he shapes many of the events into improvised comedy. This concept—life-as-comedy—realized dramatically, will come into its own toward the end of the century, but it is clearly potentially exploitable in school drama from the mid-century.

Gascoigne's *Supposes* (1556), a translation of Ariosto's *I Suppositi*, is in most ways as close to romantic comedy as *The Comedy of Errors*, which is discussed below. Ariosto's play is New Comedy; its plot is similar to the Bianca plot of *The Taming of the Shrew*, which was in fact, based upon it. It focusses upon intrigue, however, not love or even wooing. The happy couple has long been consummating their love in secret, and their problem is to head off, by a tangle of intrigue, the rival, a rich *senex* who is bidding high for the girl's hand. Eventually the usual coincidences untangle, a lost son is found, identities are established, and the hasty lovers are forgiven and allowed to marry.

Providence, we are told, has guided the outcome. In the denouement Cleandro, who has found his son, says,

> You, Philogano, may thinke that God in heaven above hath ordained your comming hither at this present to the ende I might recover my lost sonne, whom by no other meanes I coulde ever have founde oute.
>
> *Philogano.* Surely, sir, I thinke no lesse; for I think that not so much as a leafe falleth from the tree without the ordinance of God.[7] (5.8.14–23)

These remarks (which are also in Ariosto's original) could conceivably be played for ridicule of the two old men, but taken as a comment on the action they imply a contrast between the bewildered human view of the complex action and the clear design of Providence. It is the same contrast, as Robert Durling has pointed out, that Ariosto uses quite explicitly in *Orlando Furioso*.[8] The comedy has been very largely the spectacle of human beings in a maze, their view of reality distorted by passion or mere human limitation (e.g., Cleandro doesn't recognize his son because he hasn't seen him since he was a baby). The title of the play underlines the human necessity to act upon assumptions, usually false, and the marginal notes to Gascoigne's translation point these out (e.g., "a pleasant suppose").

The reference to Providence, furthermore, implies an analogy between life and a comedy (the point is made explicitly by one of the characters) on two specific counts: the contrast between the characters' view of the action (mistaken, bewildered, seeing only chance at work) and the well-thought-out design of the actual plot, corresponds to the contrast between the human view of events and God's. Secondly, the author, like Providence, has led his characters to a happy ending. Both points of resemblance, it may be noted, are commonly made explicit in the *commedia grave*, which flourished in the last half of the century. Louise George Chubb remarks,

"In play after play like Castelletti's *Furbo* and Curzio Gonzaga's *Inganni*, it is expressly stated that the seeming chaos and confusion of the intrigue is, in fact, part of a plan above change, a divine pattern, implicitly or explicitly Christian, guiding characters through innumerable *intrichi*, *inganni*, *laberinti*, and *errori* to perfect order. The very pattern of seemingly unresolvable complexities worked out to an unexpectedly simple and satisfying conclusion, the structural ideal of the writers of *commedia grave*, was held to be a reflection of the workings of Providence. And, as the theological virtue of hope depends on faith in God's Providence, the meaning of the design was tied back into the tissue of moral lesson. As Oddi says in the second prologue to *Prigione d'amore*, *commedia grave* teaches people, especially lovers, not to despair, by showing that in times of darkest confusion the pattern of their happiness is taking shape." [9]

The dramatic use of Providence, of course, was not new to the English stage. It was implicit, sometimes explicit, in the craft cycles. It is more or less explicit in a number of moralities and hybrid moralities such as *The Castle of Perseverance*, Bale's *King John*, and *Respublica*, and in these plays it is often incorporated into the dramatic structure of innocence, fall, and redemption, which reflects the divine plan for mankind and nations as well as individuals. Ariosto's structural analogy, however, seems to be new on the English stage. To what extent its introduction by Gascoigne in the Gray's Inn performance of 1566 helped audiences to recognize and accept it or encouraged playwrights to use it can only be conjectured, since most of the dramatic texts that would help us chart the story have disappeared. One can say, however, that here is one fairly clear piece of evidence that Inns of Court audiences were being made receptive to this structural analogy as early as 1566. The next extant text to use it, or something close to it, is Lyly's *Mother Bombie* (c. 1589), and then *The Comedy of Errors* (c. 1590–94). By then romantic comedy is well established.

Dramatized love stories with happy endings apparently became common during the seventies and early eighties, but these—again apparently—were usually romances of adventure like *Sir Clyomon and Clamydes*, the kind that Sidney and Gosson sneered at. They are not comedies. Nor, unless I seriously misread it, is *The Rare Triumphs of Love and Fortune*, a wildly romantic play which is in some ways very much like Lyly's and which was performed at court by Derby's men in 1582. It contains comic interludes involving a couple of clowns, but the tribulations of the lovers seem intended to be played straight. The play is tragi-comedy, both in Fletcher's sense, "in respect it wants death, which is enough to make it no tragedy, yet brings some near it, which is enough to make it no comedy," and in Una Ellis-Fermor's, who defines the mood of tragi-comedy as lying "somewhere between the light-heartedness of unshadowed comedy and the apprehension and mystery which attend a tragic catastrophe." [10]

One feature of it calls for special attention, however. That is its concern, mentioned above, with the behind-the-scenes power of Providence. In a series of scenes somewhat like Italian *intermedii* the goddesses Love and Fortune debate their relative power, and each seeks to prove her might by influencing events in the main plot, Love assisting the lovers and Fortune crossing them. At length Jupiter intervenes (to help the lovers), and it is made clear that "wisdom ruleth love and fortune both." The result is apparently still another structural metaphor of the theme of Providence, but adapted to the structure of romance; it suggests again the interest in and availability of that theme for dramatic use.

ii.

John Lyly's plays are comedies, and when he deals with love, love is—in some measure and fashion—comic. Further, different loves are comic in different ways. There are many kinds of love; they must be analyzed, distinguished, and properly—endlessly—

evaluated. But even in the noblest, like Endymion's for Cynthia, there lurks something of that absurd irrationality which is fit matter for his comedy.

Not all his plays are concerned with love, and those that are deal with other stuff as well. *Midas* is moral and political satire very much, *mutatis mutandis*, like *Magnificence* or *Respublica*, and the other plays place love in a context of discussion and action which enforces a much wider theme. There is also the formerly much-vexed possibility of topical allegory; it is impossible to disregard entirely the tendency of Elizabethan Politic Would-be's to carve gossip out of the plays, but meanings as recondite as most of those suggested are fortunately outside the scope of this book. The obvious allegory of Spanish policy in *Midas* is an exception, and there are a few clear allusions in the other plays, but these are almost all particular illustrations of generalizations, and it is with the generalizations that we are concerned now.

To return to these, Lyly's treatment of them can be seen at its simplest in his two earliest plays, *Campaspe*, the first, and *Sapho and Phao*, the second, both probably produced early in 1584. They too have the general and quite simple plot structure of a social morality like *Magnificence* or *Respublica*, love replacing the master vice as the disrupting force in king and country. In each the sovereign is assaulted by an almost overwhelming love for a subject and, after high comedy of inner struggle, overcomes it. Alexander the Great, who has fallen in love with the captive maid Campaspe, yields to the rival claim of the painter Apelles, and resumes his march toward world conquest. Queen Sapho of Syracuse (probably in a flattering reference to Elizabeth) supplants Venus as the Queen of Love. In both plays love, which is ridiculous because irrational and almost irrepressible, is the center of the comedy, but more matters for a May morning are aligned with it, and, in morality fashion, interspersed in the action.

In *Sapho and Phao* these are mainly the pretensions of court and college. The issue is opened by the courtier addressing the newly-arrived scholar:

"In universities vertues and vices are but shadowed in colours, white and blacke, in courtes shewed to life, good and bad. There, times past are read of in old bookes, times present set downe by new devices, times to come conjectured at by aime, by prophesie, or chaunce: here, are times in perfection, not by device, as fables, but in execution, as trueths. Believe me, Pandion, in Athens you have but tombs, we in court the bodies, you the pictures of Venus and the wise Goddesses, we the persons and the vertues." (1.2.12–20)

It is prologue to the presentation of the great world of the court, the real world as opposed to that shadow world of the schools, which is further mocked by the witty logic-chopping of the scholar's servant. But this real world is also gently ridiculed for its idleness, expense, and dissembling, and both are placed in ironic contrast to the shrewd common sense of a blacksmith and his master Vulcan, while Vulcan, in turn, a rough and genial artisan, is gently mocked, and mocks himself, as the fool of Venus and the cuckold of Mars. The wheel of folly thus comes full circle. The result is a picture of society, still satiric, as in the social moralities, but gently and humorously so. Its world is to be enjoyed with amusement; it is not to be reformed.

Campaspe surrounds its central figures with an even wider and more richly varied scene: philosophers, soldiers, prostitutes, witty servant boys, and citizens. Plato and Aristotle debate the existence of God; Diogenes argues for reducing wants to the little that Nature needs; a general argues for military conquest; hungry servant boys praise food and liberty; Apelles lectures on painting; Alexander ponders the relation between mastering oneself and mastering the world; three boys sing, dance and tumble.

The structure that holds this gallimaufrey together is the familiar tripartite pattern. In the opening section all is well; in the middle section the protagonist falls and the social order is corrupted; at the end both make an at least partial recovery. Scene is linked to scene, furthermore, as in many moralities, less by causal sequence than by the simple juxtaposition of thematic statements.[11] Like the almost contemporary *Three Ladies of London*, however, the play uses old patterns to some new ends.

It opens with the praise of Alexander; he is the ideal ruler—victorious in war and merciful in victory. The point is exemplified as he assures honorable treatment for two captive women. He then announces his resolve:

"*Hephestion*, it resteth now that we have as great care to governe in peace, as conquer in war; that whilest armes cease, artes may flourish, and joyning letters with launces, we endeavor to be as good philosophers as soldiers, knowing it no lesse praise to be wise, than commendable to be vailliant." (1.1.80–84)

The speech at once defines the scope of the play—the ruler and his realm—and establishes the Platonic ideal—the rule of the philosopher king—by which the comic reality is to be judged. Hephestion in replying emphasizes the point:

". . . needs must that commonwealth be fortunate, whose captain is a philosopher, and whose philosopher is a captain." (1.1.86–88)

Alexander's fall, as subsequent scenes present it, is a falling in love; psychologically it is a loss of rational control, and this psychological disorder is writ large in the "Athenian" society. On neither level does the disorder threaten tragedy. Lyly is writing comedy, after all. The tone of the dialogue permits the audience to remain detached and amused, "smoking," in Brecht's phrase. Yet the dramatic lesson is clear: this is *not* the rule of the philosopher king. The king is infatuated; the society is idle, aimless, and pleasure-seeking. Diogenes denounces it:

"Yee wicked and beewitched Atheneans, whose bodies make the earth to groane, and whose breathes infect the aire with stench. . . . Your lives dissolute, not fearing death, will prove your deaths desperate, not hoping for life: what do you els in Athens but sleepe in the day, and surfeite in the night: back Gods in the morning with pride, in the evening belly Gods with gluttonie! You flatter kings and call them Gods: speake trueth of your selves, & confesse you are divels! From the Bee you have taken not the honney, but the wax to make your religion, framing it to the time not to the trueth. Your filthy luste you colour under a courtly colour of love, injuries abroad under the title of pollicies at home, and secrete malice creepeth under the name of publick justice. You have caused Alexander to dry up springs & plant Vines, to sow roket and weede endiffe, to sheare sheepe, and shrine foxes. Al conscience is sealed at Athens. . . . O times! O menne! O coruption in manners! Remember that greene grasse must turn to dry hay. When you sleep, you are not sure to wake; and when you rise, not certeine to lye downe. Looke you never so hie, your heads must lye levell with your feete.   (4.1.21–51)

This is a familiar jeremiad of tract and pulpit, and on one level it is criticism of London and the London audience which has heard it so often that it can accept the criticism as truism. But it is also familiar as the speech of the reforming virtue-figure in moralities; coming in the fourth act, it reinforces the apparent morality pattern in which it should climax the triumph of vice and foreshadow the return to virtue and order. But Lyly mocks our expectations. The speech itself, in the first place, is distanced by its incorporation in a practical joke. Diogenes has served notice that he will fly and, when the Athenians assemble to watch him, he harangues them instead. He explains: "Thus have I flown over your disordered lives." (4.1.51–52) The indignant citizens jeer, and the servant boys laugh at the spectacle. In the second place the jeremiad is given little dramatic substantiation. There is a report that Alexander's army is rotting in peaceful ease; there is a scene of a courtesan and two soldiers, and there is one in which a fatuous father displays to a revolted Diogenes the vaudeville talents of his sons. There is also the ambiance of leisured, cultured idleness, a kind of Renaissance Heartbreak House. But by morality play standards, these things are follies, not crimes, and— Diogenes aside—they are sported with here.

Peter Saccio, in his very careful analysis of the play, argues that they are specifically improprieties, failures, that is, of the characters to realize their proper roles in society. He argues the close relationship of Lyly's paratactic style and dramatic structure. Both typically juxtapose elements—statements on the one hand, dramatized anecdotes on the other—which define the normative characteristics of the various roles: prince, philosophers, soldiers, painter, cynic, and maiden. Both style and structure, therefore, focus upon propriety: what is proper to the prince, philosopher, and so on. That is the theme of the play, and it at once explains the near absence of plot and provides what plot there is. Alexander, forgetful of his role as prince, plays the truant and dallies with love while his army neglects martial discipline and basks in pleasant vices. Other improprieties are displayed: Apelles, made desperate by Alexander's rivalry, blemishes the portrait he is painting; an erstwhile cynic turns beggar; the citizens are vicious; the father has corrupted his sons. It is as a consequence of these improprieties that the world of the play falls into disorder.[12]

"On the most philosophical level, when men fail to fulfill their functions simply as men, human life in general is corrupted. Hence Diogenes' harangue. . . . On a national level, when a warrior-king neglects his career to dally with a lowly virgin, the army for which he is responsible degenerates. . . . On the individual level, when the dalliance results in the disorderly situation of the king in rivalry with a painter, the painter takes to blemishing his own works. . . . When the king realizes the situation and, with royal magnanimity, unites the girl and the painter, the order based on status is restored, the painter kneels to utter his thanks, and the army is called back to its job."[13]

Saccio's thesis is a reasonable Elizabethan interpretation.[14] Furthermore, it is, I think, theatrically valid; that is, it could be staged —could have been staged—to work. The staging of the finale, for instance, can reinforce it greatly. At the very end, after Alexander has conquered his passion and yielded Campaspe to Apelles and the two lovers have thanked him and made their exit, he turns to a page,

> "Page, goe warne *Clitus* and *Parmenio* and the other Lordes to be in a readines, let the trumpet sound, strike up the drumme, and I will presently into Persia. How now *Hephestion,* is *Alexander* able to resiste love as he list?
> *Hephestion.* The conquering of Thebes was not so honourable as the subdueing of these thoughts.

Alexander. It were a shame *Alexander* should desire to commaund the world, if he could not commaund himselfe. But come, let us go, I wil try whether I can better beare my hand with my hart, then I could with mine eie. And good *Hephestion* when al the world is woone, and euery countrey is thine and mine, either find me out an other to subdue, or of my word I will fall in love.

Exeunt." (5.4.144–55)

An *exeunt* accompanied by the drums and trumpets that the lines suggest and staged with banners and as many marching soldiers as the combined boys' companies could muster would obviously provide a strong chord of resolution, probably strong enough to override with sheer theatricalism any doubts or any questions that spectators might otherwise feel unanswered.

A quieter ending, on the other hand, played casually for the pleasantly wry concession of the last line might suggest that the return of Alexander to his role of warrior-king, though it gets his army out of bed and restores the lovers to each other, leaves other affairs still disordered. The Athenian citizens, presumably, are as wicked as ever; the servant boys still hungry, the courtesan still active, the three "corrupted" boys still, presumably, dancing, tumbling, and singing, and Plato and Aristotle still debating the existence of God. But the play has opened wider issues than these. The theme of propriety, in the sense of what is proper to a given occupation, is widened to the theme of what is proper to man. Alexander, Diogenes, and the two lovers represent quite different points of view and ways of life in conflict with each other, and this conflict too is unresolved.

We are clearly asked to admire Diogenes as the uncorruptible reformer, and we are asked too to admire his sententious replies familiar from our copy-books:

Sylvius. Farwell *Diogenes*, thou needest not have scraped rootes, if thou wouldest have followed *Alexander*.
Diogenes. Nor thou have followed Alexander, if thou hadst scraped roots. (5.1.61–64)

117

Alexander admires him, again in the copy-book phrase, "were I not Alexander, I would wish to be Diogenes," and the general Hephestion grants him his due: "He is dogged, but discrete; I cannot tell how sharp, with a kind of sweetness, full of wit, yet too too wayward." (2.2.148–51) But the copy-book wisdom is placed in a dramatic context that questions it. Diogenes himself is given a slightly currish, certainly clownish personality, and his view is not the only one presented sympathetically nor the last. He is pitted not only against the general viciousness and folly of Athens, against a courtesan and a doltish father, but also against the romantic passion of Apelles and Campaspe, and the aspirations of Alexander, and the wit, the common sense, and the hunger of the servant boys.

Apelles' view is defined by the metaphor of his occupation as painter. He is concerned with the shadows of things (or, in the probably relevant Platonic terms, with the shadows of shadows), not their substance.[15] His love at least begins with the love of appearances; he falls in love with Campaspe by painting her picture, and there is much pretty talk about whether he will possess only her shadow, which he comes to find unsatisfying, or her substance. In winning her he seems to possess substance, but his victory is also the defeat of his reason, even in his own rhetoric: "Art must yield to nature, reason to appetite, wisdom to affection" (3.5.19–20), or "Dispute not the cause, wretch, but yield to it: for better it is to melt with desire than wrestle with love" (5.2.11–12). It is a defeat mocked also, of course, by the ascetic scorn of Diogenes and, finally, by Alexander, who has conquered his own passion:

"Two loving wormes, *Hephestion!* I perceive *Alexander* cannot subdue the affections of men, though he conquer their countries. Love falleth like dew aswel upon the low grass, as upon the high Cæder. Sparkes have their heate, Antes their gall, Flyes their splene. Well, enjoy one an other, I give her thee franckly, *Apelles.* Thou shalt see that *Alexander* maketh but a toye of love, and leadeth affection in fetters; using fancy as a foole to make him sport, or a minstrell to make him mery. It is not the amorous glaunce of an eie can settle an idle thought in the heart; no, no, it is childrens game, a life for seamsters and scholers; the one pricking in cloutes have nothing els to thinke on, the other picking fancies out of books, have little els to mervaile at. Go, *Apelles*, take with you your Campaspe, *Alexander* is cloied with looking on that which thou wondrest at." (5.4.127–140).

Yet the true love, though irrationally comic and though rooted in the eye's sensuous apprehension, is granted full dramatic sympathy. Timid, shamefaced, irrepressible despite the fear of tyrannic reprisal, the humble couple receives it finally as their highest bliss:

Apelles. Thankes to your majestie on bended knee, you have honored *Apelles*.
Campaspe. Thankes with bowed heart, you have blessed *Campaspe*. (5.4.141–43)

The question is raised of who has the shadow, who the substance. Alexander speaks like a Stoic in suppressing his passion, but he turns immediately to the worldly ambition that Diogenes has mocked throughout and which, he has just reminded him, must finally be contented with a grave plot. The witty servant boys, in turn, who praise the pleasures of good cheer, comment also upon the respective vanities of Diogenes and Apelles. The former feeds his hapless starveling (Manes) with a "gallymafrey" of sayings instead of meat, and the latter feeds his (Psyllus) with the paintings of food. He "telles of birdes that have beene fatted by painted grapes in winter: and how many have so fed their eies with their mistresse picture, that they never desired to take food, being glutted with the delight in their favours." (1.2.64–67) Only the servant of Plato, "that reads in the morning in the schoole, and at noon in the kitchen," feeds well. Yet Alexander, who has at least the dramatic benefit of drums and trumpets and the last word on the stage, turns his back upon both good cheer and philosophy.

The spectator, as Lyly seems to suggest in prologue and epilogue, may find in the play one or other viewpoint more firmly emphasized than the others; but the balance among them seems nearly perfect. The comedy rests in amused contemplation of the unresolved problem posed by a world in which various worldly aims and the ascetic contempt of the world seem alike persuasive and ridiculous. Diogenes speaks truths. If we had scraped roots we need not have followed Alexander. *Natura paucis contenta.* To learn to be content one must unlearn to covet. But Diogenes is also ridiculous, a dog-man, and the demands of nature, however small, include appetites like love which conflict with the rationality of his Cynicism. His hatred of love and women, though rational, is unnatural. As Alexander says, "In mine opinion thou wert never born of a woman, that thou thinkest so hardly of women" (5.4.68–69). Love, as the play "proves," is irrationally absurd but certainly natural and of almost overwhelming force. Only an Alexander can rise above it, but even Alexander is bent on a conquest which reason ridicules.

The result is a comedy of human nature, damned to be funny alike in its irrationality and its striving to be rational. This is the comic "problem." Lyly may have intended to suggest a religious answer to it, I think, even in this play, and part of his answer lies certainly in the good-humored mercy that Alexander shows to his captives, to a traitor, and to the lovers, but part also lies in the release of laughter which comes from recognizing the problem—and ourselves—as comic.

In various ways all of Lyly's later comedies except *Midas* exploit the same theme of the comic absurdity of human nature. The *Woman in the Moon,* for instance, presents the story of a woman who is influenced by each of the seven planets in succession, becoming in turn melancholy, proud, belligerent, genial, amorous, deceitful, and lunatic. Her servant and the shepherd swains who surround her alternately suffer and enjoy her moods, mistreatment, deception, and advances. Finally she is translated to the moon, to rule it. This entertaining and lively story, mixing fantasy, high comedy, farce, intrigue, and adventure, is a thoroughgoing allegory. Near the surface there is a metaphorical representation of the planets as bickering human beings, but the heart of the matter is in the fact that the woman is Pandora, universal Woman. Her translation to the moon sums up in one symbol the mutability which is the meaning of her career and which defines the nature of women. Thenceforth, at Nature's command, she will rule over women's nuptials and birth, making them

> mutable in all their loves,
> Fantasticall, childish, and folish, in their desires,
> Demaunding toyes:
> And starke madde when they cannot have their will.
>
> (5.1.323–26)

But the ending also summarizes the human condition. At the beginning of the play, when women were as yet uncreated, the shepherds had prayed to Nature for a mate, and Pandora is Nature's answer. They are bound to it by the decrees of Nature, and the final lunar trinity defines the fated human condition as the eternal comic triangle: the foolish lover, the tortured husband, and the fantastical wife. The only possible reaction is laughter.

Laughter alone is frail shelter in so bleak a world, and if one does not accept the play as jocular, it is tinged with bitterness. That the play was probably played as jocular should be clear, I think, from the tone of the dialogue and the episodes of pleasantly fantastic farce, but for most Elizabethans the joke would be a half-truth, not a lie. It defines the condition of fallen human nature with some accuracy. Transposed into a different key, it is the acrid domestic comedy that Milton's Adam and Eve play out in the last part of Book IX, a short and funny view of the hell to which men and women are bound by their nature. What is lacking, of course, is the divine rescue through forgiveness and charity, the story Milton tells in the remaining books.

In some of his other plays Lyly presents a more nearly complete view of the human situation. Characters are equally the victims of their natures, and their love is equally ridiculous; but they find rescue and forgiveness, and their love, ridiculous as it is, leads to harmony in the end.

Thus *Gallathea* opens—as common theory prescribed—with the

threat of tragedy. The land, we learn in the opening scene, is under the doom of an angry god, Neptune, who has demanded the periodic sacrifice of the fairest maiden to a sea monster. Led by their natural paternal affection, the fathers of the fair Gallathea and Phillida disguise their daughters as men. The two girls meet and "naturally" fall in love, each deceived by the male dress of the other. Their foolish irrationality, however, defined as in the common morality metaphor by the comic deception, is not uniquely theirs: it is generalized by the wholesale falling in love of Diana's nymphs. Cupid has gotten among them and mischievously stricken them with love for the two girls, whom they mistake for men. Diana is of course outraged and points out to them the sorry truth:

"Cast before your eyes the loves of *Venus* truls, their fortune, theyr fancies, their ends. What are they els but *Silenus* pictures; without Lambes and Doves, within, Apes and Owles: who like *Ixion* imbrace clowdes for *Iuno*, the shadowes of vertue in steede of the substance." (3.4.41–44)

Her imagery, it may be noted, widens the scope of the folly. We are again reminded of the truth symbolized by Silenus's "pictures" (*imagunculae*, usually described as small images or figures): the *inevitable* opposition, as Renaissance satirists and moralists saw it, between the visible surface of things and the inner reality, the values prized by the world and those discerned by the wise man. Ixion's embrace, which was almost as proverbial, figured the same opposition, contrasting the unsubstantial show of worldly good with its failure to bring satisfaction and its evanescence—"behind a dream." [16]

Meanwhile, other kinds of human folly are surveyed as four boys, in carefully spaced scenes that counterpoint the pastoral action, hold up to mockery the jargon and pretensions of a mariner, an alchemist, and an astrologer. As Saccio has argued, it is the prideful ambition of these men and their attempt to realize it by "absurdly complicated rational systems, over-eleborate, over-measured, ridiculously subdivided," that makes them ridiculous.[17] Despite their vaulting language, the mariner is nearly drowned, the alchemist starves, and the astrologer falls backward into a pond. They too, like Ixion, have thought to embrace Juno and have grasped a cloud.

The comic action is not merely the spectacle of absurd irrationality, however. For the two girls, their fathers, and the nymphs, it is also the breaking of divine law—Neptune's and Diana's—and the wrath of the gods hangs over them. Yet the play emphasizes this law-breaking, not as a malevolent or criminal act, like the seduction of Mankind by Covetous, but as natural and irresistible. Nature has made the girls fair and has made their fathers "kind." Gallathea laments that Nature gave a Phillida so fair a face and to herself "a fortune so hard" (2.4.8–9). Phillida complains to Gallathea "that Nature framed you not a woman" (3.2.1). An erring nymph replies to Diana's angry rebuke,

"Madame, if love were not a thing beyonde reason, we might then give a reason of our doings, but so devine is his force, that it worketh effects as contrarie to that wee wishe, as unreasonable against that wee ought." (3.4.54–57)

In a court performance the erring nymphs and their mistress must have suggested to spectators the obvious analogy of irrepressible ladies-in-waiting and *their* chaste, severe, and royal mistress. That is certainly one level of meaning and for some spectators perhaps the only one beside the literal surface of pastoral mythology. Renaissance mythology, however, was dense with potential significance (surely the statement needs no defense and illustration at this date), and for spectators educated in the lore of the mythographers other meanings can be postulated. Saccio, who has examined the mythological implications very carefully, has argued that Neptune can be taken quite seriously as "primary image of divinity in the play." [18] For spectators who were acquainted with common Christian teaching, furthermore, the opening situation is analogous to the generalized condition of natural man. It is a metaphor, a stage picture, of a world burdened by guilt and living under the doom of an angry god. It is also the comedy (for it is funny) of men born under one law, to another bound, driven by their natures to break the laws—Neptune's decree, Diana's rule of chastity—that bind them. This is the state of mankind under the Old Law as it was commonly understood, and it is the state of unredeemed man at all times. The analogy is reinforced by the association of the virgin sacrifice to the sea monster, a version of the myth variously told of Andromeda, Hesione, the daughter of Erectheus, and the princess rescued by St. George —all of whom were interpreted as imaging man's state before the redemption.

From that state the characters are rescued and harmony is restored as in real life by the forgivenesss of the angry god, here Neptune. He reconciles the irreconcilable Venus and Diana, and he remits the sacrifice he has demanded. Venus then promises to make either Gallathea or Phillida a man so that they will be happy, "for never shall it be said that Nature or Fortune shall over-throwe Love and Fayth" (5.3.132–33).

It is possible that this last solution of the insoluble is the dramatist's deliberately insouciant use of the *deus ex machina*, like the ending of *The Beggar's Opera*, and perhaps that is one of the effects Lyly aimed at. But the possibility that it makes sense in an Elizabethan context should not be disregarded. Saccio sees its significance in the fact that the reconciliation of love and chastity (Venus and Diana) "is impossible for human beings." Huppé points out that Lyly's Christian spectators would have concluded that this human impossibility was possible only as Christian mystery.[19] This seems clear. The play is coherent as a statement about the human condition as the Christian teaching known to most of the audience described it; because of the limitation of fallen human nature and because passionate man subjects himself to Fortune, he can achieve happiness only through the divine suspension of natural law. That suspension, an actual historical event, has made human happiness possible.

It should perhaps be stressed again that "meaning" here must be counted a statistical generalization, more or less probable for an indeterminate but significant part of the audience, as that audience is defined by its ascertainable learning and training. In this case the relevant knowledge of Christian doctrine can be estimated as very nearly universal; that of the allegorical interpretation of mythology, roughly, as demanding about as much education as Shakespeare had received.[20] Skills and interests such as Sidney apparently expected of readers of *The Arcadia*, Spenser, of readers of the *Faerie Queene*, or Lyly himself, very obviously, of the audiences of *Endymion*, are relevant, and these instances, as well as the circumstances of production by Paul's Boys, suggest a limited but substantial coterie audience with the requisite literary training. The themes of the tenor are familiar from mysteries and moralities; the disparity between vehicle and tenor seems to be no greater than many of the examples cited in chapter I, and the consistency of the vehicle-tenor relationship seems relatively high. On balance, it seems reasonably probable that a significant number of spectators might be expected to be conscious of such a meaning.

Mother Bombie, Endymion, and *Love's Metamorphosis*, in exploiting similar themes, all use love in much the same way, as the prime exemplar of inevitable human folly, and all exemplify forgiveness directly. In expressing other ideas, however, they use several different metaphors.

Mother Bombie states the theme by putting to novel use the familiar gags and devices of Roman comedy. There are four distinguishable actions. Two stern fathers try to marry off the young lovers for money and are, of course, outwitted. Two other fathers, also impelled by avarice, try to conceal the fact that their children are "naturals"—morons—in order to marry them off. They too are outwitted. A boy and girl who believe themselves brother and sister confess with horror that they love each other. The witty serving boys, who have been involved in the first two plots, cheat a hackneyman, a sergeant, and a scrivener and are threatened with arrest.

In the denouement an old nurse reveals that the morons are really brother and sister (her own children) and the supposed brother and sister are unrelated, the children of the second pair of fathers, and may therefore marry. She had changed them in the cradle. The not-so-stern parents forgive the children who have out-witted them, and all forgive and pay the fines of the witty serving boys.

Lyly gives coherence to this odd mixture of plot scraps by insisting that the play is about nature, law, and folly, or more precisely, about man's natural folly which leads him to violate laws of one sort or another. The words *law, nature, fool,* and related words are key terms in the dialogue. They gloss the action, making us constantly aware of behavior as natural or unnatural, lawful or unlawful, according to the law of nature or the law of man, foolish or clever or foolish although clever. *Fool, folly, foolish* and their synonyms, at first applied literally to the two naturals, spread and attach themselves to the fools' reputed fathers, to the clever young lovers, and finally to the witty, mischief-loving servant boys. All are judged on the scale that measures wit and folly, and all are found in some way natural fools, like the two naturals. The concept of nature expands in much the same way. The play opens with pleasantry about the naturals, sly allusions to their folly deriving naturally from their reputed fathers, a clever twisting of the Horatian phrase, *naturam expellas furca, tamen usque recurret,* and of *Quod natura dedit, tollere nemo potest.* The rebellious young lady complains of her father that Nature made her his child, not his slave, and the father of the rebellious young man complains that his son has learned to hate against Nature, and he threatens to make him stoop or his own mind will break the laws of Nature. The reputed brother and sister lament their "affections beyond nature" and their "unnatural" love and rejoice that at least they have not become "monsters," but they also argue that "that which nature warrenteth laws forbid." The wisewoman, Mother Bombie, tells them they will be married,

> By the lawes of God, Nature, and the land,
> Your parents shall be glad, and give you their lande,
> You shal each of you displace a foole.
> And both together must releeve a foole.
> If this be not true, call me olde foole.
>
> (3.2.41–45)

She tells the nurse who has changed the children,

> In studying to be overnaturall,
> Thou art like to be unnaturall,
> And all about a naturall.
>
> (5.3.16–18)

When the nurse confesses to the parents, she offers in excuse that "nature wrought with me" (5.3.281). Then she shows that she can remove the artificial birthmarks from the changelings, but not from the true children, for "no herb can undo that nature hath done" (5.3.309).

The laws of nature have been threatened in one case, believed threatened in another; the laws of the land have been violated and mocked; parents have neglected their responsibilities; children have flouted the authority of their parents, and servants that of their masters. (One can make this sound very much like *Lear*.) Only pardon can bring matters to a happy ending, and pardon is granted. Facing the nurse, one of the fathers she has cheated tells her, "Vicinia, thy fact is pardoned; though the law would see it punished" (5.4.342). Then the two bilked fathers offer to continue to keep the poor naturals whom they have reared. But pardon is not merely granted; it is granted with good humor, a shame-faced grin of fellow feeling for the natural impulse that requires forgiveness. As one of the not-so-stern fathers remarks when about to forgive the rebellious youngsters, "in truth their love stirs up nature in me."

At the beginning of the play the four fathers were lamenting their lots; at the end, having seen their own folly and forgiven the others, they announce four days of feasting. It is nature, not malevolence that needs to be forgiven, and once forgiven it ceases to be lamentable and becomes a source of joy. The point is familiar, not only from homilies and tracts, but also from mystery and morality. The novelty of the play consists rather in the vehicle, the New Comedy intrigue of clever-foolish old men and their clever-foolish offspring, borrowed from Roman comedy, or perhaps from the contemporary *commedia grave*, which was reshaping the older *commedia erudita* into a philosophical and religious vehicle.[21]

One other feature may be mentioned: the theme of Providence noted above. Although *Mother Bombie* contains no such specific reference to Providence as in *The Supposes*, it employs the concept in much the same way, that is by building up a situation of great complexity, which none of the characters involved in it can see clearly or see through to a solution, and simultaneously implying behind this tangle a clear rational pattern and a happy outcome. It does this chiefly by the figure of Mother Bombie, the wise woman whom the other characters consult from time to time and who predicts the future. We are constantly made aware that the tangle is not a tangle and that for these people of good will suffering only from their inescapable human nature, it will have a happy ending. That is a loose definition of the operation of Providence.

Both *Endymion* and *Love's Metamorphosis* are built, like *Gallathea* and *Sapho*, upon fantastic myth, and they employ many of the motifs, such as the wandering in the wilderness, the magic transformation, and the test of true love, which are staples of the romantic drama early and late. In both plays Lyly assumes as usual that all men fall in love and that love is in some way foolish. This is basic, the inevitable result of man's fallen nature. Both plays, however, not only contrast the ideal of a rational, ordered love, but also present the imperfect love in a tableau which is in itself a symbolic picture of the human condition.

The central character in *Endymion* is Cynthia, clearly presented as a metaphor of both the moon and Elizabeth. The hapless Endymion, in love with her, is cast into enchanted slumber by order of the fair but jealous Tellus. He experiences a mysterious dream vision and becomes an old man in his slumber. Cynthia puts Tellus under the guard of Corsites, a strong man who falls in love with his beautiful charge. Victimized by her charms he too is cast asleep and is covered with ugly spots. Meanwhile Sir Tophas, an amusing *miles gloriosus* who consorts with the inevitable clever servant boys, is smitten with love of the grotesque witch Dipsas. He too falls asleep and experiences a comic dream vision. Endymion's faithful friend Eumenides, scorned by the fair Semele, discovers the cure for Endymion's sleep with the help of the old man Geron. It is a kiss from Cynthia, and once that is graciously given, all the other lovers obtain their loves. Endymion himself becomes young again, and even old Geron, who has been divorced and banished by Dipsas, is taken back happily by his repentant wife.

The play demands interpretation. For the interpretive critic it has the irresistible comehither of *Finnegan's Wake*. Lyly himself, one suspects, must have planned such an effect; everything in it points tantalizingly to a larger or further significance. Only one great truth, however, the beauty, justice, and mercy of the queen —is immediately apparent and universally recognized, and one other point, first suggested by Huppé, that Endymion's dream implies the debate and final agreement of Justice and Mercy, seems to be gaining a consensus.[22] These two points are accepted as basic in the discussion that follows.

To go beyond them, one may find a plausible Elizabethan interpretation if one accepts the debate of Justice and Mercy as related to its usual concern: the condemnation and forgiveness of humanity, both simply *qua* human kind and as it errs and repents. The play as a whole then figures the human condition, which is shown at the beginning as comic frustration and at the end as joy after liberation from the threat of justice by the mirror of divine mercy (a familiar role for Elizabeth). Fallen human nature is not only shown in action; it is symbolized by the enchanted old man Geron (Γερων), the Old Man whom St. Paul urges men to put off, and by the old age which comes upon the enchanted Endymion. The specific irrationality of human nature is symbolized by sleep, as in the Wit and Science plays or the lost *Cradle of Security*. Endymion, Corsites, and Sir Tophas all sleep on stage, Endymion and Corsites through the enchantment of Tellus, the lovely earth. Sir Tophas, who is a natural fool, sleeps "naturally." Corsites, who has erred through actual desire of Tellus, is spotted, like Wit in *Wit and Science* or Conscience in

The Three Ladies of London. Redemption comes from the un-
selfish brotherly love of Eumenides and from Cynthia's love and
forgiveness. Her chaste kiss awakens the sleeping Endymion, and
her grant of favor enables him to "put off the Old Man." She
grants happiness, indeed, to all, resolves all conflicts, and forgives
the sins or infirmities of each.

The significance of the ending, like that of the whole play, is
likely to be dual for most spectators, political and theological. On
the one hand, Cynthia-Elizabeth acts as a ruler should, imitating
the Divinity whose deputy she is, forgiving her subjects their
transgressions and enlisting their loyalty. But Cynthia (like the
Queen herself) is also a metaphor of divinity. On this level the
play presents, just as in the moralities, the predicament of mankind, foolish, irrational, and condemned, but forgiven, and
granted whatever "bliss" he chooses.

The bliss chosen is of various sorts. At one extreme is
Endymion's love, defined both by his turning away from the
earth, Tellus, and by his humble adoration of Cynthia as mirror
of divinity and meeting point, as suggested in the first scene of
the play, of the sublunary and transient with the transcendant
and eternal. From this height the scale of love and lovers extends
downward through gradations of increasingly mundane contentment. Eumenides gains the reluctant favor of his scornful courtly
mistress; Corsites, who wants the Earth, gets it; Geron rejoins the
(repentant and reformed) enchantress to whom he was wedded;
Sir Tophas' passion is undiscriminating—"so she be a wench, I
care not." He gets his wench.

The tableau ending, in short, presents a universe which, for all
its obvious differences, is the same as Dante's in that everyone gets
what he wants, and what he gets therefore defines him. It is only
superficially so many happy endings to so many plots; beneath
that surface it is a caricature of various conditions of the human
will. The vehicle of the metaphor is marriage, similar though not
identical to the marriage metaphors of the Wit and Science plays,
The Three Ladies of London (where Love is wedded to Dissimulation) or *The Three Lords and Three Ladies of London*

(which celebrates the triple marriages of Love, Lucre, and Conscience to Policy, Pomp, and Pleasure). As a means of differentiating among the characters—or the values that they represent —it probably builds more, however, upon the theatrical experience of *Campaspe*, which contrasts Alexander, Diogenes, and Apelles in the same kind of tableau, and of plays like *The Trial of Treasure*, which bring their vice and virtue characters to contrasting symbolic endings. Looking ahead, it is part of the theatrical experience that makes possible the endings of *Twelfth Night* and *As You Like It*.

Love's Metamorphosis moves to a slightly different kind of conclusion. Its problem, set by the opening scene, is no less than the existence of evil, made specific in three major questions about love: how can love be thought to have created a world in which there is so little love?; how can love be said to be divine when it drives men to such earthly and transient ends?; and what course is open to men, "being in their own natures more miserable than beasts," except to "pursue their owne ruines" by yielding to the unruly powers of their blood? (1.1.1–16). The questions are solemn, but the scene should obviously be played for a light tone, close to the wistful, smiling irony of Rosalind and Celia meeting Corin and Silvius in the forest of Arden. Lyly's disputants, three amorous foresters, resolve to "bee constant in the worlds errours and seeke oure owne torments" (1.1.19–20). Their resolution is one of humorous despair, but it is based upon and reminds the audience of the ideal of rational control and its impossibility, since men are doomed by their natures to the misery of passionate turmoil.

The characters exemplify or symbolize various reactions to the problem posed by the first scene. With the possible exception of the atheistic self-lover Erisicthon who tries to destroy the nymph Fidelia ("the expresse patterne of chastitie"), all are characterized by the attitudes they take toward love—fickle, coy, lustful, meretricious, disdainful, and so on. By the end of the fourth act all are in trouble: enchanted, betrayed, starved, or forsaken. They are rescued, as in *Endymion*, by the selfless love of a mortal, the tenderhearted Protea, and by the intervention of a god, Cupid. The significance of the intervention derives from the significance of Cupid himself in the play. Although his costuming and appearance are not indicated in the printed text, it seems clear, as both Saccio and Parnell have pointed out, that Lyly did not intend the visual image of a mischievous little boy out of Moschus. He was probably at least as tall as the other boy actors; he has his own temple at which the other characters, including the goddess Ceres, assemble and present their offerings, and in the denouement it is he who interrogates the erring nymphs, threatens punishments, and assigns mates. As Saccio remarks, he is "the presiding deity" in the play, and he is so on two levels: on the human level, where he instructs the other characters in love and courtship, and on the cosmic level, as the "great god" that he claims to be, more powerful than Jupiter, representing, in Saccio's words, "the love which orders and preserves the world, whose power is absolute and whose realm is everywhere."[23] He himself defines his power thus:

"What is love, divine love, but the quintescens of chastitie, and affections binding by heavenly motions, that cannot be undone by earthly meanes and must not be comptrolled by any man?" (2.1.123–126)

It is both divine love and human affection; it joins *l'amor che move il sole e l'altre stella* with the human love between the sexes. Cupid is thus a visible refutation of the scepticism of the play's opening lines: "I cannot see . . . why it is fain'd by the Poets, that Love sat upon the Chaos and created the world; since in the world there is so little love" (1.1.1–3). Such a concept can be taken as Christian Neoplatonism, as Saccio points out,[24] but it will also make sense in terms of more widespread Christian teaching. Cupid's intervention, in either case, becomes a metaphor of God's love of man and of His pardon for man's errors. All the characters are forgiven, including the repentant Erisicthon, and all granted the happiness of obtaining the love they desire.

In this ending, unlike that of *Endymion*, Lyly marks only lightly the differences in the kinds of happiness the lovers achieve, emphasizing instead the bitter-sweetness won by all three foresters and their loves. Although Cupid can say in conclusion, "there is none but is happy," Lyly makes comic capital out of the limitations of happiness in human love. The three nymphs whom Cupid has changed into a rock, a rose, and a bird to symbolize their attitudes toward love, he now changes back into their proper forms, and he bids them yield to the foresters. All three at first refuse, alleging that the vexations of love on earth are bitterer than their transformed existences. The lass who has been a rock says, "rather had I been worn with the continual beating of waves, than dulled with the importunities of men, whose open flatteries make way to their secret lusts" (5.4.60–63). She who has been a rose says,

"more good commeth of the rose, than can by love: when it is fresh, it hath a sweete savour; love, a sour taste; the Rose when it is old, loseth not his vertue; love, when it is stale, waxeth loathsome. . . . In the rose, how ever it be, there is sweetness; in love nothing but bitternesse." (5.4.78–84)

She who has been a bird laments that "in the heavens I saw an orderly course, in the earth nothing but disorderly love, and pievishnesse" (5.4.96–98).

Such lines must be spoken with flippant gaiety, but they make their point and they keep the scene from dissolving into a vision of saccharine delight. They are reinforced, moreover, by the terms on which the nymphs finally yield. The rock-nymph, for instance, stipulates, "I am content so as *Ramis*, when hee finds me cold in love, or hard in beliefe, hee attribute it to his owne folly; in that I retain some nature of the Rocke he changed me into (5.4.133–35). Similarly the ex-rose warns that as a result of her former prickles her love may find her slightly shrewish, and the ex-bird warns that her vestigial feathers may appear as a tendency to gad. Clearly the happiness-ever-after into which the lovers are moving is severely limited by the human nature that it is rooted in. But it is also directed, controlled, and ordered by the "divine love," the "heavenly motions" of which it is part. The point is stated in theatrical terms. Cupid, representing the love that has created the world, is in visible command of the scene, kneeled to and commanding. The harmony that results, imperfect as it is, is worked out under his direction, and he takes credit for it, announcing at the end, "I will soare up into heaven, to settle the loves of the gods, that in earth have dispos'd the affections of men" (5.4.168–70). The scene thus represents an answer to the questions raised in the opening scene and denies the atheism which was Erisicthon's answer to them. Divine love indeed guides the world, forgiving, reconciling, and granting to men the kind of happiness they desire. It is men, not God, who deny love on earth, as it is men who by their desires have limited the satisfactions—the happiness—of which they are capable. Granted furthermore, that the inescapable nature of man renders him to some degree ridiculous, that fact can be turned to the pleasure of laughter. Human love can therefore be rejoiced in (Erisicthon invites everyone to a wedding feast); the foresters have not, as they predicted, "more miserably than beasts pursue[d] their own ruins" (1.1.16); indeed, as Cupid has indicated by threatening to turn the reluctant nymphs into monsters, it is only the denial of love that makes men monsters "to all men odious and . . . to . . . themselves . . . loathsome" (5.4.106–9).

Much of Lyly's contribution to the development of comedy must be passed over here, his use of witty dialogue, for instance, or devices like the clever servant boys. To sum up the main points noticed in the preceding discussion, however, he developed subject matters, dramatic metaphors, and themes which enabled audiences and playwrights to proceed to the romantic comedies that followed. He borrowed subjects from Roman comedy, from popular dramatic romance, from myth, and apparently from semidramatic forms like Heywood's dialogues or the Italian *trattati d'amore*. He exploited the potential metaphors of myth, as the allegorical interpretations of the fashionable mythographers presumably taught him to do, and by mixing myth and romance, he gave the latter a significance it had lacked on the popular stage. But it is above all his exploitation of new comic themes that, it seems to me, must have forced him, his successors, and their au-

134

diences to widen their concept of the comic on the level of vehicle as well as tenor. The new themes are related to the notion of man as comic in his very nature as opposed to the notion of man as comic in his correctable or reformable vice and folly. They mark a real shift in dramatic concern, a shift symbolized by the difference between Wager's Moros, or the sinner as fool, in *The Longer Thou Livest* and Lyly's two naturals, who represent the natural man as fool. The former as a person is guilty of crimes; since efforts to chastise and reform him fail, he is finally damned. As unreason in the soul, he is to be corrected. The latter are "guilty" only of being what they are. As persons who are caricatures of natural man, they are presented as ridiculous (since he *is* ridiculous), but they are treated mercifully and they are adopted by their foster parents. As natural depravity itself they cannot be reformed. They are inevitable; they must be forgiven, lived with, and in the assurance of hope, they can be laughed at. We are funny because of them.

V.

Friar Bacon and Friar Bungay.

Greene's *Friar Bacon and Friar Bungay*, although it was probably written before Lyly's last plays and although it shows very little of Lyly's influence, in the usual sense of that term, is apparently the first public theater play which exploits the concept of romantic comedy that Lyly had explored. In other ways it belongs to a group of plays like *George a Greene, The Shoemakers' Holiday*, and *The Merry Devil of Edmonton* which mingle kind hearts and coronets in praise of merry England and true love. It accepts such values, but by relating them to a comprehensive view of the world, demonstrates that the loose genre which embodies them is capable of significant development.

It can be most easily analyzed, I think, into three, or three and a half, main plots focussing respectively upon Prince Edward, Friar Bacon, Fair Margaret, and Miles, the foolish servant of Friar Bacon. In the semi-political action that begins and ends the play, Prince Edward takes the advice of his fool and decides to seduce Margaret by using the necromancy of Friar Bacon and the rhetoric of his friend, Earl Lacy, whom he sends to court her. Lacy, however, betrays the Prince by winning her for himself in honest marriage, and Prince Edward threatens to kill him. Then, in a sensational about-face, he masters his lust and anger, forgives Lacy and Margaret, and returns to court, where he falls in love with and marries Elinor of Castile, as his father had arranged.

Meanwhile Margaret, remaining at home while Lacy accompanies Edward to court, inadvertently causes the death of two local squires who quarrel over her and kill each other. When she receives a letter from Lacy jilting her, she renounces the world and resolves to serve God as a nun. Lacy intercepts her in time, however, and explains that his letter was only a test of her constancy. After momentary hesitation she yields to him, and they join the royal couple in the double wedding that ends the play.

In the third main plot Friar Bacon at first demonstrates his magic by merry tricks. He magically transports from a neighboring town the hostess of the inn on whom an academic colleague has been "studying"; he shows Prince Edward the love of Lacy and Margaret and interrupts their intended wedding, and he defeats the German magician Vandermast in a contest of magic before the King and the Emperor. Then, because of his own sleepiness and the stupidity of his servant Miles, he fails to perfect the brazen head which would have circled England with a wall of brass, and he inadvertently causes the death of two Oxford students. By means of his magic glass they see their fathers kill each other over fair Margaret, and they themselves then kill each other. Bacon thereupon repents his use of necromancy, abjures it, and resolves to spend the rest of his life in devotion.

Finally, in a late scene, Friar Bacon's servant Miles enters, haunted by one of the Friar's diabolic agents. He greets the devil merrily, gets from him the promise of a tapster's job in Hell, and rides happily off on his back.

The three main plots are roughly parallel: each builds to a climactic turning-point, which is also a repentance scene, and then leads its protagonist to a joyful ending. This is the pattern of the old moralities with a happy ending, like *Mind, Will, and Understanding, Magnificence*, and *Wit and Science*. Contrasts within it, like Margaret's double repentance or the different natures of the errors repented of, define the meanings precisely, but the basic pattern gives rough shape to each and to the play as a whole. Like the old moralities it is concerned with man's search for happiness, and it asserts that, though he errs ridiculously in that search, he can repent, be forgiven, and reach his goal. But it is also, like the social moralities, concerned with the social macrocosm. Edward's repentance and reform is made to imply England's happiness as well as his own.

Edward's error is obviously the classic one of lust, or lust and anger. It is conceived in the usual terms of rationalist psychology as the overthrow of reason by passion, and it is constantly realized in theatrical metaphors. Rafe, Edward's fool, acts the part of the morality play's misleading counsellor who is also the protagonist's own folly, like Fancy in *Magnificence*. Prince Edward not only follows his advice but installs him in his own place as leader of the band of retainers and dresses him in his own costume, disguising himself as one of the band. The inversion of order in the band, folly on top, reason below, thus duplicates the inversion in Edward's own psyche. The band, furthermore, then proceeds to riot, or near-riot, in the streets of Oxford, first trying to attack Bacon and Miles with their daggers, and later brawling in a tavern and almost killing the vintner. The moral significance of the disorder is reinforced by clever cross-cutting. Between the two riot scenes Greene shows Edward gazing into Bacon's glass and watching Lacy betray him by making love to Margaret. Lacy's usurpation of Edward's place parallels the inversion of the social order in the band; and both, moreover, are the result of Edward's own abdication. The abdication of his reason meanwhile is both exemplified directly and symbolized by still another means. While watching his betrayal he loses his temper and seeks to stab them through the glass:

Edward. Gogs wounds, *Bacon*, they kisse! Ile stab them.

> *Bacon.* Oh, hold your handes, my lord, it is the glasse!
> *Edward.* Coller to see the traitors gree so well,
>   Made me thinke the shadowes substances.
>
>   (742–45) [1]

His analysis is precise in the terms of rationalist phychology. When reason is dominated by a passion such as choler, it errs, mistaking shadow for substance, the show of good for good itself. To verbalize the stage metaphor, we may say that Edward views the lovers in the enchanted glass of his own passion and mistakes their murder for his good. This metaphor is an alternative statement of the moral-psychological inversion writ large in the riot scenes that precede and follow it, and it is visually related to them by the dagger and the gesture of violence, but it emphasizes the resultant error, whereas they emphasize disorder.

Edward's conquest of his passion, in the scene that follows the second riot scene, is celebrated with the same kind of rhetoric and metaphors that Lyly used for Alexander in the same situation. The opening of the scene is linked to the preceding ones by the dagger and violence with which Edward threatens Lacy, but the stage picture is of the angry tyrant about to execute his bloody justice upon kneeling lovers, and then, as he masters himself, of the true prince:

> *Edward*, art thou that famous prince of *Wales,*
> Who at *Damasco* beat the *Sarasens,*
> And broughtst home triumphe on thy launces point,
> And shall thy plumes be puld by *Venus* downe?
> Is it princely to dissever lovers leagues,
> To part such friends as glorie in their loves?
> Leave, *Ned*, and make a vertue of this fault,
> And further *Peg* and *Lacie* in their loves:
> So in subduing fancies passion,
> Conquering thy selfe, thou getst the richest spoile.
> *Lacie* rise up. Faire Peggie, heeres my hand.
>
>   (1035–45)

139

Like Alexander, Edward has here made himself as prince and conqueror the metaphor or personification of reason subduing passion. By conquering his passion he has become the prince, a point realized visually by his change of costume and of course by his ensuing action. In the next scene he joins the royal company and greets Elinor of Castile in full princely dress, his appearance emphasized by remarks of Friar Bacon and the Emperor:

> See where Prince *Edward* comes to welcome you,
> Gratious as the morning starre of heaven:
>
> (1260–61)

and,

> Is this Prince *Edward*, *Henries* royall sonne
> How martiall is the figure of his face,
> Yet lovely and beset with Amorets.
>
> (1262–64)

When Edward reforms, however, he does not become passionless; he redirects his passion as the king wishes and the country's welfare demands. He greets Elinor with a rhetoric quite as ardent as any in his scenes with Margaret, and three scenes later, his wooing done, he reenters exuberantly, Elinor on his arm, declaiming,

> Should *Paris* enter in the Courts of *Greece*,
> And not lie fettered in faire Hellens lookes?
> Or *Phoebus* scape those piercing amorits
> That *Daphne* glaunsed at his deitie?
> Can *Edward*, then, sit by a flame and freeze,
> Whose heat puts *Hellen* and faire *Daphne* downe?
> Now, Monarcks, aske the ladie if we gree.
>
> (1666–72)

We must be clear, incidentally, about the mode of drama here. Interpreted as psychological realism, it shows Edward as the sort of hypocrite and political opportunist that some critics try to make of Prince Hall, and it makes nonsense of the play. We need not expect psychological realism. Edward's sudden mastery of his passion and redirection of it are not utterly implausible, but

140

they are presented by symbolic shorthand rather than naturalistic representation. Edward has not new-linked his old lust to political avarice; he has redirected his passion as it should be. He is a hero, and his gesture of rational control in his scene with Lacy and Margaret is repeated in the magnified terms of the social metaphor when he joins the royal party. As son and subject he is now controlled by his father and king. Passion is directed by the symbol of reason common to family and kingdom and, so directed, serves the great cause of peace among nations.

This, in turn, is symbolized by the tableau of the Emperor and the kings of Castile and England and reinforced by Friar Bacon's closing prophesy of the peace to come under Elizabeth:

> But then the stormy threats of wars shall cease;
> The horse shall stampe as carelesse of the pike,
> Drums shall be turn'd to timbrels of delight; . . .
> And peace from heaven shall harbour in these leaves,
> That gorgeous beatifies this matchlesse flower.
>
> (2076–82)

The play opens with an orthodox "beginning in sorrow" which is also a question. Lacy asks Edward, "Why looks my lord like to a troubled sky?" and Edward's frank avowal of passion implies the further question—"how can his passion be cured?" He begins with the fool's answer, but by the end of the play he has discarded that answer, and arrived at the real one; the orthodox "ending in joy" is achieved. The significance of the question and answers, however, has broadened with the movement of the play to include the general problem of passionate misery and its cure and to include the problem of social order.

If the foregoing remarks about the Prince Edward plot have some measure of truth, they are also obviously false in at least one respect, for they neglect entirely the spirit of holiday revelry which is a very marked feature of the play and, what concerns us now, of those scenes in which Edward's friends and retainers appear. Thus although it is true that, with the fool at their head, with their quick violence, their tough nonchalance, and their ready, irreverent laughter, they clearly imply both social and moral-psychological disorder, it is also true that, unlike their morality-play counterparts, they are not really vicious. They are only out for sport and are happy, when the game has gone far enough, to cry halt and pay damages. They accept Rafe as their head in the same spirit that young gentlemen accepted a lord of misrule at Christmas, and that tradition—of the Christmas Prince or the May Day Lord—is as clearly evident in their scenes as the morality tradition. They are in play, not earnest; they are not vices themselves; they enact, in sport, the roles of vices.

The resultant relaxed and festive tone of their scenes not only contributes to the festive nature of the play as a whole, but offers constant reassurance that the play will end happily and that we need not "worry about" even Edward, despite his very real dereliction, that indeed he may be the better, as he is certainly the more appealing, for his foolish passion. Greene is also able, as a consequence, to end his play and reform his hero without risking a scene like the repudiation of Falstaff.

Friar Bacon's error corresponding to Edward's is his lust for glory, and the personification of his folly corresponding to Rafe is his foolish servant Miles. His desire for glory is clearly established in his first scene when a colleague points out that,

> if thy cunning worke these myracles,
> *England* and *Europe* shall admire thy fame,
> And *Oxford* shall in characters of brasse,
> And statues such as were built up in *Rome*,
> Eternize Frier *Bacon* for his art.
>
> (210–14)

He wins glory for England in his contest with Vandermast, and he loses his glory when the brazen head is broken. That is the burden of his lament—"My life, my fame, my glorie, all are past" —and the shattered head lying on the floor is an obvious symbol, like Richard II's mirror, of that brittle, shattered glory.

Miles is associated with him from the beginning as a low-comic parody of him, not like the servant boys in Lyly's plays who consciously mock their masters with superior wit, but as an ally. His jeers at the unlucky Friar Burden and the rioting courtiers, for instance, are slapstick versions of Bacon's more polished sarcasm, and they are delivered under the protection of Bacon's magic. He is, in fact, a kind of comic extension of Bacon. While Bacon entertains Prince Edward, Miles entertains the other courtiers. He sets a mock feast for the royal visitors before Bacon invites them to his sumptuous banquet, and in the scene with the brazen head he takes Bacon's place just as, earlier, Rafe takes Edward's.

Bacon's reform takes place in two stages. In the first, the scene with the brazen head, he dismisses Miles and calls on "some fiend" to torment him, but he does not recant his desire for glory or his magic. He is still lamenting his departed glory in his next scene, and he allows the two students to put his enchanted glass to its last, fatal employment. It is only then that he realizes its evil and his own sin, repents, and resolves to spend the rest of his life "in pure devotion, praying to my God" (1851). As he breaks the glass, he says,

> So fade the glasse, and end with it the showes,
> That Nigromancie did infuse the christall with.
>
> (1826–27)

The blow clearly symbolizes Bacon's renunciation, but the glass has simultaneously become the symbol of the enticing "shows" which have misled the various characters. For Bacon these are earthly glory, for Edward, as for the two rival suitors, they are beauty, and for their wretched sons they are anger or revenge. The satisfactions offered by all these things are illusory, like shows, "fading," like the glass. They are also enticing, like necromancy, the work of the devil.

Margaret's sin, as she confesses it, is that of loving Lacy more than God and, beyond that apparently, of loving the world. Like Edward and Bacon she repents, but then, though she does not recant her repentance, she decides to yield to the frailty she acknowledges and marry Lacy instead of entering a nunnery. Her action, as it parallels and modifies the others, helps to define the comic vision that they have outlined.

She defines, first of all, a kind of love, chaste, pure, self-sacrificing, not altering when it alteration finds or bending with the remover to remove, that obviously differs from Edward's lust and that is not dramatized in the other characters—including Lacy—that we see. She offers her life to save Lacy's from the wrath of the Prince; she keeps her wealthy suitors at arm's length while Lacy is away, and, rather than marry another man when she thinks Lacy has jilted her, she resolves to enter the nunnery. This resolve, however, is phrased in a rhetoric that goes far beyond the demands of demonstrating her loyalty to Lacy:

> The world shal be to her as vanitie,
> Wealth, trash; love, hate; pleasure, dispaire:
> For I will straight to stately Fremingham,
> And in the abby there be shorne a Nun,
> And yeld my loves and libertie to God.
>
> (1515–19)

Greene gives her a chance, furthermore, for a very lengthy display of this kind of speech by setting up a scene in which first her father, and then Lacy, seek to dissuade her from her vows. She answers eloquently, using the traditional phrases and imagery *de contemptu mundi:*

> A, father, when the hermonie of heaven
> Soundeth the measures of a lively faith,
> The vaine Illusions of this flattering world
> Seemes odious to the thoughts of Margret.
> I loved once, Lord Lacie was my love;
> And now I hate my selfe for that I lovd,
> And doated more on him than on my God.
> For this I scourge my selfe with sharpe repents.
> But now the touch of such aspiring sinnes
> Tels me all love is lust but love of heavens;
> That beautie usde for love is vanitie:

The world containes nought but alluring baites,
Pride, flatterie, and inconstant thoughts. . . .
    Now farewell, world, the engin of all woe!
Farewell to friends and father! welcome Christ!
Adew to daintie robes! this base attire
Better befits an humble minde to God
Than all the shew of rich abilliments. . . .
Lord *Lacie*, thinking of my former misse,
How fond the prime of wanton yeares were spent
In love, (Oh fie uppon that fond conceite,
Whose hap and essence hangeth in the eye!),
I leave both love and loves content at once,
Betaking me to him that is true love,
And leaving all the world for love of him.
                                    (1860–1915)

One function of this speech is to lay the groundwork for relief and laughter when Margaret changes her mind and yields to Lacy. She surrenders with a charming admission of weakness:

The flesh is frayle; my Lord doth know it well,
That when he comes with his inchanting face,
What so ere betyde, I cannot say him nay.
                                    (1937–39)

One of the retainers jests, "To see the nature of women, that be they never so neare God, yet they love to die in a mans armes." But the jest is sweet, mingled with the simple-minded joy of see-ing the ballad heroine married to the handsome nobleman. Her condemnation of the world's vanities is not turned to the services of bitter cynicism, as Chapman might have turned it; it remains an eloquent statement of an ideal which Margaret does not have quite the strength to commit herself to. We may, as ballad audi-ence, be thankful, and we may, as Protestants, rejoice that she has not been taken in by "the show of holy nuns," but we have been reminded emphatically and at length of a point of view which we have been taught to take seriously, been taught, indeed, is true.

It is also the point of view that an audience of the time would have assumed lay behind Friar Bacon's decision to abjure the world and spend his hours in pure devotion praying to his God. Indeed the two renunciations are furthermore identified by the arrangement of the scenes. The slaughter scene, identifying Bacon's power of magic with Margaret's, or love of beauty,[2] is immediately followed by Bacon's repentance, and that, in turn, by Margaret's speeches just quoted. The inevitable effect is to enforce the similarity of the two resolutions. Margaret, like Bacon, has unintentional blood upon her hands and *therefore*, in the logic of the theater, cause for repentance. She too, in renouncing "the vain illusions of this flattering world," is renouncing "the shows that nigromancy did infuse the crystal with." The dead suitors and the shattered glass lie at her feet as well as Bacon's, and her cry that

> The world containes nought but alluring baites,
> Pride, flatterie, and inconstant thoughts,
>
> (1871–72)

is given weight by the tragedy we have just witnessed.

It is a measure of the comprehensiveness of Greene's comic vision that he can include such a point of view without ridiculing it, as it is, indeed, that he can include four killings onstage. Even the Elizabethans do not usually find slaughter fit subject for comedy, and there seems to be an obvious contradiction between the statement that life's bliss is vanity and that life is jolly and to be celebrated. Yet this latter statement is made even more frequently and with greater emphasis than the former. Not only does the play end with an orthodox happy ending, a procession to the *gamos*, the wedding feast, but five times before the end the characters have exited to feasts of celebration. Words like *jocund*, *brisk*, *frolic*, *revel*, *cheer*, *sport*, *scapes*, and *blithe* stud the dialogue. Fressingfield is almost always "merry," and the friars "jolly." The action, too, of many scenes clearly must be carried off with a holiday gaiety that anticipates such scenes as the sheep-shearing festival in *The Winter's Tale* or the jollity of Simon

Eyre. Lacy woos Margaret, for instance, against the background of Harleston fair, which Margaret introduces with words that define the mood as pure holiday:

> When we have turnd our butter to the salt,
> And set our cheese safely upon the rackes,
> Then let our fathers price it as they please.
> We countrie sluts of merry *Fresingfield*
> Come to buy needlesse noughts to make us fine,
> And looke that yong-men should be francke this day,
> And court us with such fairings as they can.
> *Phoebus* is blythe and frolicke lookes from heaven,
> As when he courted lovely *Semele*,
> Swearing the pedlers shall have emptie packs,
> If that faire wether may make chapmen buy.
>
> (352–62)

The wooing is counterpointed presumably by music and by the coming and going of Joan, Thomas, "and other clowns," and by their talk of fairings and true loves and "a pint of wine or two" and Goodman Cob of Beccles. Or there is the mock feast set by Miles, who clowns through the scene speaking macaronic Skeltonics and upsets food, decorum, and royalty in wild slapstick. Or there is the scene in which Prince Edward's retainers, under the misrule of Rafe, are haled before the college authorities by the constable. After excellent fooling they reveal themselves, are merrily forgiven, and are of course invited to dinner.

The play, in short, insistently celebrates earthly pleasures—despite its killings and despite its reminder of the vanity of earthly pleasure—to a degree that few Elizabethan comedies can equal. Whatever it is *about*, it asserts that life is at least potentially merry.

If we do not find this simultaneous exploitation of apparent irreconcilables merely inept, we may be tempted to explain it by the first available cliché, that is, as an instance of *carpe diem* sentiment, contrasting *nox perpetua* and *brevis lux*. Certainly this was a well-known idea at the time, but it does not serve very well to

147

explain the coherence of the play. The issue for Friar Bacon and Margaret lies rather between transitory shows on the one hand and their eternal destination (bale or bliss) on the other. Bacon is betrayed by his necromantic art and the lust for glory it represents, and he is terrified of "the wrath of hie Jehovahs ire" (line 1848). Margaret, before she yields, asks Lacy,

> Is not heavens joy before earths fading blisse,
> And life above sweeter than life in love?
>
> (1926-27)

The four slain bodies, furthermore, bear bitter witness to the tragic potentialities of love, beauty, and glory even in this life. If the play succeeds, it must somehow reconcile these too with its festivity. The problem solved by Catullus is quite different.

The play makes coherent sense on the assumption that an awareness of the limitations and dangers of earthly delights enables one to appreciate them properly—without committing oneself to them. The point—a Renaissance commonplace—may bear some exploration; it is frequently important to the understanding of Renaissance comedies, and it is not, at least in its Renaissance form, a commonplace today.

It is the *commitment* to the transitory that is tragic, the blind heart-and-soul devotion to the beauty that wrinkles will devour. That way lies the bitterness of satiation or betrayal or restless dissatisfaction, and beyond these, of course, damnation. Tragedy can be avoided and life realized as comedy only if its pleasures are accepted as helpful to a further, final end. In Augustine's famous analogy of life to a journey, he urged that we view temporal pleasures "not with an abiding but with a transitory love and delight like that in a road or in vehicles [non quasi mansoria quadam dilectione et delectione, sed transitoria potius, tamquam viae, tamquam vehiculorum] . . . so that we love those things by which we are carried along for the sake of that toward which we are carried." [3]

So general a principle allows of course a wide variation of application, from the austerely utilitarian view of such necessities

as food and clothing—allowing nature only what nature needs—
to a broader view of human necessity that includes such psychological aids to life's journey as recreation and delight. The more
liberal view was not universal in the Renaissance, but it was commonly taught, and its professors were not all merry-making prelates looking for a pretext for revelry. They included, for instance, Calvin and most Calvinists. Thus Calvin himself, who
grants the good intentions of the severer sort:

". . . there have bene some, that otherwyse were good and
holy men, whiche when they sawe intemperance and ryot continually to range with unbridled lust, unlesse it be sharply re-
strained, and wer desirous to corret so great a mischiefe, thei
could finde none other way, but suffred man to use the benefites
of the earth, so far as necessitie required. This was in dede a
Godly counsell, but they were to severe. For (whiche is a very
perilous thyng) they did put streighter bondes upon consciences,
than those wherewith they were bounde by the worde of God.
And they expounde necessitie, to absteine from all thinges whiche
a man may be without. And so by their opinion, a man might
scarcelye take any more foode than bread and water. . . .

Let this be a principle: that the use of Gods giftes swarveth
not out of the way, when it is referred to that ende, wherunto the
authour him selfe hath created and apointed them for us, for as
muche as he hathe created them for our good and not for our
hurt. Therfore no man can kepe a tighter way, than he that shal
diligently loke unto this end. Now if we consider to what end he
hath created meates, we shall finde that he meant to make pro-
vision not only for necessitie but also for delite and pleasure. So
in apparell, beside necessitie he apointed an other ende, whiche is
comlinesse and honestie. In herbes, trees, and frutes, beside diverse
profitable uses, there is also a pleasantnesse of sight, and swetenesse
of smell. For if this were not true, the Prophet would not recken
among the benefites of God that wyne maketh glad the heart of
man, and that oyle maketh his face to shine: the Scripture woulde
not echewhere, to set fourth his liberalitie, rehearse that he hath
geven all suche thinges to men. And the very naturall qualities of

thinges do sufficiently shew, to what end and howe far we may use them. Shall the Lorde have set in floures so great a beutie, as presenteth it selfe to our eies: shall he have geven so great a swetenesse of savour as naturally floweth into our smelling: and shall it be unlawfull either for our eies to take the use of that beutie, or for our smelling to feele that swetenesse of savour? what? Hath he not so made difference of colours, that he hathe made some more acceptable than other? what? Hath he not geven to gold and silver, to ivorie and marble, a speciall grace whereby they might be made more precious than other metalles or stones? Finally hath he not made many thinges commendable unto us without necessary use?

Therfore away with that unnaturall Philosophie, whiche in granting us of the creatures no use but for necessitie, not only doth niggardly bereve us of the lawful use of Gods liberalitie, but also can not take place, unlesse it first have spoiled man of al his senses and made him a blok." [4]

The *Homilie Against Excesse of Apparrell* in the Second Book of homilies offers similar advice:

"If we consider the end and purpose whereunto Almighty GOD hath ordayned his creatures, we shall easily perceive that he alloweth us apparell, not only for necessities sake, but also for an honest comelinesse. Even as in herbes, trees, and sundry fruites, we have not onely divers necessary uses, but also the pleasant sight and sweet smell, to delight us withall, wherein wee may behold the singular love of GOD towards mankinde, in that hee hath provided both to releeve our necessities, and also to refresh our senses with an honest and moderate recreation. Therefore *David* in the hundred and fourth Psalme, confessing GODS carefull providence, sheweth that GOD not only provideth things necessary for men, as hearbs and other meats, but also such things as may rejoyce and comfort, as wine to make glad the heart, oyles and oyntments to make the face to shine. So that they are altogether past the limites of humanity, who yeelding only to necessity, forbid the lawful fruition of GODS benefits." [5]

Since, however, everyone agreed on the very real dangers of

excessive delight in earthly pleasures, the problem of finding the proper mean remained. It was especially acute for laymen, who necessarily lived among the world's delights and distractions: how to live in the world without becoming of it?

The usual answer, implied by Augustine's analogy, was to keep constantly in mind the transient nature of these delights and the eternal destination to which one's soul was journeying. It was to this purpose that public art frequently employed visual reminders of death and earth's vanity and echoed the admonition, *respice finem*. Thus a medieval commentator on St. Paul's paradoxical advice to rejoice as though not rejoicing (1 Cor. 7:30) explains, "He rejoices as though he does not rejoice who delights [*hilarescit*] in temporal goods in such a way that he always contemplates eternal torments." [6] Similarly, Cornelius a Lapide, the Jesuit commentator, remarks of the succeeding verse, which advises using the world as though not using it, "A thing is to be used for what it is. The world, therefore, being fleeting [*fluxo*], is to be used fleetingly [*fluxe*] and as if in passing, as if you did not use it." [7] Calvin, on the same passage, makes the same point:

"Whatsoever things belong to the use of this present lyfe, they are the holy gyftes of God, but we pollute them by abusing them. If the cause be demaunded, we shall fynde it to be this, by cause we dreame alwayes of a perpetuitie in the world: For hereof it commeth that those things which should be helpes unto us to passe forward, are shackelles and snares to kepe us backe. The Apostle therefore uppon good consideration calleth us backe to the remembrance of the shortnesse of this lyfe." [8]

The point is not simply *respice finem;* it is rather that unless man constantly looks to his end, he cannot achieve the genuine pleasure which a loving God has granted him in such things as wine to gladden his heart and oil to make his face to shine.

To return to the play: we were considering the violent contrasts of festive merrymaking with Friar Bacon's and Margaret's solemn talk of their spiritual destination and with the four slaughtered corpses. These contrasts are understandable in the light of the teaching just discussed. The festivity, it should be noted, is not uncontrolled orgy; it is controlled and decorous or, if briefly riotous (for example, the behavior of the Prince's companions at Oxford), it is emphatically brought under control. It should obviously be staged not merely to win the audience's approval but to draw the audience too into happy celebration.[9] It can be of this sort precisely because the festivity is presented in the wider context of the images of mortality and transience that give it its precise significance.

In the light of this teaching, Margaret's final attitude when she capitulates to Lacy becomes a view of her life as comedy. She has become aware of the ultimate vanity of the world, and she confesses, with humorous detachment, the frailty of her own flesh. She is aware of her frailty and she is aware that it is frailty and therefore, although she yields to it—with humor—she does not do so blindly or with complete irrationality. She is placed in human contrast to the reformed young rake and the reformed magician, the one now become the ideal figure of the active life, the other of the contemplative life, both rationally disciplined as ordinary mortals cannot hope to be. Margaret, on the other hand, joins us in her amiable folly as a member of the foolish human race, and in her ability to see herself she joins us as a member of the audience. In so doing she exemplifies the highest wisdom and the best happiness which, in the world of the play, ordinary mortals can achieve.

This wisdom and happiness are also contrasted with those of Miles, who choses to ride off to Hell on the devil's back. One function of this scene, of course, is to reinforce the motif of *respice finem*. It is a literal representation of that threat of Hell which we are enjoined to contemplate in the midst of our delights. But now, in the penultimate scene, it is a joke, a scene of farce. The principals—the Prince, Bacon, and Margaret—have all moved safely past the danger of blind surrender to such delights, and Hell has ceased to be a serious threat in the world of the play.

Staged as farce, furthermore, the scene is not even seriously concerned with "the fate of Miles" as it would be if he were dragged off to Hell like Faustus. It is in the mode, rather, of the end of *The Woman in the Moon* or Gryll's choice at the end of the Bower of Bliss episode in *The Faerie Queene*. Lyly's Gunophilus chooses to live with the fickle Pandora because her mutability is his bliss; Spenser's Gryll, one of Acrasia's transformed suitors, wants to remain a pig. Similarly, the focus here is upon Miles' choice as a symbolic caricature of the bliss desired by some men. This bliss and the wisdom of it mark the lower end of the scale in the tableau of happiness with which Greene closes his play.

VI.

The Comedy of Errors.

Shakespeare's closest approach to Roman comedy, *The Comedy of Errors*, probably followed and was perhaps inspired by Lyly's Roman comedy, *Mother Bombie*. In some ways it is a cleverer play than *Mother Bombie*, and it is also more pedantic, the sort of thing we might expect, remembering Beeston's report to Aubrey, of a brilliant young schoolmaster. Shakespeare adapts Plautus and imitates him and outdoes him, doubling the mistaken identities and combining scenes from different plays. He observes the unities of time and place; he uses the five-act structure that sixteenth-century editors had imposed on Plautus and Terence; he observes, at least as well as Plautus the definition of comedy as ridiculing folly; and he fulfills with engaging literalism the requirement that comedies, which end happily, should begin by threatening tragedy. He begins with a judgment scene condemning a man to death.

Such a display of technique provides conversation for afficionados and points to an audience, or Shakespeare's anticipation of an audience, trained to appreciate it in the schools, the universities, the Inns of Court, and the private theaters. His handling of his themes suggests the same kind of anticipation, as if he were counting on an audience trained to understand Lyly's comedy of human nature and had decided to use its themes and to dazzle by a pyrotechnical display of technique. This conjecture, indeed, whatever its historical truth, provides us with an hypothesis which explains the play as the coherent and unified development of an idea. Lyly's comedy had shown human nature as damned by justice, pardoned by mercy, and funny in its error. That is the premise of *The Comedy of Errors*.

We may consider first the most general consideration. The opening scene invites pity for Aegeon, a quite ordinary man who has made a very natural blunder; he has unwittingly entered a hostile city, and his life is forfeit. Thenceforward the play invites laughter at quite ordinary people who make very natural mistakes; they confuse identical twins. The victims of both the farce and the "tragedy" are strikingly guiltless of the sort of serious faults that suggest their plight is deserved. Aegeon's plight, as he points out, has been "wrought by nature, not by vile offense"; he has acted as any man would and has been terribly unlucky. The other characters also, with the possible exception of "good Doctor Pinch," meet their slapstick doom without exhibiting any of those vivid absurdities of manners or morals which in some moralities or the comedies of Jonson direct the ridicule to an obvious target. It is true that they are not quite without absurdities. The play mocks Adriana gently for her mild shrewishness and Antipholus of Syracuse for his superstitious apprehensions; Antipholus of Ephesus can be played here and there for comic prosiness. By realistic standards all are dim-witted. But all are presented as normal beings, not humor characters. Their mistakes are funny, not because they spring from an exaggerated twist of the psyche, but because they are the almost automatic responses of human nature.

This kind of farce or comedy of situation, revolving around mistaken identities, always, or almost always, I suppose, implies that human beings are by their nature rather foolish, deceived by appearances, and funny in their folly. The point may be given topical significance or it may rest generalized, as here, a commentary on the whole human race. It is a generalization that no censor will object to and which the lightest farce will support.

But this play also asks us to see a human being threatened with the legal judgment of death, and the total concept of human nature implied by the play must somehow include this view too. More specifically, we see Aegeon condemned unless he can procure ransom. The law that condemns him, furthermore, is established as perfectly just by the Duke who judges him, although its rigor is untempered by the mercy that theorists praised in the ideal Christian prince. It is blood for blood retribution:

> The enmity and discord which of late
> Sprung from the rancorous outrage of your duke
> To merchants our well-dealing countrymen,
> Who, wanting guilders to redeem their lives,
> Have seal'd his rigorous statutes with their bloods,
> Excludes all pity from our threat'ning looks.
>
> (1.1.5–10) [1]

Then Aegeon proceeds to tell a tale so woeful and so full of improbable misfortunes that the Duke himself pities him. Yet by the law he must die unless he can procure the heavy ransom of a thousand marks.

> Thy substance, valued at the highest rate,
> Cannot amount unto a hundred marks.
> Therefore by law thou art condemn'd to die.
>
> (1.1.23–25)

Now I think it may be allowed that there is little point in trying to account for this judgment by analyzing Aegeon's character for a tragic flaw or the situation for social significance. These are potential themes, but the play does not develop them and Aegeon himself emphasizes that he is guiltless of any crime:

> . . . that the world may witness that my end
> Was wrought by nature, not by vile offence,
> I'll utter what my sorrow gives me leave.
>
> (1.1.32–35)

He stands condemned *qua* human being, for original sin, for nature, not for vile offense. Furthermore, he is pitiable, in need of ransom, and he does not have it.

Clearly the relevant concept of human nature is the one Lyly had exploited, the one common at the time, taught in catechism, sermon, and treatise, which saw man as condemned by justice for his corrupt and fallen nature to a death from which only a ransom he could not meet could save him. It saw him also as doomed by that nature to err, and comic in that error.

Shakespeare of course stresses the tragic threat of man's condemnation more than Lyly does, even in *Gallathea*. The threat is not quite so serious, however, as analysis may make it seem. Although the first scene clothes the exposition of Aegeon's plight with the most solemn trappings of tragedy, it lacks the tragic significance of, say, Richard II's deposition scene, not only because it reveals no conflict within the protagonist, but also because it suggests that Aegeon will be ransomed. Presumably the spectators knew at least that the play was to be a comedy, and the intricate exposition, dull as it is, suggests that Shakespeare thought them sufficiently seasoned playgoers to realize its relevance to the action that follows, to use it, for instance, to identify Dromio of Ephesus when he enters in the next scene. When Aegeon is doomed, when he tells of losing his family, when he speaks of twins, presumably the audience scents the happy ending, the family reunion, and the farce of mistaken identities. Except for the progenitors of Partridge, the opening scene does not really threaten tragedy. Aegeon's plight is pseudo-tragic; he will not really die.

The effect is not uncommon in the sleazier kinds of melodrama. We know from the depths of our theatrical sophistication that the wicked mortgage bond will be cancelled, the marines will arrive in time for the rescue, the last improbable and heroic blow will topple the villain from the church-spire, skyscraper, canyon, or cliff. Virtue wins. But this easy reassurance that all is right, at least in two-gun fairyland, finds an intellectually respectable counterpart in the Christian scheme of salvation. It is indeed true that man stands condemned by justice. "Consider this," Portia will say, "that in the course of justice, none of us should see salvation." "Alas, alas," cries Isabella, "Why, all the souls that were were forfeit once," but she continues, "he that might the vantage best have took found out the remedy." Man's ransom has been paid. His fallen nature renders him ridiculous and it condemns him, but the Christian does not suffer the death which the eye-for-eye justice of the Old Law demands. His plight is pseudo-tragic. In a more than formal sense this comedy is of the sort defined by Dante, and by more than formal means it seeks to yoke that comedy with that which shows man as amiable and erring fool.

This double comedy of fallen man is developed by means of a series of fantastic improbabilities, and it may be well to bear in mind their dramatic implication. Shakespeare has done much to increase them. He has not simply added another pair of twins and thereby doubled the comic mixups; he has brought both mother and father of the sons coincidentally to the same never-never Duchy of Ephesus, making the mother a wildly improbable holy abbess, and landing the father in coincidental jeopardy on the very day in that town in which . . . and so on. Obviously things do not happen this way; nor do people enter, meet, and miss with the pat, comic fortuity that they do here, nor express themselves with the slapstick antics that these lines seem to call for.

The fantasy is established in the first scene. Ostensibly this is a court; the Duke is pronouncing sentence. Though law and procedure may be unusual, it would be idle to quibble about them. But as Aegeon begins his tale of double twins, shipwreck and separation, the outlines of reality as we know it begin to dissolve. This is the shape of Greek romance, not fact. It is the wildest of fantasy, and the Duke's bland acceptance of it is the signal that we have passed through the looking-glass.

There are two main ways, I think, of taking such art as this. We may merely suspend disbelief and accept it as children are said to accept fairy tales, with devout and devoted literalism. This is tempting. It offers all the pleasures of mental relaxation, and it assures a momentary thrill of tragic feeling. But we are not really little boys who never grew up, and, as reality inevitably closes in upon us, our return from this Parnassus leaves it faded.

I would not, however, argue that such an approach is utterly without value. It certainly has charm; it is an important step toward any further understanding, and it may be (though I do not think so) the only way to watch a show in progress. Nor would I argue that there are not Elizabethan plays that reward no further scrutiny of meaning or that there were not, in the Gray's Inn audience of Innocents Day 1594, many who were willing to rest in delighted enjoyment of the surface. But most members of that audience had learned playgoing by watching moralities and hybrid moralities in which much of the interest lay in the exploitation of more or less ingenious dramatic metaphors. Many of them had also seen the plays of Lyly as well as pageants and entertainments in which such metaphors, often elaborate, were designed to puzzle the viewer and tease him into thought. Fantasy here, as in the moralities and entertainments, at least suggests a meaning beyond the surface meaning and a metaphorical bridge between the two.

Because the beast fable obviously does not refer to actual animals, it invites the attempt to find a reality it does refer to. This is no less true of Lilliput or the stories of Kafka or such emperors as we read of in the *Gesta Romanorum*. One of them, for instance, decides to travel to Jerusalem:

"The Emperour tooke his ship, and when he was in the midst of the sea, the Master of the ship tooke the Emperour and threw him overboard into the sea. . . . This Emperour . . . had learned in his youth to swim, and swam to an Iland in the sea. . . ." [2]

Clearly, emperors like this never existed. We suspect some significance behind his adventures, and we later learn that "by this Emperour wee may understand every Christian man that pur-

159

poseth to visit the Citie of Jerusalem, that is, to get everlasting life through faith" (H 3ᵛ). Like caricature, fantasy is a symbolic device; our feeling that the looking-glass has closed behind us is the signal and invitation to catch the significance of its reflections.

The Comedy of Errors is not so full-blown a fantasy as *Gallathea* or *Endymion*, and its invitation is not so obvious. Yet that the invitation is there seems to me an almost inescapable conclusion. If the opening scene does not offer it, that scene is really nonsense, and although *that* unhappy conclusion is not on *a priori* grounds to be excluded, it must be proved. We assume that a work, any work, *Finnegans Wake* or The Song of Solomon, makes sense until we prove it guilty. If here this presumptive invitation leads to chaos and inanity, it does not exist, or is only a pretence, the husk of a riddle without the grain. But the burden of proof rests upon us, to show that it leads to nonsense.

I have suggested that it makes sense in terms of man's nature, as most people professed to see it. Aegeon's fantastic plight, generalized, is man's, and on this level it is the soberest sort of commonplace. People do not actually get caught in situations like this while searching for double twins, but as an outward and visible sign, it illustrates man's hopelessness and adumbrates his hope.

What dramatic interest the first scene possesses focuses upon this pseudo-tragic situation and the theme of justice and ransom that it presents. But linked to this are two other concerns upon which the narrative speeches pile their emphasis. These are the hazards of fortune and the scattering of Aegeon's family. Both are central to the play. The plot development is presented as a series of fortuitous events, and it is partially motivated by, and works toward, the reunion of the family. Now if Aegeon's situation is indeed seen as a dramatic metaphor of the condemnation of man's fallen nature, then its thematic relation to these other matters is clear, and the thematic integrity of the play is clear also. For Fortune, which has brought Aegeon to his plight, is an illusion which man sees as a result of his imperfect, fallen vision. Behind the apparently chance concatenation of events, stands the controlling reality of Providence. These misfortunes, we know, will end happily, and our assurance finds its intellectual substance in the concept of Providential guidance.

We know, furthermore, that the happy ending will not only redeem Aegeon's life, but will reunite him with his family. At its vaguest this reunion is roughly comparable to his redemption. Both events will "make him happy." They are also alike in a more specific way, although this is not immediately apparent in the opening scene. As the play progresses, hilarious stupidity, misunderstanding all mischances, keeps the family from reuniting. This is the caricature of human error, and we see it here as the cause of a disharmony that is consistently presented in terms of family relationships. The masters beat their servants; husband and wife are set at odds; the husband visits a courtesan, and the son denies his father. The reunion is the end to all this, the restoration of the order disrupted by the errors of fallen human nature—from which Aegeon also is redeemed.

That is the significance suggested by Aemilia's last speech, when she invites the company to a feast. It is to be a "gossips' feast," a baptismal feast; it celebrates man's redemption. "Thirty-three years," she says,

> have I but gone in travail
> Of you, my sons, and till this present hour
> My heavy burthen ne'er delivered.
> The Duke, my husband, and my children both,
> And you, the calendars of their nativity,
> Go to a gossips' feast, and joy with me,
> After so long grief, such nativity!
> (5.1.400–406)

Her speech points backward to the thirty-three years of grief as well as forward to the feast. These are her period of travail, and that too, as, in the opening scene, Aegeon's casual and too-florid metaphor ("the pleasing punishment that women bear" [1.1.46]) reminds us, is a punishment for the Fall. The long years of wandering and loss and error are like the pain of childbirth, punishment deserved by human nature. But they are not genuinely tragic; by appointed and inevitable process they end in joy.

The significance of the play is shaped by its general movement from sorrow into joy. The characters avoid tragedy, however, not only because their happy ending is clearly in the cards, but also because they are all—except Aegeon—farcically absurd. Adriana, for instance, is by no means a mere stage shrew, for she is given a quite convincingly pathetic eloquence; but she misdirects it:

> How comes it now, my husband, O, how comes it,
> That thou art then estranged from thyself?
> Thyself I call it, being strange to me,
> That, undividable incorporate,
> Am better than thy dear self's better part.
> Ah, do not tear away thyself from me!
> For know, my love, as easy mayst thou fall
> A drop of water in the breaking gulf
> And take unmingled thence that drop again
> Without addition or diminishing
> As take from me thyself, and not me too.
> How dearly would it touch thee to the quick,
> Shouldst thou but hear I were licentious
> And that this body, consecrate to thee,
> By ruffian lust should be contaminate!
> Wouldst thou not spit at me and spurn at me,
> And hurl the name of husband in my face,
> And tear the stain'd skin off my harlot brow,
> And from my false hand cut the wedding ring
> And break it with a deep-divorcing vow?
> I know thou canst; and therefore see thou do it.
> I am possess'd with an adulterate blot,
> My blood is mingled with the crime of lust;
> For, if we two be one, and thou play false,
> I do digest the poison of thy flesh,
> Being strumpeted by thy contagion.
> (2.2.121–46)

162

Clearly this is not stuff for a Restoration virago; it is too sympathetically appealing, and it has too much intellectual substance. But it is not for the Amanda of *Love's Last Shift* either. Adriana is talking to her bewildered brother-in-law, a total stranger. The effect is to make us feel the funny and distressful aspects of her situation simultaneously.

This sort of scene makes its point in a highly theatrical fashion. We quite literally *see* what Adriana cannot see, and her blind error frames, as it were, in comedy, the rise and fall of her jealous and pathetic monody. This kind of passion, it implies, is blind and absurd. Why it should be so has been suggested five minutes before by Luciana in a little homily on wifely obedience. The husband, she tells Adriana, is "the bridle of your will" (2.1.13). Adriana is rebellious, her will unbridled; she is acting irrationally.

Yet her mistake—after all, Antipholus of Syracuse looks exactly like her husand—is inevitable; anyone would make it. Precisely so (through Griselda might have waited at home); Adriana's error is only human. Human beings err by nature; their wills are naturally unbridled, mistaken, led by passion.[3]

The slapstick action implies the same absurdity. In the second scene of Act I, Dromio of Ephesus is beaten by Antipholus of Syracuse; in the next, by Adriana; in the next, Antipholus beats his hapless twin. It seems a far remove from Meredith's thoughtful comedy, and one may be tempted to acknowledge the delighted response to "mere farce." Again, this is certainly possible, yet even the simplest Bergsonian analysis acknowledges that the machine-like responses of Adriana and Antipholus are laughed *at* here. They are, we may notice, a machine powered and directed by passion in its most theatrically emphatic form; temper made visible. The hand rises and the blow falls. It is also explosively comic, and comic not only because of whatever risible shock of timing, leer, or gesture the actors may bring to it, but also because the temper acts as a machine does—blindly. Everybody mistakes identity. Again, this is quite natural; anybody would. This is human passion and human blindness.

Like this hot temper, the romantic ardor of Antipholus of

Syracuse is blind and funny. It is presented with a good deal of sympathy, and I do not mean to suggest that the actor plays the wooing scene as if he were Malvolio. But Luciana handles him with a coolness (rather more than we might expect her to show toward a declaration she thinks incestuous) that makes a straight romantic interpretation of the role quite inappropriate:

> O, soft, sir! hold you still!
> I'll fetch my sister to get her good will.
>
> (3.2.70–71)

If the scene is played for comedy, its point I think is clear. Antipholus is completely bewildered and simultaneously dizzy with love. The two giddinesses are knotted in his speech intrinsicately as one:

> Sweet mistress (what your name is else, I know not,
>   Nor by what wonder you do hit of mine),
> Less in your knowledge and your grace you show not
>   Than our earth's wonder, more than earth divine.
> Teach me, dear creature, how to think and speak.
>   Lay open to my earthy gross conceit,
> Smoth'red in errors, feeble, shallow, weak,
>   The folded meaning of your words' deceit.
> Against my soul's pure truth why labour you,
>   To make it wander in an unknown field?
> Are you a god? Would you create me new?
>   Transform me then, and to your pow'r I'll yield.
>
> (3.2.29–40)

Love is a species of comic error. But there is also his comic struggle with and surrender to his passion. He has shown timorous qualms before, and they later almost overwhelm him, but here he surrenders to the danger he senses with the happy recklessness of a dyspeptic reaching for mince pie:

> O, train me not, sweet mermaid, with thy note,
>   To drown me in thy sister's flood of tears.

Sing, siren, for thyself, and I will dote.
 Spread o'er the silver waves thy golden hairs,
And as a bed I'll take them, and there lie
 And in that glorious supposition think
He gains by death that hath such means to die.

(3.2.45–51)

But even this struggle is in part a comic blundering. Luciana is not, we know, the siren that he calls her; he is not, as he fears, enchanted by witches. His dizziness, however caricatured, is only the feeble conceit of human kind, earthly gross and smothered in errors, and it is funny as the folly of all men is.

His twin, too, snared by the casual coils of farce, is guiltless of any serious offence. The text carefully provides him with a chaperone when he leaves to dine with the courtesan, and he strikes out, when he does, only as any man might. Yet he is locked out of his house, arrested, accused of being possessed, and shut, bound, in a dark room; and he is ridiculous.

Human nature errs and it is funny. But it is also pathetic; it gets into trouble, and it needs rescue—ransom. This aspect too can be taken lightly. When Antipholus of Ephesus is arrested, he sends Dromio home to Adriana for bail. Like his father, Antipholus needs ransom, and Dromio seizes upon the inevitable analogy. In his report to Adriana the arresting sergeant becomes the "devil . . . a fiend, a fury, pitiless and rough; . . . One that before the Judgment carries poor souls to hell" (4.2.33–40), and the bail money (or Adriana, in the Second Folio reading) is "redemption." In the next scene Dromio, rushing back to his master with the bail money, meets Antipholus of Syracuse walking at liberty and expresses his surprise by asking, "What, have you got the picture of old Adam new-apparell'd?" (4.3.13) His meaning, as I have argued elsewhere, is roughly equivalent to "Ah, set free from sin, I see!" [4] The arresting sergeant here has become the picture of Old Adam (unregenerate human nature), and the new apparel is the new garment of regeneration. But Antipholus of Syracuse is only bewildered by the present of bail money, and he ends the dialogue and once more points the eternal jest with the lines,

> The fellow is distract, and so am I,
> And here we wander in illusions.
> Some blessed power deliver us from hence!
>
> (4.3.42–44)

The lines come near to being an epigraph for the play as a whole. At the same time, as delivered by Antipholus, they illustrate neatly the comic irony implicit in the human situation as the play assumes it. For Antipholus's words, we *see*, are true in another sense from that he means. He is wandering in illusions, but they are natural, the illusions in which all men wander. Like all men he needs deliverance through some blessed power, though not from the witchcraft he fears. His prayer is answered ironically by the entrance of the courtesan "in gay apparell," and he flees her fearing she is Satan.

The fifth act, however, recalls momentarily, before the final comic lightening, the tragic consequences that threaten. Adriana's plea for the release of her husband rings with an uncomic anguish, and Aemilia's refusal to release him suggests again, soberly, the thematic concern with irrationality:

> Be patient; for I will not let him stir
> Till I have us'd the approved means I have,
> With wholesome syrups, drugs, and holy prayers
> To make of him a formal man again.
> It is a branch and parcel of mine oath,
> A charitable duty of my order.
>
> (5.1.102–7)

Then Aegeon enters, bareheaded, in his melancholy procession to the block. He is a visible reminder of the potential tragedy which blind and funny human beings, beguiled by fortune, face. The Duke proclaims justice:

> If any friend will pay the sum for him,
> He shall not die, so much we tender him.
>
> (5.1.131–32)

And the cry for justice rises. Adriana pleads, "Justice, most sacred Duke against the Abbess!" (5.1.133) and her husband counters, "Justice, most gracious Duke! O, grant me justice! . . . even for the blood / That . . . I lost for thee, now grant me justice! . . . Justice, sweet prince, against that woman there!" (5.1.190–97). But justice is entangled both comically and tragically. After five minutes of crossfire of accusation, corroboration, denial, and counterclaim, the Duke has only reached bewilderment: "I think you are all mated or stark mad" (5.1.281). The relationships are snarled beyond all straightening, and Aegeon's last hope fades: his lost son fails to recognize him. If justice be their plea, they are all condemned. For a long moment, as Aegeon's pitiful amazement unrolls,

> Not know my voice? O time's extremity,
> Hast thou so crack'd and splitted my poor tongue
> In seven short years that here my only son. . . .
>
> (5.1.307–9)

The tragic tableau is fixed, and the audience sees the symbols of the human doom before the bar of justice. Comic and tragic plots are now at length shown simultaneously, lit by and reflecting the same lamp. The "errors" are comic, but Antipholus's error means his father's death.

Then the other twins enter with Aemilia, and the expected magic happens. The facts are clarified; the family is reunited, and Aegeon is freed.

Now these events are presented on the stage as parts of one action. They occur simultaneously; they are immediate and visible results of Aemilia's entrance, and they are themselves closely related. Theatrically they are equivalent and indistinguishable.

The theatrical identity is also thematic. Most obviously the events constitute a happy ending. They do this by their theatrically sensational denial of the still raw tragi-comic nightmare which has threatened these human beings with perpetual farce, or death. Clarity has succeeded error; harmony, discord; and mercy has tempered justice. By the law Aegeon is still condemned, but when Antipholus offers to pay his ransom, the Duke replies, "It shall not need. Thy father hath his life" (5.1.390). This is again fantasy, at least in effect. The legal point is avoided. The one point relevant is made: Aegeon is set free. Man will not die for his nature. Charity has replaced justice. The Old Law is dead. That is why gossips' feasts are held.

The events, then, reflect three aspects of the central fact of man's redemption, which, within the Christian scheme of things, is what makes comedy with a happy ending possible. The ending is still within the human situation, however. It is not Dante's ending, only the imperfect earthly analogue of it. Though Aegeon's recognition, liberation, and reunion, like the end of *The Winter's Tale* or *Pericles*, moves to the music of solemn joy, set against this is the laughter of polite amusement. Confusion has not quite ended. The chance of error still remains;

> *Duke.* Antipholus, thou cam'st from Corinth first.
> *S. Ant.* No, sir, not I! I came from Syracuse.
> *Duke.* Stay, stand apart. I know not which is which. . . .
> *Adr.* Which of you did dine with me to-day?
> *S. Ant.* I, gentle mistress.
> *Adr.* And are not you my husband?
> *E. Ant.* No; I say nay to that.
> *S. Ant.* And so do I.
>
> (5.1.362–72)

This sort of mistaking is no longer dangerous, but it is there, and it is comic. Human beings may be saved from the tragic consequences of their nature, but they remain human and fallible and funny.[5]

VII.

The Taming of the Shrew.

Though *The Taming of the Shrew* may not be later than *The Comedy of Errors*, it is more complex in both its structure and its thematic development. It is intellectually more interesting for that reason, yet also more difficult to analyze, and statements about its meaning fall that much farther short of indicating the totality of meanings and their relationships.

Perhaps it is easiest to begin by noting that the play is framed by two large-scale theatrical metaphors comparing life to a dream and to a play. On the basis of extant evidence, both metaphors are new to the stage; at least they are new in anything like their elaboration in *The Taming of the Shrew*. The dream metaphor had been used once before, in Wager's *Longer Thou Livest*, when Moros awakens thinking that perhaps he has only dreamed his former greatness. Something close to it had been used in the standard scene of the young man rocked to slumber in his leman's lap and awakening to perceive his folly. The play metaphor had not, I think, been used except in the general sense in which the stage was said to be a mirror of life. This was a critical assumption of all drama, but some plays of the time used it very self-consciously. Edwards's *Damon and Pythias*, for instance, as has been pointed out, stages the magnanimous contest of the two friends as a "tragedy" from which Dionysius can profit. In a different way Hieronimo's polyglot play in *The Spanish Tragedy* symbolizes the Babylonian corruption and fall of the court before which it is staged. Greene's *Friar Bacon*, as noted above, comes close to realizing the metaphor, as does his *James IV*. But though such devices may have helped prepare the ground for Shakespeare's use of the analogy, none precisely matches it.

Shakespeare not only developed the two metaphors extensively; he linked them. The linkage is not surprising, since it was common in non-dramatic literature, although our own ready acceptance of it may rather reflect our memory of it in Shakespeare —in these two very plays, for instance, or Hamlet's identification of the player's speech as "a dream of passion," or Prospero's equation of "this insubstantial pageant" with "such stuff as dreams are made on." Shakespeare's own *Gestalten*, after all, have affected ours. But since antiquity the dream and the play, when life was compared to them, had symbolized the transient and illusory nature of earthly glory, wealth, and pleasure. The major examples of the analogy of life to a play have been traced from Lucian to Calderon. Erasmus, in *The Praise of Folly*, gave it wide currency in the sixteenth century, and by Cervantes's time it had become trite and boring to Sancho Panza.[1] The dream analogy probably had even wider currency, although it was not usually developed at any length. In the specific form, however, that it takes in the induction to *The Taming of the Shrew*, that of a drunken beggar installed in momentary lordship by a nobleman, there are several narrative versions. It is apparently of oriental origin, but during the sixteenth and seventeenth centuries it became popular in Europe and was told as an historical incident, usually about a beggar found by Philip of Burgundy. Three English versions, of the same period, but slightly later than *The*

Taming of the Shrew, are extant. Shakespeare's source is not known. It might have been Heuterus's Latin chronicle *De Rebus Burgundicis* (1584), which quotes an account by Vives, but more probably it has disappeared. In any event, it almost certainly carried the moralization which all the other versions do and which, indeed, granted familiarity with an other-worldly scheme of values, is as nearly implicit as a meaning can be. That moralization, of course, is that glory, wealth, and pleasure, the *summum bonum* of worldlings, are precisely as evanescent and hallucinatory as the experience of the besotted beggar.

Heuterus, for instance, remarks of the drunken man when the Duke and his followers find him in the street. "In eo visum est experiri quale esset, vitae nostrae ludicrum, de quo illi interdum essent collucuti." At the end, he adds, "Quid interest inter diem illius et nostros aliquot annos? Nihil penitus, nisi quod hoc est paulo diuturnius somnium, at si quis unum duntaxat horam, alter vero decem somniasset." [2] Edward Grimeston's translation (1607) of Simon Goulart's French version (c. 1606), which in turn follows Heuterus closely, begins in the same way: "It pleased the Prince in this Artisan to make triall of the vanity of our life, wherof he had before discoursed with his familiar friends," and he concludes that, of the artisan, "his goodly day, and the years of a wicked life differ nothing, but in more and lesse. He slept foure and twenty houres, other wicked men some-times foure and twenty thousands of houres. It is a little or a great dreame: and nothing more." [3] Sir Richard Barckley's *Discourse of the Felicity of Man: His Summum Bonum* (1598) uses the story in support of his argument that man's *summum bonum* does not consist in pleasure, and points the moral especially for carousers. [4] The anonymous "Waking Man's Dream," a fragment of about 1620, moralizes at great length, using imagery in itself significant:

"Our life is compared unto those, who sleeping dreame that they eate, and waking find themselves empty and hungry; and who is he that doth not find this experimented in himselfe, as often as he revolves in his memory the time which is past? Who can in these passages of this world distinguish the things which have been done from those that have beene dreamed? vanities, delights, riches, pleasures and all are past and gone; are they not dreames? What hath our pride and pompe availed us? say those poore miserable soules shut up in the infernall prisons: where is our bravery become, and the glorious show of our magnificence? all these things are passed like a flying shadow, or as a post who hastens to his journeyes end. This is it which caused the ancient Comick Poet to say that the world was nothing but an universall Comedy, because all the passages thereof serve but to make the wisest laugh: and, according to the opinion of Democritus, all that is acted on this great Theater of the whole world, when it is ended, differs in nothing from what hath bin acted on a Players stage." [5]

It should be noticed that the two metaphors, of the stage and the dream, are equated by Heuterus's phrase, "vitae nostrae *ludicrum,*" which Grimeston, following Goulart, renders as "the vanity of our life," and equated also by the elaborate theater imagery in the last quotation. In all versions except Barckley's, furthermore, the drunkard watches a comedy while enjoying the delusory pleasures of lordship.

We may take the vanity of worldly delights, then, as a reasonable sixteenth-century meaning of the induction, reasonable in the sense that it is a meaning commonly attributed to the story at that time, and many people—not all—might be expected to grasp it. That Sly, the transformed beggar, should watch a comedy has the same potential meaning, though it is less insistent. The comedy he watches is an illusion like the *ludicrum* (in Heuterus's phrase) of our life represented by the little play in which he is unwittingly a character. But Sly in his waking dream of bliss is merely a symbol of all men, of us in fact, who are enjoying a slightly longer dream. That, like us he should be watching a comedy, emphasizes the parallel. We too are involved in a *ludicrum* while we watch one. It is equally important, however, that we are simply made aware of the play that Sly sees, as a play, an artifact. Like the patently fictional nature of Aegeon's expository narrative in *The Comedy of Errors,* the framing device helps to keep us alert to the unreality of the play, a fiction that veils and is analogous to reality.

Then there is the play itself. It has two plots: Petruchio's taming of Katherine, and Lucentio's winning of Bianca. Shakespeare has linked the plots by giving them mutually shared characters and by making Bianca's marriage contingent upon Katherine's. But he has also recast the Lucentio plot, which he borrowed from Ariosto, into a wooing contest where the prize falls to the cleverest deceiver; he has thus graded Bianca's three suitors on an ascending scale of cleverness, and he has ranked Petruchio in relation to them as the cleverest of all. The cleverness and avarice of Baptista, Bianca's father, is the obstacle to all three of her suitors, and among them, Gremio's cleverness (hiring a "tutor" to plead his case) is overmatched by Hortensio's (getting himself hired as a tutor), and that in turn is surpassed by Lucentio's (getting himself hired and actually winning the girl). Lucentio's cleverness, finally, is not so much surpassed, as supplied, by that of his clever servant Tranio, who really devises the scheme by which he wins Bianca. Petruchio's aim of winning Katherine has meanwhile been established as foolish, since Katherine, in contrast to the mild Bianca, is a shrew; but he is shown to have been the wisest of the wooers when he finally proves that Katherine is more obedient than Bianca or the widow Hortensio has married.

This is the fable, as patterned as a folktale in the telling, which Shakespeare has fused out of two separate plays. The result on the stage lacks the insipid patness of its outline because of the farcical extravagance of its gestures and because it makes almost no claim on pathos. The action is distanced esthetically throughout; we are never asked to feel strongly for anybody.

The contrast between Petruchio and Bianca's suitors, however, is not one of surprising good luck and bad luck. Shakespeare gives it significance which can be grasped if we examine Lucentio, who alone of Bianca's suitors is given a motivation which is made clear to the audience. His basic folly, directing his cleverness, is the fact that he is in love. The point is established at the very beginning, even as Sly quiets himself reluctantly beside his "lady," the disguised servant boy. Lucentio enters with Tranio; he sounds a flourish of rhetoric and announces that he has come to Verona to study

> Virtue and that part of philosophy
> Will I apply that treats of happiness
> By virtue specially to be achiev'd.
>
> (1.1.18–20)

The lines admit the caricature pose of the idealist—chin thrust forward and cloak flung back, one foot advanced and planted firmly on a small dragon—which prepares nicely for the comic lightning that is imminent. But the phrases also place the scene in the context of the philosophical treatises, from Plato onwards, of the happy life, the good life, man's *summum bonum*, and related topics *de finibus*. Treatises of this sort, written in, or translated into English, had become popular during the latter years of the century—Barckley's *Discourse of the Felicity of Man* is typical—and literate members of the audience, not merely university men, could well be expected to be familiar with the sort of studies Lucentio refers to.

The popular treatises use various styles, emphases, and methods of organization, but they teach the same basic points and use most of the same arguments and even imagery. They are Christian (Calvinist and Catholic agreeing on the vast bulk of the teaching); though they depend heavily upon Stoic arguments and illustrations, they reject Stoic passivity and the Stoic confidence in the wise man's ability to achieve happiness by himself. All agree that happiness is to be defined as a state of tranquillity and that the things of earth do not offer it. Thus, for instance, Edward Smyth introduces his translation of Jean de L'Espines's *Discourse touching the Tranquillity and Contentation of the Mind* by remarking that:

"Every man naturally endeavoreth by all means possible to live quietly, and seeketh continually to settle himself in that estate which he imagineth to be most to his liking and contentation . . . Some thinking felicity to consist in riches, do seek for nothing else as long as they live but to gather wealth; others hunt after

honor and promotion, and some after pleasure and delight: . . .
But there is no man so fortunate as to find that which he seeketh,
neither is there any but complaineth of his own estate and condition. . . . The reason whereof is this: they seek for that in
this world which cannot possibly be found: for this tranquillity
and repose of the mind is laid up in heaven. . . . And yet I will
not say, but that it may appear in some sort and be attained unto
even in this life: and that true and unfained Christians, being
illuminated and regenerated, perceiving the vanity of this world
and corruption of all things therein, may find such quiet and assured rest, as they could never before attain unto." [6]

The insistence that man can attain only an imperfect, though
still worthwhile, happiness on earth is typical. So is the insistence
that the vanity of the things of this earth must be recognized before the happiness of the tranquil mind can be achieved. Pierre de
La Primaudaye, the first part of whose *French Academy* was
Englished in 1584, emphasizes the same points:

"The Philosophers teach us by their writings, and experience
doth better shew it unto us, that to covet and desire is proper to
the soule, and that from thence all the affections and desires of
men proceed, which drawe them hither and thither diversly, that
they may attaine to that thing, whiche they thinke is able to leade
them to the enjoying of some good, whereby they may live a contented and happie life. Which felicitie, the most part of men,
through a false opinion, or ignorance rather of that which is good,
and by following the inclination of their corrupt nature, doe seek
and labour to find in humane and earthly things, as in riches,
glory, honour, and pleasure. But for as much as the enjoying of
these things doth not bring with it sufficient cause of contentation,
they perceive themselves alwaies deprived of the ende of their
desires, and are constrained to wander all their life time beyond all
bounds and measure according to their rashness and inconstancie
of their lusts. . . . Briefly, all men whose hearts are set upon
worldly goods, . . . this mischiefe of continuall, uncertaine, and
unsatiable lustes and desires doeth more and more kindle in them.
. . . But they, who through the studie of Wisedome are furnished

with skill and understanding, and know that all humane and earthly things are uncertaine, deceitfull, slipperie, . . . they I say, do lay a farre better and more certaine foundation of their chiefe *Good*, contentation, and felicitie. . . .

. . . Albeit our soveraign and chiefe *Good*, our perfect contentation and absolute felicitie be onely in heaven in the enjoying of that divine light, yet wee must not in the meanewhile, (albeit wee cannot fully possess that) leave off to seeke without ceasing . . . that good and infallible way of vertue, which causing us to passe over quietly, . . . and appeasing the perturbations of our souls, . . . will teach us to leade a pleasant, peaceable, and quiet life." [7]

The general drift of the argument is common from Plato through the Renaissance, of course, but granted its logic, some results follow which are surprising to expectations nurtured on more materialistic notions of good. The book of Ecclesiastes, for instance, becomes a guide to happiness, not in spite of, but because of its refrain of *vanitas vanitatis*. This again is medieval teaching, but it is well to hear it in popular Renaissance phrasing:

"I take the principall ende of this discourse to be, OF THE CHIEF, OR, SOVEREIGNE GOOD. . . . It is altogether needeful that there should be extant a plaine doctrine of Felicitie, whereuppon we might certainely rest: least in stead of true happiness, we laye holde upon the shew and shadow of happiness. . . . For when as Felicitie or happiness is the principall and cheefe ende of oure whole life, and that all men with the whole labour and endeavour of their willes and studies are caried thereunto . . . and yet in the mean season the greatest part of men are led far and wide away from *Felicitie or happinesse*. . . .

"First [Solomon] teacheth that happinesse is no where to be found in things of the world, *viz.* hee sheweth, *what happiness is not*, against the arguments of man his reason, dreaming falsly of a vaine shew of happiness. Then . . . hee teacheth *what felicitie or happiness is*. . . . hee doeth altogether place it . . . in the true knowledge of the true God, and in his diligent and earnest service." [8]

People were happy, it was explained, or as happy as they could be, when they turned from the world to God because then their insatiable passions no longer drove them to seek the things of the world. As Parsons, the Jesuit, says,

"From this slaverie then [to the passions] are the vertuous delivered, by the power of Christ, and his assistance, insomuch, as they rule over their passions in sensualitie, and are not ruled thereby. . . . After this priviledge of freedom, followeth another of no lesse importance than this, and that is a certain heavenly peace and tranquillity of mind. . . . But the wicked men, not having mortified the saide passions, are tossed and troubled with the same, as with vehement and contrary windes, And therefore their state and condition is compared by Esai to a tempestuous sea, that never is quiet: and by St. James, to a citie or countrey, where the inhabitants are at warre and sedition among themselves." [9]

The specific faculty which should rule the passions and sensuality is, of course, reason, as commonly and loosely defined, but reason illuminated by grace, so that it can perceive not only the vanity of the world's goods but also the true good. This traditional dual function of reason, as both the eye of the mind and governor of the passions, Jean De Serres finds implied in Ecclesiastes, for although, "the wit of man is blind even in the viewing of the things of this worlde, untill that it be enlightened with the true light of the knowledge of God," [C5] yet it is reason that must nevertheless guide and control us. "There hath beene nothing given unto man by God, more excellent than the minde. This also is manifest, that nothing is so great an enimie unto this heavenly present and gifte as pleasure, as the which quencheth all the light of the minde, and doeth, as it were dazel the eyes of the minde, a foe doubtlesse unto reason, and having nothing to doe with vertue: for where pleasure beareth rule, what place, I pray you, can there be for reason or vertue? The government of reason being banished, what other thing can there range in the minde of man, than mere madnesse, with a blinde violence running unto his owne destruction?" [E8] The metaphors are noteworthy: reason is both eye—it can be blinded or enlightened or dazzled—and governor. "Pleasure," on the other hand is both dazzler and anarch.[10]

The kind of thinking here illustrated, which it would be easy, though perhaps painful, to illustrate much more extensively, represents clichés and truisms of the time. What Lucentio is talking about and what he intends, or thinks he intends, to do, therefore, should be clear to an overwhelming majority in the Elizabethan audience. Pursuing his studies, he will perceive the vain show of earthly pleasures, and, with God's help subdue his passions to his reason and thereby achieve, so far as is humanly possible, that tranquillity of mind which is the true felicity of man on earth. Tranio, in mock alarm warns against the dangers of Stoicism: "Let's be no Stoics nor no stocks, I pray." Then Bianca enters, and the comedy is on.

On one level it is the perennial comedy of pride going before a falling in love. On another level it is the more significant comedy of the man who, boasting that he will scorn the vain shows of the world, promptly falls for one of the most obvious of them, and who, boasting that he will master his passions, is immediately subdued by them. His love is dramatized as sudden, overwhelming, and as eye-love, as springing from the mere visible. His comedy and Sly's, though the dramatic metaphors differ, are identical.

Petruchio contrasts with Lucentio as the rational man to the irrational. There is, however, one apparent difficulty in the contrast which must be considered. Petruchio, by his own assertion, is led by avarice, or perhaps even avarice and lust, just as Lucentio is led by his eye-love:

> I come to wive it wealthily in Padua;
> If wealthily, then happily in Padua.
>
> (1.2.75–76)

By the same moral-psychology he is therefore, for all his carefully reasoned plan of taming Katherine, quite as much dominated by passion, quite as irrational, as Lucentio. His reason merely serves his passion. But he is certainly not ridiculous because of this irrational avarice. If there is one thing unequivocally clear in

178

the play, it is that Petruchio is triumphant and that the ending of the play is a happy one for him. The signs that mark and seal his happy triumph are Katherine's obedience and his acquisition of wealth, and Shakespeare emphasizes wealth as a sign of triumph by staging the wager scene in which Petruchio wins two hundred crowns and an additional gift of twenty thousand. An interpretation of the play, therefore, which sees men mocked because they mistake *temporalia* for true good and because they are dominated by the passions, which must include avarice, is nonsense.

Such an argument cannot be dismissed. There are highly intelligent people, trained by a certain kind of literary experience and trained to accept certain kinds of values, to whom it will remain convincing. There must have been some, Stephen Gosson, possibly, among the original audience. For such people the contrast between a rational and an irrational man will exist if and only if avarice is to be regarded as rational. Since for many such people avarice is not rational, Petruchio and Lucentio are equally irrational.

So much may be granted as an empirical fact. There are such people and there is such a meaning to the play. Obviously there are other people for whom the meaning is different, but it remains to be argued that their interpretation is reasonable.

In the first place, dialogue does not build up Petruchio as an avaricious man in the sense that it does so build up the character Avarice in *Respublica*, or Worldly Man in *Enough is as Good as a Feast* or even old Damon, the money-loving father in Ariosto's play, who corresponds to Baptista in Shakespeare's. Shakespeare gives Petruchio few lines requiring that his bride be, above all, wealthy, and these are near the beginning of the play. I have never heard of an actor playing Petruchio for avarice, and I think he would find the task difficult if he tried. Most actors concentrate, quite rightly I think, upon emphasizing those qualities in Petruchio which the lines seem to yield more easily: a rough and merry boisterousness, abounding energy, shrewdness which includes the ability to act a role, and an underlying geniality. Certainly the lines easily yield such an interpretation, which, in turn, keeps the rough business of the taming from becoming bitter or sadistic and keeps the ending sweet; to try to suggest on the stage that Petruchio is much concerned with money is to create a quite irrelevant or even distracting consideration.

Petruchio's avowal of purpose, then, serves the function, not of establishing through the quick, easy lines of caricature, his dominating aim, like the opening soliloquy of Richard III, but of giving the simplest possible explanation, very much in the manner of some folk-tales, of his determination to woo Katherine. It is the simplest explanation, and it keeps him human, in the sense of unsaintlike. He is given a quite mundane motive, but he is aware of it and he is not dominated by it.

The last point is all-important, since it is domination by passion that, in the common thought of the time, made a man miserable, and domination of it that allowed him that measure of felicity which is achievable on earth. That Petruchio dominates his passion is shown clearly, I think, by his behavior throughout the play, or rather it can easily be made clear by the actor, but in any case Shakespeare allows him finally to define the concept of the *summum bonum* to which his outrageous taming of the lady can now be seen to have been tending. The moment comes in the last scene, after Katherine has demonstrated her obedience, and Hortensio, struck with wonder, asks, "I wonder what it bodes." Petruchio answers,

> Marry, peace it bodes, and love, and quiet life,
> An awful rule, and right supremacy,
> And, to be short, what not that's sweet and happy.
>   (5.2.108–10)

This is a respectable definition of earthly felicity and a rational aim to which any moralist of the time would have been glad to subscribe.

Petruchio contrasts with Lucentio, then, as the man whose reason both sees his good and controls his passions, contrasts with the amiable youngster whose vision is beguiled by love and whose clever, scheming reason serves it. This contrast is visibly realized in the tableau at the end. Petruchio with the obedient Katherine stands over against Lucentio and Hortensio with their disobedient wives. The scene evokes the mild pleasure and pseudo-astonishment common at the end of fairy tales: the mild sister has turned out to be shrewish and the shrewish one mild. But beyond this contrast, there is the further point that Petruchio's reason has brought him to the tranquil life, while Lucentio's passion has deceived him and gained him turbulence. This psychological statement, however, is externalized in the traditional metaphor of the family, in which the husband stands for reason and the wife for will or passion, obedient on the one side, rebellious on the other.

Although the thematic contrast between Petruchio and Lucentio is spelled out in the final scene, it is implied throughout in the evident contrast of the two men. On the simplest naturalistic level Lucentio is ardent and usually a little stupid, often in need of prompting by his clever servant. Petruchio, on the other hand, is involved in an elaborate make-believe in which he counterfeits whatever emotions—rapture at Katherine's "mildness," anger at the servants' "negligence"—the pretended situation demands. All these emotions are simulated; none control him. Furthermore he devises his own strategy, and he is a brilliant strategist.

Katherine, in the meantime, exemplifies the change from one mental state to another, from passion-ridden fury brutally bent on domination to the happy mistress of her emotions who submits cheerfully. It should be noticed incidentally that her submission must be played as sincere, as the evidence of Fletcher's *The Tamer Tamed* shows it was originally.[11] Any suggestion that she is only biding her time or that she is merely continuing, as, indeed, she began, to resign herself to a bad situation will shatter the closing scene into a hundred irrelevancies. Her passion is really mastered; hence, in the time's psychology, her entry into the freedom and gaiety which she shares with Petruchio. It is a self-mastery which is indicated, like Petruchio's, by her sudden ability to simulate emotion, here the joy and wonder of seeing a beautiful maiden when Petruchio orders her to greet old Vincentio:

Young budding virgin, fair and fresh and sweet,
Whither away? or where is thy abode?
Happy the parents of so fair a child!
Happier the man whom favourable stars
Allot thee for his lovely bedfellow!

(4.5.37–41)

It marks one of the funniest moments in the theater and one of
the most poignant. Henceforth she acts her part consciously, with
exaggeration and humor, as when she places her hand beneath
Petruchio's foot.

For those trained in morality techniques the naturalistic level
of action also carries a reinforcing moral-psychological tenor.
They may see the inverted master and servant relationship, for
instance, like that in *Friar Bacon*, as a mirror of Lucentio's mental
inversion, his reason dethroned and serving his will. I do not think
that Shakespeare paid much attention to this possibility if, indeed,
he noticed it. He borrowed the situation from Ariosto's play,
where it seems to have no metaphorical meaning, and he did not
noticeably emphasize its potential meaning as metaphor. The
most that can be said for it is that it "works" in a general way
for those who look for it.

Katherine's taming by Petruchio, on the other hand, reflects
the submission of her will to reason with great precision. That
the analogy was traditional may have helped to emphasize it for
members of the audience, but the analogy itself is simply "there,"
like a good, close rhyme. In the moral psychology of the time
Katherine's will, inflamed by her passions, is rebellious to her reason exactly as she is rebellious against her husband, and it submits
exactly as she does. Indeed, as I have already remarked, on the
naturalistic level she submits to Petruchio *because* her will has
submitted to reason. The taming can be seen, therefore, as a
humorous allegory, very much like one of the "Wit and Science"
plays, of the mind's struggle with itself; the Will on the rampage,
tamed by a mad wag of a Reason. The action writes large most
obviously the struggle and conquest of Katherine's psyche, but if

the actor so wills it, it is also a metaphor of Petruchio's wild psychic ride upon his bucking will to the tranquillity he foresees at the end. It also narrates the fight for and accomplishment of the aim—happiness by virtue to be achieved—which Lucentio bravely professes and comically falls short of. Or more precisely, it presents Lucentio with a lesson in that subject which he has come to Padua to study.

Other similar manipulations of this theme and metaphor in the play will suggest themselves. One can only guess at the extent to which Shakespeare or his audiences may have been conscious of them, but it is a measure of the play's thematic coherence that the same patterns reappear as the play is turned in the hand.

Finally with the usual qualifications about audiences and their expectations, the play compares life to a play or comedy. Most obviously it does this by presenting the life of Petruchio, Lucentio, Katherine, and the rest *as* a comedy watched by Sly, but the comparison is reinforced by the fact that it is closely linked to the dream metaphor of the Sly story, that Sly's beguilers turn actors to beguile him, that the play is one of the illusions of his dream of lordship, and that Sly, who as delighted worldling represents us, is himself a character in a comedy.

Now one half of the comedy that Sly watches is a comedy of deceits or illusions or mistakes; Ariosto called it *I Suppositi*, Gascoigne *The Supposes*. These supposes, as they occur throughout the play, make everyone but Lucentio and Tranio look foolish, and Lucentio also is finally revealed to be duped. The characters are like people who are unknowingly playing in a play and mistaking its illusions—the properties and costumes and titles and offices of the various roles—for reality. It is this illusory, deceptive nature of dramatic production that forms the basis of the traditional comparison of life to a play from Lucian on. Thus, for instance, Pierre Boaistuau uses it—though his rhetoric is more solemn—in his *Theatrum Mundi* (Englished 1566):

"What else is this world but a Theatre? Whereas some playe or use the state of Artificers and men of base condition and calling, and others do represent the state of kings, Dukes, Earls, Mar-

quises, Barons, and others, constituted in dignities. And nevertheless when al these have cast of their visards and masking garments, and that death commeth and maketh an end of this bloudie
tragedy, then they acknowledge themselves al to be mortal men.
And then the Lord that is in heaven laugheth at their foolish en-
terprises and vanities." [12]

In short, if we see these people as like characters unwittingly in
a play, they are the exact counterparts of Sly in his, the alternative metaphor of life as dream.

Petruchio, however, is an exception. (So, perhaps, is Tranio,
but Shakespeare makes nothing of the fact.) He is not duped; he
does not mistake the appearances of the comedy for reality. He is
an actor who remains emotionally detached from the role which
he is playing, amused by it as he is amused by the other characters,
especially Katherine, in the comedy of which he is author, director, and co-star. I have remarked on this characteristic as it indicates his emotional control, but it is also important as it distinguishes him within the comic metaphor. He enjoys playing his
role and can step out of it. He addresses the audience twice, explaining and laughing at his strategy, once (2.1.169–82) before
the wooing, once (4.1.182–205) on the wedding night. His wooing is a contest in the improvisation of wit and the tricks of combat which certainly he, and perhaps Katherine, enjoys as an
exercise in skill. The flamboyant tatters of his wedding dress, his
robust and witty bravado as he carries off the bride, and his
playful-whimsical naming of the hours and sun and moon bespeak
the artist's delight in the skill of the doing that is quite distinct
from mere determination to get the thing done. It is an effect that
most actors wisely play for. As a result, Petruchio is shown
enjoying the comedy of which he is a part in a way that the
other characters rarely do and that Katherine, though the wooing
scene can suggest her capabilities, only learns to do as she tames
herself.

This kind of character, laughing at and easily stepping outside
the comedy and his role in it, was familiar to audiences and playwrights from the vice in later moralities, who characteristically

takes the audience into his confidence, exults in his own cleverness, and laughs at his victims when they leave the scene: for
example, Courage in *The Tide Tarrieth*, Covetousness in *Enough
is as Good as a Feast*, their descendants like Richard III, Iago, and
Edmund, and their less malevolent counterparts like Jack Juggler,
Diccon the Bedlam, or the servant boys of *Mother Bombie*. By
playing such a character in a play seen as a play, however, Shakespeare creates a novel kind of actor-hero. He is analogous to the
moralists' ideal man in the active life, who is in the world but not
of it; he is in the comedy, wooing and taming Katherine and winning wealth, but conscious of the fact that he is acting a role in
the comedy, amused by it, and able to step out from it. He is thus
like the man who engages in the pursuits of his worldly fellow
men but is undominated by their concerns and able to view the
whole scene, including himself, with Lucianic humor. This is es-
sentially the kind of attitude which Erasmus seems to recommend
in the famous and influential passage of *The Praise of Folly* where
he makes his comparison of life to a play:

"I praie you, who is he that confessith not a prince to be bothe
riche, and a great lorde? but set case he hath no good qualitees
of the mynde, nor with all those gooddes he hath, can be satisfied:
now is he not riche, but poorer than the poorest. Than againe
admit he be gevin to sundrie vices: now is he no lorde, but more
subjecte than a servaunt: and after this rate maie ye skanne also
the others. But this is enough for exemple. Now it maie be, ye
muse what I meane hereby, but geve me leave yet a little further.
If one at a solemne stage plaie, woulde take upon hym to plucke
of the plaiers garmentes, whiles they were saiying theyr partes,
and so disciphre unto the lokers on, the true and native faces of
eche of the plaiers, shoulde he not (trow ye) marre all the mattier?
and well deserve for a madman to be peltid out of the place with
stones? ye shoulde see yet straightwaies a new transmutacion in
thynges: that who before plaied the woman, shoulde than appeare
to be a man: who seemed youth, should shew his hore heares: who
countrefaited the kynge, shulde tourne to a rascall, and who plaied
god almightie, shulde become a cobler as he was before. Yet take

awaie this errour, and as soone take awaie all togethers, in as muche as the feignyng and counterfaityng is it, that so delighteth the beholders. So likewise, all this life of mortall men, what is it els, but a certaine kynde of stage plaie? wheras men come foorthe disguised one in one arraie, an other in an other, eche plaiyng his parte, till at last the maker of the plaie, or bokebearer causeth theim to avoyde the skaffolde, and yet sometyme maketh one man come in, two or three tymes, with sundrie partes and apparaile, as who before represented a kynge, beyng clothed all in purpre, havyng no more but shyfted hym selfe a little, shoulde shew hym self againe lyke an woobegon myser. And all this is dooen under a certaine veile or shadow, whiche taken awaie ones, the plaie can no more be plaied.

"Here nowe if one of these wisemen, come (I wene) from heaven, did sodeinly appeare, and saie, *howe evin this great prince, whom all men honor as their god and soveraigne, deserveth skarce to be called man, seyng like the brute beastes, he is trained by affections, and is none other than a servaunt of the basest sort, seyng willyngly he obeith so many, and so vile vices his maisters. Or than againe, woulde bidde some other, who mourned for his fathers or friendes decease, rather to laughe, and be merie, because suche diyng to this worlde is the beginnyng of a better life, wheras this here, is but a maner death as it were. Furthermore, wolde call an other gloriyng in his armes and auncestrie, bothe a villaine, and a bastarde, because he is so many discentes disalied from vertue, whiche is the onely roote of true nobilitee.* And in suche lyke sorte woulde raile upon all the rest. I praie you, what shulde he prevaile therby, but make men take him for frantike and distraught? For surely as nothing can be more foolisshe than wisedome out of place, so is nothyng more fonde than prudence out of season. And dooeth he not out of season (trow ye) that plieth not him selfe as the world goeth? . . . On the other side, it is a verie wysemans part to coveite to know nothyng beyond his bandes, and either as the whole multitude of other men dooe, to dissemble gladly, or to erre, and be deceived with the most. But evin this is Foly (saie thei). And in good faieth I will not much

186

denie it, upon condicion againe they graunt me, that to dissemble, or erre so, is the right plaiyng of the pageantes of this life." [13]

Now it is true that Folly's counsel of prudence here is shot through with that dazzling irony that makes reading *The Praise of Folly* an experience at once delightful and exasperating. One can never be quite sure of Erasmus's intentions. Certainly if Folly's advice is pushed to extremes, it becomes the counsel of sycophancy, as More's friend Hythloday argues in the first book of *Utopia*. More has been seeking to meet Hythloday's contention that philosophy has no place in court, and he uses the image of the theater:

"There is another philosophy more civil, which knoweth, as ye would say, her own stage, and thereafter, ordering and behaving herself in the play that she hath in hand, playeth her part accordingly with comeliness, uttering nothing out of due order and fashion. And this is the philosophy that you must use. Or else whiles a comedy of Plautus is playing, and the vile bondmen scoffing and trifling among themselves, if you should suddenly come upon the stage in a philosopher's apparel, and rehearse out of *Octavia* the place wherein Seneca disputeth with Nero, had it nor been better for you to have played the dumb person, than, by rehearsing that which served neither for the time nor place, to have made such a tragical comedy or gallimaufrey? For by bringing in other stuff that nothing appertaineth to the present matter, you must needs mar and pervert the play that is in hand, though the stuff that you bring in be much better. What part soever you have taken upon you, play that as well as you can and make the best of it. . . .

"So the case standeth in a commonwealth, and so it is in the consultations of kings and princes. If evil opinions and naughty persuasions cannot be utterly and quite plucked out of their hearts, if you cannot even as you would remedy which use and custom hath confirmed, yet for this cause you must not leave and foresake the commonwealth. You must with a crafty wile and a subtle train study and endeavor yourself, as much as in you lieth, to handle the matter wittily and handsomely for the purpose;

and that which you cannot turn to good, so to order it that it be not very bad." [14]

At this Hythloday is shocked, replying that "whiles that I go about to remedy the madness of others I should be even as mad as they." He jeers that "preachers, sly and wily men, following your counsel (as I suppose) because they saw men evil willing to frame their manners to Christ's rule, they have wrested and wried His doctrine." He denies that crafty wiles and subtle trains are of use to the reformer, for "there is not place to dissemble in nor to wink in. Naughty counsels must be openly allowed and very pestilent desires must be approved." [15]

Hythloday's shock is More's salutary reminder that there are limits to playing along with the comedy, and years later More proved that he knew them. But within those limits he was celebrated for acting his part with mirth and good humor and for the amusement with which he observed the comedy about him—giving his wife imitation jewelry, for instance, and persuading her of its worth and rarity. Erasmus's Folly tells the story and adds that the lady was overjoyed, guarding the glass carefully, that More saved money, and that he had the further pleasure of enjoying her delusion.

Within the limits of comedy, in short, Hythloday is wrong. At least it could be so argued. Hythloday's argument is absolutist; it demands all or nothing. One must strip the masks, whip abuses, cleanse the foul body of the infected world, or retire and be silent, as Hythloday, in disgust and despair, has determined to do. On the contrary, it is possible to be in the world but not of it. One can act in the comedy without being deceived by its illusions; one can perceive it as illusion and as funny.

To return to Petruchio. By accident or design he comes very close to being the Erasmian spectator-actor, and as such he presents a new antithesis to the simple-minded worldlings, Plato's cave-dwellers, the Lucentios spellbound by the shadows on the wall. The traditional stage antithesis had opposed to vice the clear-sighted virtue figure, Wisdom who is Christ, Lady Verity, Old Honesty, Jonson's Crites, who unmasked the rogues and undeceived the cheated innocents, or who, if powerless, like King John or Simplicity, or Lady Conscience, suffered. It is true that there were also other traditional antitheses which were not explicitly moral, like that of wit to tediousness in *Wit and Science*, or clownish cowardice to romantic heroism in *Sir Clyomon and Sir Clamydes*, but Lyly, while still very much concerned with moral issues, had scrutinized instead of, or in addition to, vice, the inherent and ridiculous weakness that leads to vice. This makes difficult the tidy contrast of black to white and leads to such scaled gradations of imperfection—sometimes capped by perfection—as that which forms the closing tableau in *Endymion*, or to the amused and non-committal balancing of Alexander, Diogenes, and the lovers in *Campaspe*. Greene, working in the older fashion, had matched the vice of Bacon and of Edward with the virtue of their reformation, but he balanced Margaret's frailty —not vice—with her own awareness of it and of the vain shows to which, when Lacy presses her, she returns. She thus anticipates (if Greene's play is the earlier) such self-conscious heroes as Petruchio and Berowne, and in respect to her awareness of her frailty, she is a more complex character than Petruchio.

Petruchio, however, gradually takes command of the audience's point of view as Margaret does not, so that we do not merely sympathize with him, or find him engaging, or admire him, but can share his vision. It is the comic vision of our situation and our weakness as human beings—moving unwittingly in the illusions which are figured as those of the stage or the dream, our reason blinded and all but mastered by emotions which make fools of us.

The play does not call us to reform ourselves; certainly it does not call very loudly. Nor does it, unlike Calderon's plays on the same metaphors, preach that we must act well our parts, or accept what Providence has in store for us, or restrain our unregenerate and beastlike natures from the passionate lunge at the tempting satisfactions of the dream. Granted that it suggests taming the shrew, within as well as without, the suggestion is made in the tongue-in-cheek language of farce which suspends belief in, or even denies, its affirmations as it makes them. Whether it is possible to tame a shrew or control oneself is not really said, and is not relevant to the comedy of the taming. The ideal as ideal is taken for granted, but its attainment is not discussed. Instead the play suggests, as a way of getting along with our blindness and passionate irrationality, that awareness of the comedy which Petruchio has from the beginning and which Katherine comes to. The audience also, spectators of life presented as dream and comedy, shares it.

VIII.

A Midsummer Night's Dream.

A Midsummer Night's Dream is far more complex than *The Taming of the Shrew*, and any one pattern or action provides only an arbitrary starting point for analysis. The play does fall "naturally," however, into three parts as it moves from court and town to grove and back again, a movement which, as C. L. Barber points out, reproduces that of the May game and also indicates the mental progress of the four lovers, from dissatisfaction to chaos, to harmony; or from waking, to dreaming, to waking again.[1] These divisions provide an adequate and convenient approach.

The first part opens with what turns out to be a frame or prologue to the main action; the exposition of the coming marriage of Theseus and Hippolyta and of the state of their love, and the announcement, implied in Theseus's speech, of the general nature of the show we are to witness:

> Stir up the Athenian youth to merriments,
> Awake the pert and nimble spirit of mirth,

and

> (1.1.12–13)

> I will wed thee in another key,
> With pomp, with triumph, and with revelling.
>
> (1.1.18–19)

The play is to be joyful, as is appropriate for a wedding, and there *is to be* a wedding. Theseus's stormy wooing,

> I woo'd thee with my sword,
> And won thy love doing thee injuries;
>
> (1.1.16–17)

is about to culminate in marriage. The love of the pair is now ordered, controlled, and brought to an harmonious close. The point is emphasized in part by the human impatience that Theseus shows:

> our nuptial hour
> Draws on apace. Four happy days bring in
> Another moon; but, O, methinks, how slow
> This old moon wanes! She lingers my desires,
> Like to a stepdame or a dowager,
> Long withering out a young man's revenue.
>
> (1.1.1–6)

and by Hippolyta's charming words of restraint:

> Four days will quickly steep themselves in night;
> Four nights will quickly dream away the time;
> And then the moon, like to a silver bow
> New-bent in heaven, shall behold the night
> Of our solemnities.
>
> (1.1.7–11)

It is the impatience that gives occasion to show us that it is being controlled. The staging of the scene also emphasizes the point, pleasantly ceremonious, lifting the royal couple above and apart from the brabbling disorder among their subjects. For those in the audience with some education, furthermore, Shakespeare's choice of Hippolyta and Theseus for the royal bride and bridegroom reinforces the point. Hippolyta as queen of the Amazons was the archetype of all women uncontrolled by men, in the common allegory, the passionate will uncontrolled by reason. Theseus's conquest was a psychomachia. She is tamed now, like Katherine. The mind's order is restored. Hence joy.[2]

In a sense, the rest of the play is flashback, a review of the *sturm und drang*, social and psychic, which came before. It begins immediately with the turbulent entry, the complaints, and the recriminations of Egeus, Hermia, Lysander, and Demetrius. Egeus is intemperate himself, and his failure to control himself is reflected both in his failure to control his daughter and, if we like, in her disobedience. Theseus points out her error:

> To you your father should be as a god;
> One that compos'd your beauties; yea, and one
> To whom you are but as a form in wax,
> By him imprinted, and within his power
> To leave the figure, or disfigure it.
>
> (1.1.47–51)

Her duty is to "master her blood," either by conforming to her father's wishes or by becoming a nun in Diana's service:

> Therefore, fair Hermia, question your desires,
> Know of your youth, examine well your blood,
> Whether, if you yield not to your father's choice,
> You can endure the livery of a nun. . . .
> Thrice blessed they that master so their blood
> To undergo such maiden pilgrimage;
> But earthlier happier is the rose distill'd.
>
> (1.1.67–76)

The penalty for not mastering her blood is death, of course, by an Athenian law which, like that of Ephesus in *The Comedy of Errors*, is analogous to the Old Law, condemning man simply for his nature. By any realistic Elizabethan standards it is a fantastic law, just as Egeus's willingness to invoke it is fantastic, and Theseus's description of filial duty is fantastic overstatement. Partly for that reason, partly because the play has been announced as comedy, the audience knows that the threat is sham, like the seeming threat of the Old Law for men of good will. Man runs his comic course against the dark background of the doom that he deserves, but merely as man he does not suffer it. His end is happiness.

Meanwhile we witness in the jeering petulance of the quarrel. Egeus against Hermia and Lysander, Lysander against Demetrius, Demetrius against Hermina, and finally Helena against Demetrius, the evidence of unmastered blood in all the characters, not simply Hermina. Both mind and society are disordered. Hence, misery.

We are led first to focus upon the misery of Hermia and Lysander and then, as they generalize in their lovely duet upon that of all lovers:

> *Lys.* Ay me! for aught that I could ever read,
> Could ever hear by tale or history,
> The course of true love never did run smooth;
> But, either it was different in blood—
> *Her.* O cross! too high to be enthrall'd to low!
> *Lys.* Or else misgraffed in respect of years—
> *Her.* O spite! too old to be engag'd to young!
> *Lys.* Or else it stood upon the choice of friends—
> *Her.* O hell! to choose love by another's eyes!
> *Lys.* Or, if there were a sympathy in choice,
> War, death, or sickness did lay siege to it,
> Making it momentany as a sound,
> Swift as a shadow, short as any dream,
> Brief as the lightning in the collied night,
> That, in a spleen, unfolds both heaven and earth,
> And ere a man hath power to say 'Behold!'
> The jaws of darkness do devour it up:
> So quick bright things come to confusion.
>
> (1.1.132–149)

This is one of the first great lyric show-stoppers in Shakespeare's career. It is not decorative song, however. It makes the lovers' plight representative, first of the whims of circumstance to which the satisfactions of love are subject, and then, in a daring extension, of the transiency of love and, indeed, all beauty: "So quick bright things come to confusion." This is to the tune of "Beauty is but a flower which wrinkles will devour," or "Wanton pleasure, doting love, are but shadows flying." To the modern ear, at least, it is an odd emphasis in a play written for a wedding celebration, but it is part of the general recognition of the evanescent and illusory nature of earthly pleasure which is one of the premises of the action.

After finishing their duet, the unhappy lovers plot to meet in the wood and to flee from the sharp Athenian law. They are joined in their lamenting by the wretched Helena, who is understandably, though still politely, envious of Hermia. Hermia, however, after telling of their plans to flee remarks,

> Before the time I did Lysander see,
> Seem'd Athens as a paradise to me.
> O, then, what graces in my love do dwell
> That he hath turn'd a heaven unto a hell!
>
> (1.1.204–7)

Sense can be made of the last couplet, but the paradox strikes first, underlining the touching absurdity of Hermia's love. The idea is not new; it is a variation on the sonneteers' conceit of the sweet torment, or on the resolution of Lyly's foresters in *Love's Metamorphosis* to pursue their own ruins, and it is based on the commonplace that the seeming-sweet of passion is really misery. As an expression of the lovers' passionate unreason, then, it suggests that they are fleeing to the hell they seek to escape, and it foreshadows the chaotic distress of the night in the wood.

Demetrius and Helena are also engaged in this same absurd pursuit of pain. Hermia complains of Demetrius, "the more I hate, the more he follows me." Helena confesses to pursuing him though she knows he hates her, and, when Lysander and Hermia leave, she resolves to tell him of their plan though she knows he will immediately follow Hermia: "herein mean I to enrich my pain." The flight and pursuit to the wood, then, becomes a figure of lovers' flight to and pursuit of the torment of passionate turmoil. As Helena has reminded us, it is obvious error:

> And as [Demetrius] errs, doting on Hermia's eyes,
> So I, admiring of his qualities.
> Things base and vile, holding no quantity,
> Love can transpose to form and dignity.
>
> (1.1.230–33)

Yet, of course, she follows.

Needless to say, the scene must be played for comedy, high comedy, a mood to be broken by the farce that follows, but funny. We are made to smile at this silly, wrangling, irrational pursuit of the evanescent and painful. We are also asked to sympathize with the lovers, driven irresistibly, both in their pain and in their wishes, which we share even as we are made to laugh at them.

When Helena leaves, a short scene introduces the artisans and their plan to meet in the wood. Then the second part begins, opened by Puck and a fairy, who introduce Titania and Oberon and their quarrel.

In general, the second part dramatizes in ampler action and more fully developed theatrical metaphors the situations and themes lightly sketched in the first part. For instance, in the first part, the lovers told who loved whom, who was pursuer, who pursued. Now they act out the relationships established verbally in the first part. Demetrius enters in visible pursuit of Hermia and visibly pursued by Helena, whom he spurns. This is straight exemplification, but the action modulates into a metaphorical statement a few minutes later when Lysander and Hermia enter, their distress realized theatrically as fatigue and their irrational confusion, just as in Dante or Spenser or Dekker's *Old Fortunatus*, as their loss of their way in the wood. The compulsive nature of their loves is similarly realized as like the effect of magic juice;

the moral inversion of the love is exemplified by the paradoxical hatred to which it leads, and the rational or moral blindness of Demetrius and Lysander is compared to their bewildered following of Puck's voice. The theme of disordered love is extended, furthermore, by the parallel quarrel of Titania and Oberon, where we see marriage in disharmony, and through Titania's whimsical explanation of the bad weather, it is extended to the larger order of nature. Bottom's transformation, the flight of the artisans, and Titania's infatuation are, of course, variations of the central statement. These are all fairly obvious and elementary stage metaphors, linked together very much, though within the comic mode, as in *Lear* or *Hymenaei*.

Like the anti-masque-like scene in *Hymenaei* the second part presents the disorder of passionate unreason by way of fantastic allegory, and like that scene it reveals and then avoids the ultimate danger of such unreason in the threat of violence. Lysander and Demetrius pursue each other in blind rage, their swords drawn, ready for death and tragedy. This is the goal to which unreason speeds. Although we see how tragedy can happen, safe in the knowledge that it will not happen we are made to laugh at it. As Puck and Oberon have befuddled the lovers, set them at odds, and lured the two young men into danger, so they also save them.

That action, in turn, helps to define Puck and Oberon. Oberon is a fairy, of course, and Puck is Puck or Robin Goodfellow, and there will always be spectators—perhaps there were some in the sixteenth century—who smilingly resist the notion that they represent anything else, except possibly a vague impish embodiment of the spirit of J. M. Barrie. For the rest, it may be noted that they are not close transcriptions of the figures of popular belief; rather they are sophisticated literary, or dramatic, variations on those figures, and Shakespeare, as Mr. Barber has pointed out, delicately spoofs the "reality" of their existence.[3]

Their main function—Puck's sole function—is to work on the minds of other characters, and as they do this they are like the externalized impulses, emotions, and faculties of the moralities. Specifically, as they set the others at odds, they are like the vices, but they differ from them in their benignity. They are mischievous in the modern sense, not wicked.

This is also the chief difference between Oberon and the fairies of popular belief, who were usually thought to be diabolic. He is not diabolic or infernal and Shakespeare thought the point worth emphasis. Thus Puck warns him:

> . . . yonder shines Aurora's harbinger;
> At whose approach ghosts, wand'ring here and there,
> Troop home to churchyards; damned spirits all,
> That in crossways and floods have burial,
> Already to their wormy beds are gone.
> For fear lest day should look their shames upon,
> They wilfully themselves exile from light,
> And must for aye consort with black-brow'd night.

Oberon replies,

> But we are spirits of another sort.
> I with the Morning's love have oft made sport;
> And, like a forester, the groves may tread
> Even till the eastern gate, all fiery red,
> Opening on Neptune, with fair blessed beams
> Turns into yellow gold his salt green streams.
> But notwithstanding, haste.
>
> (3.2.380–394)

The assertion also distinguishes him from the lord of misrule as seen by Puritans like Stubbes:
"Against May, Whitsunday, or other time all the young men and maids, old men and wives, run gadding over night to the woods, groves, hills, and mountains, where they spend all the night in pleasant pastimes . . . And no marvel, for there is a great Lord present amongst them, as superintendent and Lord over their pastimes and sports, namely, Satan, prince of hell." [4] As Barber, again, points out, "in making Oberon, prince of fairies, into the May king, Shakespeare urbanely plays with the notion of a supernatural power at work in holiday." [5] It is a

playing with the notion. Oberson is *like* a May king or lord of night-rule. Puck is like his jester. They are like supernatural powers or vices or even devils, but they are also unlike these things, and their actions do not constitute a statement about such beings. The actions rather serve to explain, to make funny, and to evaluate what "gets into" people when they fall in love. In this respect they are precisely like the actions of Cupid and Venus in *Gallathea*. The crazy business of youthful falling in and out of love, to reverse the metaphor, is not only like losing one's way in a forest at night, like being enchanted by magic juice, or the lunacies of going a-maying. It is also as if one were under the power of a benevolent May lord or fairy king or a merry and undiabolic devil or misled by an unvicious Vice. The experience is funny to the onlooker and, though it skirts the very rim of chaos and bloodshed, it can be guided past to that order in mar-riage of which its passion is the substance ordered. In Milton's phrase, "the passions within us . . . rightly tempered are the very ingredients of virtue."

As misleaders and leaders—or misrulers and rulers—then, Puck and Oberon externalize both the apparent and the real, the ap-parent misguidance of chance and passion to which all men are subject and the real guidance of a larger, benign purpose. In this respect they are like the appearance of Fortune, whose caprices, dominating passionate men, mask the reality of Providential de-sign, and within this analogy the four lovers are like generic man-kind. They are significant, that is, not because of sharply indi-vidual characters, actions, or fates, but because they exemplify the passionate silliness and the happy ending of man as man. That they are so little characterized as to be almost indistinguishable, therefore, is not the dramatic disaster it might be. Like Gallathea and Phillida or Diana's nymphs in *Gallathea*, they exist as identical manifestations of a natural tendency.

Finally, the experiences of the lovers, of Titania, and of Bottom are like dreams. The point needs little demonstration. The dream-like nature of the action itself aside, the analogy is made explicit in the dialogue, and when Theseus and his hunting party discover them sleeping, the lovers actually wake as from a dream and allude to their experience as if it had been one. So do Titania and Bottom.

Bottom's dream is like Sly's, a dream of the transient bliss of this world, but the other dreams are unpleasant, of bale, not bliss. They are dreams of passion, however; passion, not reason, had led the will, directing it to the objects of sense—what the eye sees. Such is the life of the worldling in woe and perturbation as well as in imagined bliss, or specifically, such is the life of the lover, a dream of passion from which, like young Wit after his whirl with Wantonness, the mind awakens at the call of reason.

The play's third part, which begins with this awakening, brings the lovers to harmony. Their awakening is preceded by the entrance of the hunting party and the lyric duet of Theseus and Hippolyta hymning the baying of their hounds. This curious and lovely piece would be a dramatic monstrosity in some kinds of theater. It motivates the royal entrance, to be sure, but its emphasis on music is irrelevant to that purpose and it is needlessly long:

> *The.* . . . since we have the vaward of the day,
> My love shall hear the music of my hounds.
> Uncouple in the western valley; let them go.
> Dispatch, I say, and find the forester.
> We will, fair Queen, up to the mountain's top
> And mark the musical confusion
> Of hounds and echo in conjunction.
> *Hip.* I was with Hercules in Cadmus once
> When in a wood of Crete they bay'd the bear
> With hounds of Sparta. Never did I hear
> Such gallant chiding; for, besides the groves,
> The skies, the fountains, every region near
> Seem'd all one mutual cry. I never heard
> So musical a discord, such sweet thunder.
> *The.* My hounds are bred out of the Spartan kind;
> So flew'd, so sanded; and their heads are hung
> With ears that sweep away the morning dew;

Crook-knee'd, and dew-lapp'd like Thessalian bulls;
Slow in pursuit, but match'd in mouth like bells,
Each under each. A cry more tuneable
Was never holloa'd to nor cheer'd with horn
In Crete, in Sparta, nor in Thessaly.
Judge when you hear. But, soft! What nymphs are these?
                                             (4.1.108–30)

This is delightful but static. It makes dramatic sense, however, if we view it as a sort of musical-comedy prelude to the last act, implying the resolution of the preceding passionate discord in harmony. We have been watching disorder and listening to cacophony; we now prepare for concord. Theseus's surprised question assumes the analogy and carries it forward:

. . . I pray you all, stand up.
I know you two are rival enemies.
How comes this gentle concord in the world
That hatred is so far from jealousy
To sleep by hate and fear no enmity?
                                             (4.1.144–48)

Obviously, we can expect concord now, but the imagery in the duet implies not merely concord after discord, but a concord of the hitherto discordant notes themselves, a "musical discord," "sweet thunder," or "the musical confusion of hounds and echo in conjunction." This is the *discordia concors* by analogy to which theologians explained the existence of apparent evil within a comprehensive divine harmony. Such a theological implication is not wholly irrelevant here, but the more immediate paradox is that these warring passions should produce the harmony of love. Jonson, in *Hymenaei*, effects a similar shift from chaos to harmony when Reason suddenly subdues the passions. That is the usual and expected assertion of order as rational, and certainly the awakening of the lovers seems to satisfy that expectation by the use of familiar symbolism. After man's passionate dream, his reason awakens, just as in Spenser or the Wit and Science plays.

201

In the theater, what seems *is*. For many Elizabethans, I suppose, this awakening to reason must have been fact, and Shakespeare allows such people a fairly consistent, though rather crude, interpretation of the play's ending. But others, if statistical expectations hold, will notice that the lovers' awakening contrasts with, as well as parallels, the usual return to reason. Demetrius after all has the juice of love-in-idleness still in his eyes, and the ungoverned passions of Hermia, Helena, and Lysander remain unchanged, ungoverned still. It is only the bewildered lovers who *think* they now see clearly, but even they admit their bewilderment. Demetrius, for instance, explains his change as forced by an unknown power, though he also sees it as a return to health from sickness:

> . . . I wot not by what power
> (But by some power it is) my love to Hermia,
> Melted as the snow, seems to me now
> As the remembrance of an idle gaud
> Which in my childhood I did dote upon;
> And all the faith, the virtue of my heart,
> The object and the pleasure of my eye
> Is only Helena. To her my lord,
> Was I betroth'd ere I saw Hermia;
> But, like a sickness, did I loathe this food;
> But, as in health, come to my natural taste,
> Now do I wish it, love it, long for it,
> And will for evermore be true to it.
>
> (4.1.167–79)

But to the audience his assurance is ridiculous. It is both young Tweedledum's external, triumphant celebration of the unique and surpassing charms of Miss Tweedledee and the grown man's perpetual boast that he has put away his childish things and now, thank God, sees face to face. We have just seen how love really comes about and we know better. The harmony which has surprised Theseus is produced not by human reason "but by some power." As a statement about generic mankind this makes sense;

Mankind remains passionate and absurd, its goals ridiculous and its eyesight blind. It is brought into harmony by a superior power.

As individuals the lovers are obviously and simply like most people who have come through courtship to marriage. They have come through tempest to a unity and married calm that is not more rational but is less turbulent. They have joyfully accepted what luck—Fortune or Providence, Fortune's other face—has given them. And having come through the emotional tempest, they can now look back with amusement upon that passionate folly as it is staged and unconsciously parodied by the artisans. The play of Pyramus and Thisbe, like their own mad action of the night before, is a drama of romantic love, of lovers separated and of mistakes by moonlight. Like theirs it is bitter to the characters and hilarious to observers. From the safe shore of matrimony, they can now turn back to observe and laugh.

Although they are visible and audible in the last act, however, they are not the center of it, and their new-found calm and merriment is not the point or focus of the scene. Insofar as we are aware of them, it is as spectators no wiser or better than ourselves, certainly not as the erstwhile fools of passion who have now learned their lesson. Indeed, in their unseemly mockery of the honest player-artisans, they seem to provide the audience—especially the aristocratic audience of the first performance—an example to be shunned. It is "not generous, not gentle, not humble," as Holofernes told the jeering aristocrats he faced. Theseus's gentler behavior tactfully rebukes them and it also, of course, encourages the real audience to show its wonted courtesy to the Lord Chamberlain's Men, who in any case are obviously and dazzlingly superior to the amateurs *they* parody.

It is the show, not the audience, however, that claims attention, but *as* a show, something staged and watched, and we are kept aware of the watchers. Granted that the implications must have varied from performance to performance and from spectator to spectator, the mirror effect at the first performance must have been striking and obvious. In the hall itself sat the noble groom and bride, perhaps the Earl of Derby and Elizabeth Vere, surrounded by their entourage, watching the play staged for their wedding; on the stage sat Theseus and Hippolyta as bridegroom and bride amidst their entourage, watching the play staged for *their* wedding. The blessing of the bride-bed in the epilogue serves ambiguously for both the real couple and their mirror image on the stage. Spectators who missed this parallel shut their eyes.

The parallel stages the analogy of the world and the theater, and it implies further that we in the audience with the Earl of Derby are, like Theseus and his retinue, also actors in a play. They mirror us in that way too. And like them we laugh and have laughed at a "comedy" which was tragic, or near-tragic, to the characters in it. The vision the play presents is focussed by this paradox. How shall we find the concord of this discord?

We may recall from *Measure for Measure* Isabella's explanation when she speaks of proud Man, who

> Drest in a little brief authority,
> Most ignorant of what he's most assur'd,
> (His glassy essence), like an angry ape,
> Plays such fantastic tricks before high heaven
> As make the angels weep; who, with our spleens,
> Would all themselves laugh mortal.
>
> (2.2.118–23)

Man's tragic passions, here pride and anger, spring from his assumptions that his authority is something "real" instead of a costume which he is dressed in briefly and that his being is solid instead of something fragile, like glass. But the same assumptions also make him ridiculous unless one sees him from the heights of pity. This is common medieval—and Miltonic—teaching, and applied to drama it provides one explanation of Socrates' assertion that comedy and tragedy are the same. They both result from man's acceptance of temporal appearance for reality, the Platonic cave-dweller's passionate devotion to the shadows on the wall.

This is the view of life implied by the situation, the tragedy within a comedy; it is also implied by the tragedy itself, which, although it makes fun of the near tragedy of the four lovers, is of the same kind; as it makes fun of the tragedy of Romeo and Juliet, also of the same kind. They are all, that is, tragedies that spring from the passionate conviction that the appearance of good is the reality, the shadow the substance, and its loss, consequently, desolation. The chief apparent good in each play, furthermore, is the beloved. These tragedies are of this kind, of course, only within a context of otherworldly values implied by such metaphors as "life is a dream" or "all the world's a stage;" in other contexts they are quite different. Pyramus, Romeo, Demetrius, Lysander, Helena, Hermia, Thisby and Juliet are victims of the passionate delusion that bliss is union with the beloved, and that absence is the utter void. In Romeo's phrase,

> . . . Heaven is here,
> Where Juliet lives; and every cat and dog
> And little mouse, every unworthy thing,
> Live here in heaven and may look on her;
> But Romeo may not,
>
> (3.3.29–33)

and

> There is no world without Verona walls,
> But purgatory, torture, hell itself.
>
> (3.3.17–18)

Romeo in his frantic desolation is a sympathetic figure, but he is also, as Friar Laurence calls him, a "fond, mad man." In this kind of analysis "that is the trouble with" Lysander, Demetrius, Pyramus, and the rest; they all go mad because they think that heaven be in their beloveds' lips and all is dross that is not Helena —or Hermia—or Thisby. We may say that Romeo and Pyramus kill themselves because of this error or because they mistake the facts (Juliet and Thisby are not really dead). Both causes, if we analyze them, result from irrational, passionate reaction to the reports of the senses. Both, then, exemplify the same inversion of the mind; they are cousins-german, and the simple, factual mistake is symptom, symbol if we like, of the larger philosophical error.

The notion that man is caught in a potentially tragic illusion created by his own passions is thus restated in four major variations: in the night-wandering scenes themselves, in the lightly suggested projection of them as dreams, in the "tragedy" of Pyramus and Thisby, and in its projection as a play within a play. The dream and the play are alternative metaphors of the illusion, and Shakespeare also uses both to draw the audience into consciousness of its own involvement in the illusion. The spectators, seeing themselves reflected in Theseus's entourage watching a play, have been invited to imagine themselves as actors to a further audience, and at the end of the play Puck invites them to see their experience as a dream:

> If we shadows have offended,
> Think but this, and all is mended—
> That you have but slumb'red here
> While these visions did appear.
> And this weak and idle theme,
> No more yielding but a dream.
>
> (5.1.430–35)

His lines, it is true, are a conventional disclaimer of topical allusion and personal satire, echoing a similar disclaimer in the epilogue to *Endymion*, but they go beyond that function. They come at the end of a play in which the characters have, like Sly, been made to think of their experience as a dream, and thus invite the spectators to see themselves as like those characters or like Sly, their lives such stuff as dreams are made on.

So far as the play gives us to understand, the illusion—dream or play—is impenetrable to the characters in it, and one cannot escape completely from it. But one can, apparently, by realizing that it is an illusion, avoid committing oneself to it, unlike Pyramus and Thisby or the four lovers, and thus one can avoid tragedy. One will stumble, of course, and be funny in the stumbling, but one will not break one's neck. There will be a happy ending, and within the play that ending is figured as the joy of marriage.

IX.

The Merchant of Venice.

The Merchant of Venice, though it has obvious sim-
ilarities to some of the earlier comedies, emphasizes far more than they do death and the threat
of tragedy. These are touched on, to be sure, in the earlier comedies, but they are treated lightly. In *The Merchant*, as in *Measure
for Measure*, there is a sudden, unexpected tightening of the tragic
knot, and the audience is momentarily caught by its pity and
terror. This is unusual enough in the history of comedy to deserve
examination.

The text is notoriously ambiguous. Stage interpretations, which
have usually hinged on the characterization of Shylock, have
shown him as of almost as many sorts as Hamlet: as the scornful,
romantic hero, the patient and pathetic sufferer, the neurotic villain, and, in Max Reinhardt's 1921 production, as a farcical clown
who walked with flat feet.[1] In each kind there have been both
notable successes and failures. Critical interpretations have been
equally various and, again, within different frames of reference,

Elizabethan and other, they have been variously successful in achieving a view of the play as an integrated and coherent whole.

In the interests of brevity, the discussion that follows will proceed without much explicit regard or reference to other criticism. It will come as no surprise, perhaps, that *The Merchant* will be interpreted as of the same general kind of comedy as *Mother Bombie, The Comedy of Errors*, and *A Midsummer Night's Dream,* that is, as a comedy of natural man. The interpretive aim remains as explained above: a way of making coherent sense of the play which the Elizabethan playwright might reasonably have expected of a significant (*and* intelligent and educated) part of his audience. The comedy of natural man (though other formulations of the same concept might also serve) best serves, I think, this aim.

Such a concept also helps to explain why Shakespeare was attracted to the old story of the Jew and the pound of flesh, for the Jew was both example and established symbol of the natural man. While any pagan would in theory do as well, the Jew forced the Christian to face himself, as it were, in a sort of theological mirror where he saw himself as he would be if he demanded simple justice or thought to gain heaven by mere good works. For the Jew was someone living consciously under the Law which Christians also acknowledged; this Law condemned man, indeed was set forth only to make man aware of his deserving of doom; it was a living reminder of man's inborn, native corruption and of his consequent need of grace.[2]

The Jew simply as Jew served such a function: he was a ready-made symbol. If we recall the torturous and awkward way in which Shakespeare was forced to establish and handle the undramatic figure of Aegeon as such a symbol in *The Comedy of Errors*, we can better appreciate the appeal that Shylock as symbol, already in the source deeply involved in a dramatic action, must have had. He is also much more easily understood as a symbol of natural man than is Aegeon. Aegeon, after all, like Elis Heyst in Strindberg's *Easter*, is merely a metaphor of natural man. He is like natural man in several ways, but the question of whether he is or not, is not raised. Shylock as a Jew is himself unquestionably a natural man, an exemplar of the class.[3]

To see Shylock as natural man also explains, I think, some of his otherwise irrelevant characteristics and, above all, the puzzling ambivalence of attitude which the text suggests. On the one hand he is given lines which seem to demand a sympathetic reading and so to win the audience to his side. On the other hand, at least his vengeance certainly stands condemned, and an interpretation so sympathetic to him that Act IV ends as a felt tragic defeat of the hero, makes the festivity of Act V aesthetically and morally impossible. It is because Shylock represents the old Adam within us that the audience must sympathize—more precisely, empathize—with him and also find him ridiculous and abhorrent. He is a device for making the spectator view himself, with a detachment which enables him to turn from this self in relief and laughter. The detachment, with its ridicule and its moments of terror, provides the basic view of Shylock. Only intermittently and after the spectators have learned to accept him as a comic villain are they suddenly forced to recognize him as themselves. At the end of the trial scene, to the precise extent that they have sympathized with him they can—now as Christians—accept his sentence with relief and joy. They have been, in effect, "saved," and can now turn to the rejoicing of the last act.

The usual restrictions apply to this interpretation. It will not "work" for a non-Christian spectator or for a Christian who does not accept its doctrinal basis. It can of course be understood, though its tensions and satisfactions are not fully shared, by those of us who, although unbelievers, are aware of the doctrine. All that we can claim for this interpretation is that, granted spectators who accepted the commonly taught doctrine about man's natural state, it makes coherent sense of the play.

It is that nature which he shares with Christians and all men that Shylock emphasizes both by implication and explicitly in the lines so often cited and so often used by actors as the hinge to swing the sympathy of the audience. This slow turning begins in Act I:

Signior Antonio, many a time and oft
In the Rialto you have rated me
About my moneys and my usances.
Still have I borne it with a patient shrug;
For suff'rance is the badge of all our tribe.
You call me misbeliever, cutthroat dog,
And spet upon my Jewish gaberdine,
And all for use of that which is mine own.
Well then, it now appears you need my help. . . .
You that did void your rheum upon my beard
And foot me as you spurn a stranger cur
Over your threshold.

(1.3.107–20)

The rhetoric, as every actor knows, is extremely powerful, and
it is powerful precisely as an appeal to empathy, an appeal that
reaches its climax in the rhetorical questions that follow: "What
should I say to you? Should I not say/'Hath a dog money? Is it
possible . . . ?' Shall I bend low, and . . .

Say this:
'Fair sir, you spet on me on Wednesday last;
You spurn'd me such a day; another time
You call'd me dog; and for these courtesies
I'll lend you thus much moneys'?

(1.3.121–30)

The rhetorical question, after all, is preeminently an appeal for
empathy, and it is as such an appeal, to Antonio, that the speech
is dramatically justified. The common reading of it then, for full
empathy, is surely right. The rhetorical questions need no spoken
answers because the human nature that Shylock shares with us all
makes the answers obvious.

This last point is made explicit in Shylock's famous lines of
Act III, answering Salerio's uneasy assurance:

Saler. Why, I am sure, if he forfeit, thou wilt not take his flesh.
What's that good for?

Shy. To bait fish withal. If it will feed nothing else, it will feed
my revenge. He hath disgrac'd me and hind'red me half a mil-
lion; laugh'd at my losses, mock'd at my gains, scorned my nation, thwarted my bargains, cooled my friends, heated mine
enemies—and what's his reason? I am a Jew. Hath not a Jew
eyes? Hath not a Jew hands, organs, dimensions, senses, affections, passions?—fed with the same food, hurt with the same
weapons, subject to the same diseases, healed by the same
means, warmed and cooled by the same winter and summer as
a Christian is? If you prick us, do we not bleed? If you tickle
us, do we not laugh? If you poison us, do we not die? And if
you wrong us, shall we not revenge? If we are like you in the
rest, we will resemble you in that. If a Jew wrong a Christian,
what is his humility? Revenge. If a Christian wrong a Jew,
what should his sufferance be by Christian example? Why revenge. The villany you teach me I will execute, and it shall go
hard but I will better the instruction. (3.1.53–76)

Again, in the interpretation I am constructing, the popular, sympathetic reading of the lines is the right emotional direction. It is
guided by the emphasis upon the shared nature of Christians and
Jews: upon their hands, organs, dimensions, senses, affections, and
passions, upon their identical needs and reactions, including their
natural impulse to revenge. The effect has been such that, as John
Russell Brown points out, "So powerful has Shylock's justification
proved that it is sometimes forgotten that a villain is speaking. It
has to be pointed out that "what is commonly received as Shylock's plea for tolerance is in reality his justification of an inhuman
purpose." [4] This is a fair moral commentary; its use of the word
"inhuman" can be justified by Renaissance usage, and it corrects
the common tendency to overlook the evil which Shylock's speech
would justify. But "inhuman" should not be taken to imply a distinction that sets him apart from the rest of the human race or to
indicate, romantically, the corruption of basically good nature.
Shylock's speech insists that revenge is humanly natural to both
Jew and Christian; contemporary theory supported him, and it

seems fair to suppose that some spectators, recognizing their empathy with horror, would acknowledge the charge. Shylock's flippant reply, furthermore, "To bait fish withal." points to the natural human irrationality which he explicates more fully later. Early in the trial, he himself raises the question of his motivation:

> You'll ask me why I rather choose to have
> A weight of carrion flesh than to receive
> Three thousands ducats. I'll not answer that!
> But say it is my humour, is it answer'd?
> What if my house be troubled with a rat,
> And I be pleas'd to give ten thousand ducats
> To have it ban'd? What, are you answer'd yet?
> Some men there are love not a gaping pig,
> Some that are mad if they behold a cat,
> And others, when the bagpipe sings i'th' nose,
> Cannot contain their urine; for affection,
> Mistress of passion, says it to the mood
> Of what it likes or loathes. Now for your answer:
> As there is no firm reason to be rend'red
> Why he cannot abide a gaping pig,
> Why he a harmless necessary cat,
> Why he a woollen bagpipe—but of force
> Must yield to such inevitable shame
> As to offend himself, being offended;
> So can I give no reason, nor I will not,
> More than a lodg'd hate and a certain loathing
> I bear Antonio, that I follow thus
> A losing suit against him. Are you answer'd?
>
> (4.1.40–62)

The speech can usefully be made to suggest Shylock's cruelty and self-confidence, but it also professes to be a self-analysis, and whether we take it as sincere or not, it emphasizes that his motive is irrationally aimless, that it springs directly from his nature, and that in these respects it is like the whims which possess all men. These are basic points in the comedy of human nature. If we sub-

212

stitute romantic love for Shylock's hatred, the same analysis
would apply to, say, the young lovers of *Mother Bombie* or *Friar
Bacon* or *A Midsummer Night's Dream*. In *The Merchant* itself,
human irrationality is not a major theme, but it is a minor one,
and it links with Shylock both Antonio and Portia. Antonio opens
the play with his self analysis:

> In sooth, I know not why I am so sad.
> It wearies me; you say it wearies you;
> But how I caught it, found it, or came by it,
> What stuff 'tis made of, whereof it is born,
> I am to learn.
>
> (1.1.1–5)

Portia opens the second scene with hers: she too confesses to melancholy, and she rebuts Nerissa's reasoned admonition with a flat
assertion of human irrationality: "the brain may devise laws for
the blood, but a hot temper leaps o'er a cold decree" (1.2.19–21).
Shylock, as he asserts, is not alone in his whims. He is indeed like
any man or every man in his inborn, inherited nature—with the
same organs, senses, affections, and passions, subject to the same
diseases, and so on—irrational, comic and damned. This is, I think,
a sufficient "spine" for an interpretation of the play, and other
matters will fit into place easily enough around it. The play becomes a play about man's escape, or rescue from, his own nature
and situation, and the last act can be joyful because it celebrates
the escape of all the characters, including Shylock, from the justice which he invokes. Obviously this interpretation requires that
the audience accept his forced conversion as both a boon and as
likely to result in his sincere adoption of Christianity. Such an interpretation is very close to that of Nevill Coghill, who has argued that the play is about the Old Law of Justice and the New
Law of Mercy, and that only when Shylock can be seen to have
escaped from the rigor of the Old Law does the gaiety of the last
act make sense: "From Anthonio's point of view, Shylock has at
least been given his chance of eternal joy, and it is he, Anthonio,
that has given it to him. Mercy has triumphed over justice, even

if the way of mercy is a hard way." [5]

I do not see any way of determining how many of Shakespeare's spectators would have accepted it thus if they tried to apply the same criteria of value and of psychological realism which they might apply to a similar situation in real life. The fact that there were recusancy laws in England and that severer laws enforced orthodoxy on the continent suggests that some people of the time thought forced conversion less wicked and more effective than we do. But it does not seem to me that many Elizabethan spectators would be likely to apply the criteria of real life. All three main plots of the play—caskets, pound of flesh, and ring plots—are unrealistic enough to serve notice that the play is folk tale or fairy tale, as Granville-Barker once pointed out, and that its relation to life is like that of folk-tale—allusive, symbolic, or allegorical. Bassanio's choice of the leaden casket symbolizes in some way his righteousness or trueness; Portia's return of his ring and Nerissa's return of Gratiano's guarantee the fidelity and felicity of both couples. *Of course* they will live happily ever after. And so with Shylock. *Of course* he is converted. He too lives happily ever after, just as the generic unredeemed mankind, and its unregenerate nature, which he represents, are also saved and, as in *The Comedy of Errors*, new apparelled.

It is not necessary to comment on the morality of such a view of enforced conversion, except to note that it is not based on any feeling of racial superiority. This is borne out by the rest of the play. Jessica is completely accepted after her elopement and conversion and, as we shall see, the play's concept of "tribe," as distinct from Shylock's, is defined solely in terms of religious belief.

To turn to the play. Granted that Shylock represents unregenerate man and his nature, the play becomes, as I said, a story of escape from the nature and its consequences. This story is developed in four movements, marked off by short vaudeville scenes or music-hall turns, in all of which Lancelot Gobbo appears.

The first movement, which runs to Act II, scene 2, is of course expository. It establishes the two chief motivating situations and introduces all the main characters except Jessica.

The opening scene smuggles in artfully enough the usual kind of necessary information, that Antonio is a wealthy merchant, for instance, that a large part of his wealth is committed to sea, that he claims not to be worried about it, and that Gratiano is a conscious buffoon. But the scene concentrates upon Antonio's melancholy to a degree that may seem puzzling since very little is made of it thereafter. One recent production, indeed, tried to turn it somehow to account by making it the point to which Antonio (in this interpretation, a homosexual) comes full circle at the end of the play when he stands pathetically bereft of his friend Bassanio.[6] Even this desperate expedient, however, fails to make the melancholy of the opening scene significant as character revelation or as motivation. His melancholy becomes understandable, however, as a statement of his condition, from which in the normal movement of comedy we may expect him to escape.

On one level of consciousness this condition is the state of melancholy itself; at the end of the play he will be happy (in this interpretation of the play the actor does not play Antonio for sentimental wistfulness, smiling sadly at the news that his ships have come through). But his melancholy is the surface of a deeper malaise which consists in part of that natural irrationality which makes him kin to Shylock, and in part of his sense of being—despite his denial—extremely vulnerable to fortune. Shakespeare emphasizes the point heavily, and it is worth notice. Salerio and Solanio diagnose his difficulty at once:

> *Sal.* Your mind is tossing on the ocean;
>   There where your argosies with portly sail. . . .
> *Sol.* Believe me, sir, had I such venture forth,
>   The better part of my affections would
>   Be with my hopes abroad,
>
>   (1.1.8–17)

and so forth for thirty-odd lines, to which Antonio replies,

> Believe me, no. I thank my fortune for it,
> My ventures are not in one bottom trusted,
> Nor to one place; nor is my whole estate

Upon the fortune of this present year.
Therefore my merchandise makes me not sad.

$$(\text{1.1.41–45})$$

The actor can read these lines to indicate genuine assurance or whistling in the dark, but in any case they do not imply the Stoic or Boethian-Christian freedom from Fortune through contempt of Fortune's goods; rather Antonio relies, as it were, on an insurance policy. This is the protection of the normal worldling—doubly, triply, quadruply guarded against all hazard, rocked in the cradle of security, the classic set-up for disaster. Such men call their downfalls to them. Gratiano flatly accuses Antonio of worldiness:

You have too much respect upon the world—

$$(\text{1.1.74})$$

and Antonio seems to deny it:

I hold the world but as the world, Gratiano—
A stage, where every man must play a part,
And mine a sad one.

$$(\text{1.1.77–79})$$

But the denial, although it implies his self-detachment, and distinguishes his attitude from such unselfconscious immersion in the world as Shylock's or Morocco's, is at the same time his confession that he is trapped in the world and his role in it. The point is given at least negative theatrical substantiation by the fact that, unlike such actor-heroes as Petruchio or Prince Hal, Antonio does not consciously play a part (Petruchio as ardent wooer, Hal as roisterer). Nor is he, unlike Viola or Rosalind or Berowne, aware of his own folly. He is aware only of his melancholy, his insurance policy, his role, and his inability to change it.

Bassanio's situation and the direction he must move in are more easily and quickly sketched, and the speeches also fit him, thanks in part to their folktale connotations, into a highly generalized context. His famous description of Portia, beginning with the fairy-tale magic of "In Belmont dwells a lady," ends with lines that place her clearly as a heroine of a romance of which he is the hero:

> Nor is the wide world ignorant of her worth;
> For the four winds blow in from every coast
> Renowned suitors, and her sunny locks
> Hang on her temples like a golden fleece,
> Which makes her seat of Belmont Colchos' strond,
> And many Jasons come in quest of her.
> O my Antonio, had I but the means
> To hold a rival place with one of them,
> I have a mind presages me such thrift
> That I should questionless be fortunate!
>
> (1.1.167–76)

When Portia enters, her half-humorous lament, "By my troth, Nerissa, my little body is aweary of this great world," echoes Antonio's languid melancholy, and the scene quickly establishes the loose parallel. Nerissa scolds her: she has no cause of complaint, rather a surfeit of good fortune. But, though she acknowledges that Nerissa speaks reason, she confesses her inability to follow it:

"If to do were as easy as to know what were good to do, chapels had been churches, and poor men's cottages princes' palaces. It is a good divine that follows his own instructions. I can easier teach twenty what were good to be done than to be one of the twenty to follow mine own teaching. The brain may devise laws for the blood, but a hot temper leaps o'er a cold decree: such a hare is madness the youth, to skip o'er the meshes of good counsel the cripple." (1.2.13–23)

As characterization the reply cuts two ways, at once helping to build the unique complex of insouciance, impatience, strength, wit, and amused self-detachment that makes Portia Portia, and also by its generalized content, making her weakness apparent as an instance of mankind's.

She then suddenly returns to romance as she gives the exposition in the old straightforward manner and rhetoric of Lyly's heroines:

"O me, the word 'choose'! I may neither choose who I would nor refuse who I dislike, so is the will of a living daughter curb'd by the will of a dead father. Is it not hard, Nerissa, that I cannot choose one nor refuse none?" (1.2.24–29)

Nerissa, defending Portia's father ("holy men at their death have good inspirations") explains the schemes of the three caskets; as she does so, the world of Romance, of symbolic action and riddling meanings, has closed in.

How quick how many spectators were to riddle these meanings is conjectural. Even we, of course, know which casket is the right one as soon as they are named, and we know vaguely—"all that glisters is not gold"—why. Beyond this, meanings like that given the caskets in the *Gesta Romanorum* are gradually unveiled in the course of the play.[7] They are unveiled, that is, to those alert and looking for them, and, granted a significant proportion of the audience trained by, say, *Gallathea* or *Love's Metamorphoses* or the *Faery Queene* or *A Knack to Know an Honest Man* or the putative first version of *Old Fortunatus*, we might expect, and Shakespeare might expect, a scene like this to alert many spectators to look for such meanings. To alert the spectators, rather than to convey any such meaning immediately, seems to me one probable function of the scene.

Yet a meaning is beginning even here. Portia, indeed, as the undefined goal or *summum bonum* of all men, has already been fairly clearly suggested, and Bassanio as the man in search of it. This scene, by introducing the casket story, helps to build the semantic structure of this search, but it also begins to define Portia as Bassanio's (and Antonio's) counterpart. She too is like all men in her lack of self-control, but she is also like the classic figure of mankind, the enchanted princess who awaits the redeemer: Una to be rescued by the Red-Cross Knight, Andromeda by Theseus, and Hesione by Hercules. Within the dramatic tradition she is like Lyly's Gallathea and Phillida, Mankind, or Anima in *Wisdom Who is Christ*, all of whom also require rescue from the consequences of their own nature. Mankind, or some faculty of man, in Christian allegory, is like the princess rescued by Christ or by a virtue from the diabolic monster. Such a meaning, however, is only prepared for here. It does not emerge clearly until the scene when Portia, encouraging Bassanio, makes the comparison to Hesione and Hercules explicit:

> . . . Now he goes
> With no less presence, but with much more love,
> Than young Alcides when he did redeem
> The virgin tribute paid by howling Troy
> To the sea monster. I stand for sacrifice;
> The rest aloof are the Dardanian wives,
> With bleared visages come forth to view
> The issue of th' exploit. Go, Hercules!
> Live thou, I live.
> (3.2.53–61) [8]

By the end of this speech the alert Elizabethan schoolboy should be able to understand Portia as a metaphor of mankind, but the development of the mythical parallel and its significance are begun in the present scene.

Shylock is introduced in the third scene, and we are made to see four main aspects of him: that the other characters consider him a villain, indeed, as like the devil, that he is unnatural in taking usury, that he lays great emphasis on being a member of the tribe, descended from Abraham, and that he has, quite aside from Antonio's Christianity and his interference with Shylock's usury, a clearly natural motive for hating Antonio with which we can sympathize.

Shylock as villain or devil is obviously a meaning of some importance in Antonio's spiritual adventure. Like the devil he demands, merely as a matter of justice, that Antonio die. He is the ultimate monster from which Mankind—Hesione—needs to be rescued by Hercules. As he is unnatural in taking usury, he illustrates the common paradox that man's fallen nature (here his unrestrained avarice) leads him to unnatural behavior. It is the paradox of Gallathea and Phillida and also of Edmund in *Lear*. His "naturalness," on the other hand, is only briefly sketched here, something felt rather than fully conceptualized, communicated by our feeling of sympathy for him. It is linked, however, to his claim to be the descendant of Abraham and to his later insistence on judgment by the law.

Shylock's claim, it should be remembered, was only a half-truth in Christian eyes because, as St. Paul explained, though the Jews were descended from Abraham in the flesh, the Christians were the spiritual heirs of Abraham. "He is not a Jew," declared St. Paul, "which is outward in the flesh. But he is a Jew, which is one inwardly; and circumcision is that of the heart, in the spirit." (Rom. 2: 28–29) Consequently, just as Ishmael (explained by Paul allegorically as a type or figure of the errant Jews) was not, though Abraham's son, heir to the promise made to Abraham and his seed, so Shylock or any other literal Jew was not heir to the promise unless, of course, he accepted the redemption of Christ. Abraham, in Paul's phrase, "is the father of us all." According to the ordinary Christian teaching known to the audience, then, Abraham's seed consisted of those who held his faith, his spiritual descendents the Christians, and it was they, not those who thought to be saved by the law, to whom God's promise pertained. The law, indeed, only "worketh wrath" in that it defines man's sin; salvation comes to the faithful because of God's grace.[9]

These, it seems to me, are all significant assumptions of the play; they are common teachings of Shakespeare's time, and intelligent spectators might be expected to see them as relevant to Shylock's emphasis on his descent. Certainly for those who were, or are, acquainted with St. Paul's interpretation of the concept of the "sacred nation," Shylock's claim introduces these teachings as major issues of the play.

Antonio meets Shylock in the same scene, disputes with him about the morality of taking interest and finally agrees to sign the fatal bond. This encounter, part of which has already been quoted, further defines Antonio, as well as Shylock, and helps to explain his later scape with death. Antonio, like Aegeon in *The*

Comedy of Errors, is a victim of incredibly bad luck, an example of the instability of the human condition. He can of course be played simply as a passive victim of that luck and of his human nature, like one of those kings familiar in late medieval woodcuts, strapped helplessly to the bottom of the wheel of fortune. The actor, building upon his opening confession of melancholy and his later resignation ("I am a tainted wether of the flock,/Meetest for death. The weakest kind of fruit/Drops earliest to the ground, and so let me.") can create a convincing and pathetic patience on a monument, smiling wistfully at his own grief. Thus played, Antonio fits easily into the escape theme as a highly generalized mankind figure, trapped by the law simply as mankind is trapped, by nature not by vile offense.

He is in fact often played this way, and, in the sentimental humanism of most audiences he emerges paradoxically as a kind of stupid and distasteful saint. But this interpretation, besides being un-theatrically bland, is at awkward odds with the implications of this scene. His rudeness is hard to disguise. He interrupts Shylock's, "But note me, signior" with, "Mark you this, Bassanio,/ The devil can quote Scripture for his purpose," and he continues with an *ad hominem* attack which disregards Shylock's presence. He replies to Shylock's account of the insults he has given him:

> You that did void your rheum upon my beard
> And foot me as you spurn a stranger cur,
>
> (1.3.118–19)

with the assurance that he may repeat the insults again. The lines offer no chance to suggest an underlying charity of motivation, and they certainly suggest a smug self-righteousness. That they do not, however, destroy the characterization of Antonio as saint and martyr in most productions is owing largely to the fact that Shylock's stronger lines and, usually, the stronger actor speaking them, steal attention from him. The result is commonly to start building empathy for Shylock rather than dislike for Antonio. The actor playing Antonio, furthermore, plays down his potential brutality and arrogance. In consequence, most modern spectators,

I think, accept him in this scene with some embarrassment as an intended, though distasteful virtue character. His anti-Semitism is shocking, but it seems, alas, to be Shakespeare's—or perhaps the disease of his times—and one turns from it more or less consciously. But the suspicion that Antonio may have been "intended" to be deeply flawed is suppressed in view of what seem to be the norms of the play.

It is quite possible, however, to play Antonio in this scene for full brutal arrogance. The actor can reveal, not merely bigotry, but a bullying contempt for human feeling. He interrupts and disregards Shylock's attempt to speak to him, not with any show of charity, but with the casual, smug selfrighteousness of the young snob. His contempt has a social, not a moral, motivation; his opening commentary is an exercise in one-upmanship, delivered in the third person, designed to make Shylock feel excluded from the "in" group. At the same time, his belligerent hostility, as in,

> I am as like to call thee so again
> To spet on thee again, to spurn thee too,
>
> (1.3.131–32)

can also suggest the attempt to conceal and repeal the embarrassing concession which he finds that in seeking Shylock's aid he has granted.

Such an Antonio is not necessarily inconsistent with the loyal and self-sacrificing friend of Bassanio—many a snob is loyal enough to his fellow club members—and, unlike the alternative patient saint, he illustrates with convincing realism the lack of charity and the pride that justify his death under the law.

The final scene of the first movement introduces the Prince of Morocco and in so doing it helps to clarify the peculiar lottery by which Portia is to be won. It also helps, by gorgeousness of costume, by Portia's reference to his royal estate, and by the Tamburlainian vaunt of his rhetoric, to build up the worth of Portia as the inestimable prize sought by princes. Finally, it defines Morocco himself, roughly to be sure, but with sufficient precision to explain his failure. There is, first of all, the pride indicated by his boasting, which is usually though not inevitably, spoken with satiric exaggeration. In this kind of folk-tale the braggart, like Cinderella's sisters, *always* gets his come-uppance. But beyond this explanation, there is the fact that finally he sees that for him, despite his prowess, the outcome depends on fortune:

> . . . But, alas the while!
> If Hercules and Lichas play at dice
> Which is the better man, the greater throw
> May turn by fortune from the weaker hand:
> So is Alcides beaten by his page,
> And so may I, blind Fortune leading me. . . .
>
> (2.1.31–36)

So far as the audience can judge at this point, Morocco is in one sense, and on one level, right; choosing the right casket seems to be, in Portia's words, a "lottery." But our experience of folk tales confirms Nerissa's earlier statement that the apparent lottery is a device for sifting out the unworthy, that it is not at all determined by fortune, and that, in committing himself to fortune Morocco is in error. On a more intellectual level, the common teaching confirms and defines this lesson: it is worldlings alone who, in choosing the goods that Fortune can grant or deny, commit themselves to Fortune, and in so choosing they mistake their highest good. To the extent that we recognize Portia as symbolic of this felicity, then, Morocco has defined his error for us and explained his failure. His Moorishness, finally, corroborates the symbolism. In the absence of qualifying phrases (like those establishing Othello's Christianity), he is emphatically not a Christian and not a Jew—an example and easy symbol of the ignorant and vainglorious worldling.

The second movement is largely concerned with the escape, or attempted escape, of most of the principals from Venice and Shylock to the felicity of Belmont or Portia. Bassanio, Gratiano, Lorenzo and Jessica, all move from the turmoil of the one to the bliss of the other and then, as they seem to have won it, are made to wait until Antonio is also freed. The movement is begun by a kind of prologue in which Launcelot Gobbo makes a similar escape in leaving the service and house of Shylock, to which he is bound by law, for that of Bassanio, an action which carries him too to Belmont. The scene begins with a comic morality play in which Launcelot stages a debate between his conscience and the fiend about shaking off his legal indenture to Shylock. The fiend counsels him to flee, and his conscience counsels him to stay, but he sees Shylock himself as the "devil incarnation," a pretty paradox. As he resolves to flee, his blind father enters; Launcelot begs the old man's blessing and, after some comic business in which the old man, groping for his head, mistakes his hair for his beard, obtains it. Then Bassanio enters, and the old man seconds his son's request to enter Bassanio's service. Bassanio accepts him; Shylock had already preferred him.

The scene is genial foolery; it provides good farce relief and must have given Kempe a chance to exhibit his clownage. But it is not necessarily merely genial foolery. Launcelot's escape from Shylock adumbrates the general action of the movement and the play, and its semantic implications reinforce the themes which have already been introduced. The moral paradox of Launcelot's little morality play, for instance, results from the fact that the law binds him to the service of "the devil," and he must somehow escape. Similarly the comic business of the blessing is an obvious parody of blind Isaac's blessing of Jacob. This in turn, like Isaac's own receiving of God's promise to Abraham, had been explained since Patristic times as an allegory or figure of the Christians' receiving of that promise. The Christians, of course, were symbolized by Jacob, the Jews, the first-born, by Esau.[10] Like Isaac's receiving of the promise, it implies that the promise is not "through the law, but through the righteousness of faith." Hence, again, mankind like Launcelot is freed of that law which "worketh wrath," or which binds him to the service of the "devil incarnation."

If the total resultant meaning seems over-elaborate for comprehension in the swift flow of stage action, we may settle according to our capacities for something less ingenious, and one might argue plausibly that there must have been many in the original audiences who would make a similar settlement. But we should be settling for something less than the perception we might reasonably expect of the educated, trained, intelligent part of the audience whose understanding of the play we seek to know. That the scene is a parody of Isaac's blessing of Jacob is sufficiently obvious and has often been pointed out before; that the blessing had such a potential allegorical meaning for many Elizabethans, furthermore, is a simple matter of historical fact, and however loosely we apply it to the scene, it implies man's escape from the law into Christian freedom.

On the religious level this is close to the play's main theme, which is, however, a little more general, including man's escape from the world and from the consequences of his nature as well as from "the law." The second movement develops the parallel theme of romantic escape mostly by a simple staging of the flight of Bassanio, Gratiano, Lorenzo, and Jessica. The scenes of flight have little in themselves that implies a meaning beneath the romantic surface; they are compatible with it, but their implication as continued metaphors of such meaning derives from their context. This is provided in part by the great trial scene that follows, but also in part by the scenes which show the failures of Morocco and Arragon and Bassanio's contrasting success.

Morocco's failure, as we saw, has already been largely explained. He is a worldling, subjecting himself to Fortune and as we should expect, he chooses the gold, the false good that many men desire and that fortune can grant or deny. The reality beneath this false good is death. This judgment can be understood if and only if, I think, we also understand the choice as symbolizing his end in life or *summum bonum*, like Lust's fatal choice of Treasure in *The Trial of Treasure* or the choice made by the princess in the *Gesta Romanorum* version of the casket story. Morocco's reward, indeed, confirms the symbolic nature of his choice.

Arragon's error, although his pride could be said to mark him as equally a worldling, is emphasized as more sophisticated and theological. Unlike Morocco, he is not to be taken in by the outward appearance of gilded vanity. He chooses the casket which promises as much as he deserves, and assumes his own high desert. He is given a Fool's head. His error is Pelagianism, the doctrine that man deserves his own salvation. It is also, we may notice, closely related to Shylock's belief that he is blameless before the law, and therefore needs no mercy.

Bassanio's success, on the other hand, is not explained in precise, explicit terms. On the level of folk tale he is the always successful third wooer; Portia loves him; he himself is rapturously and appealingly in love, and unlike the other egoistically self-assured wooers, he is becomingly modest. He is also native, whereas they are ridiculous foreigners to that Italy to which for the afternoon the audience belongs. Such reasons not only explain the success of, but actually create, the hero of romantic adventure. To round out his portrait, he needs only to kill a monster, and Portia indeed actually sees him as the monster killer, Hercules the redeemer, come to rescue her.

His lack of pride and his love, the fact that he does not value his own prestige or merit, also go far to explain his success in obtaining the *summum bonum* that Portia as the aim of the wooers has come to represent. But in this context his rejection of the gold and silver caskets is not merely his folk-hero's intuition that all that glisters is not gold; it indicates his sane ordering of values and his sound mental process in choosing. The song that accompanies his silent musing—"tell me where is Fancy bred"—calls attention to his mind's working. The answer—"It is engend'red in the eyes,/ with gazing fed, and Fancy dies"—reminds us that something more perceptive than shallow-rooted Fancy must choose and that it must not rely upon appearance. His moralistic commentary reinforces the point that appearances are deceiving. In the world of whimsical romance this point is trivial enough, like little Buttercup's list ("skim milk masquerades as cream," and so on) which makes a nice parody of Bassanio's. But to the extent that we see him as attempting to discover the Good, the point, though elementary, is vital. In this attempt, moreover, he has shown his

willingness to give and hazard all he has. He has done so only symbolically, to be sure; he does not exemplify that willingness until he gives away his ring. But the inscription on the leaden casket makes it clear, and in the search for the Good, it is that willingness which assures success. It does so, in common Christian thinking, because it comes from the recognition that beside the Good all else is vanity. Its most familiar illustration is the gospel parable of the merchant who gave everything for the pearl of great price.

But probably the most important distinction between Bassanio and the two preceding wooers is that he is poor and has borrowed the money, while they are rich and rely on their wealth. In folk tale this fact gives him the insuperable advantage of Cinderella over her two sisters, and on the religious-moral level it distinguishes him from the pagans and Pelagians who do not acknowledge and are unaware of their need for help. Bassanio, as he confesses to Portia a moment after he has chosen rightly, says that he is

> . . . worse than nothing; for indeed
> I have engag'd myself to a dear friend,
> Engag'd my friend to his mere enemy. . . .
>
> (3.2.260–62)

He has been enabled to gain his bliss through Antonio's sacrifice just as generic mankind is so enabled through the blood sacrifice—or debt payment—of Christ. This is not to say of course that Antonio "is" Christ or a symbol of Christ; the focus is upon Bassanio here and his situation. He is, again, like the other principals in the play, a study in mankind escaping.

As the tension—half suspense and half anticipation—of Bassanio's choosing crests into rapture with his choice, the rhetoric of the lovers suggests a bliss too great to express fully, almost too great to bear:

> O love, be moderate; allay thy ecstasy;
> In measure rain thy joy; scant this excess!

I feel too much thy blessing. Make it less
For fear I surfeit!
(3.2.111–14)

and

Only my blood speaks to you in my veins;
And there is such confusion in my powers. . . .
Where every something, being blent together,
Turns to a wild of nothing, save of joy,
Express'd and not express'd.
(3.2.176–83)

Their happiness is a glimpse of the happiness-ever-after to which
the end of the comedy must deliver them, and as it suggests a bliss
beyond human capacity in this world, it is a fitting analogy of the
supreme good which they seem to have achieved. But it is only a
glimpse before the lovers and the mood they have established
bump back to the world from which they had apparently escaped.
Gratiano breaks the spell as he steps forward in fleshly geniality,
and the immediate announcement of Antonio's plight returns
them to all the frustration of humanity. Bliss must be deferred.

For spectators awake to the religious analogies of the play,
Bassanio's confession reinforces his resemblance to mankind in his
honest, guilt-striken appraisal of his unworthiness of the bliss offered him:

Rating myself at nothing, you shall see
How much I was a braggart. When I told you
My state was nothing, I should then have told you
That I was worse than nothing;
(3.2.257–60)

and there follows his acknowledgment already quoted of his
pledge to his "dear friend," pledged in turn to his "mere enemy."
This kind of feeling, though probably most familiar to us in
seventeenth-century verse, like Herbert's

Love bade me welcome, yet my soul drew back,
Guilty of dust and sin,

is common in devotional literature. The resemblance is not vital to the understanding of the play or even of the play's religious implications. It deepens the significance of Bassanio's experience, but the main outline of that significance is clear without it.

The third movement (Act IV) carries through the trial scene and Bassanio's loss of the ring. On the level of romance it frees all for frolic in the last act and lays the ground for tempering that pleasure with smiling sanity. Antonio is set free from the death penalty, and the others are unburdened of the sorrow for his condemnation—or for Shylock's heresy. On the level of man's search for the Good, the movement has the same general function, freeing Man, as represented by Antonio and Shylock, from his tragic doom and trapping him comically, as he is represented by Bassanio and Gratiano, in the minor predicament that remains. On both levels then, the movement repeats the escape themes of the second movement transposed into a more somber key. Enough has been said about both Antonio and Shylock as representatives of mankind to make further commentary superfluous. It may be noticed, however, that the trial scene emphasizes the pairing off of the two that earlier scenes have developed. Neither man—rightly, I think—is ordinarily played as wholly depraved. I have argued that Antonio should be played as a rather stupidly arrogant (perhaps slightly foppish?) young clubman, but to do so still leaves him light years this side of Iago or Richard III. He is a human being immersed within the human condition, not rising above it. He has not, so far as he is aware, broken the law, and yet the law condemns him to death. Shylock too is equally guiltless of any conscious law breaking: "What judgment shall I dread, doing no wrong?" (4.1.89). Yet the law catches him too. Nominal Christian and nominal Jew are alike condemned; for some spectators the point may be underlined by Portia's inquiry as she looks about her: "Which is the merchant here? and which the Jew?" (4.1. 174). The question can suggest their moral equality, and the visual scene itself, of course, can also be staged to suggest that they are somehow equivalent. The same truth, as Portia makes clear, applies to both:

That, in the course of justice, none of us
Should see salvation.

(4.1.199–200)

The trial is dramatization of that point, a glance of horror, as the trials of Morocco and Arragon were glances of amusement, at the tragic—or comic—world where fortune reigns.

As the tide of law suddenly swings and turns against Shylock, Gratiano leaps in to mock him, quoting his earlier praise: "O upright judge! Mark, Jew. O learned judge!" (4.1.313), and he continues to jeer at intervals. The significance of his reaction is debatable. It has, however, at least one clear function. The whole scene hinges upon Shylock's terrified recognition that the law, which he has claimed as almost a tribal possession and has relied upon to befriend him, actually condemns him. The moment marks an anagnorisis as significant and agonizing as that of *Oedipus*, and it deserves underscoring. Gratiano's remarks do this. His continued jeers, however, after Portia has advised Shylock to seek mercy, are likely to seem merely vindictive. "Beg that thou may'st have leave to hang thyself," for instance, obviously does not breathe the Christian forgiveness that Portia and the Duke commend.

His jeers can be and usually are, made to stand out harshly against the talk of mercy, and if he is made to head up a Nazi-like threatening mob, the effect is frightening. The audience almost completely identifies with Shylock of course, and, while this is relevant to the point that Christians as well as Jews are vindictive by nature, the horror and revulsion are likely to obliterate all intellectual considerations or, at best, leave only an impression that the Christian talk of mercy is the hypocritical mask of revenge. This, in turn, is clearly at odds with the interpretation I am urging. Gratiano's vindictiveness can be stressed but not to the point where it is felt actually to threaten Shylock.

On the other hand, the jeers can be made, even today, to ride the wave of the hubbub of the relieved and excited spectators, without emphasis. This has a point if the actor can so speak the

lines and the surrounding business is so directed as to make clear that revenge is quite inconceivable here. Gratiano's vindictiveness, then, serves him as a subject for his amusement just as earlier and later his lust does or his desire to wreak vengeance on the judge's clerk. He is not carried away by these passions but sports with them.

The trial scene completes the play's real denouement. It is true that another knot, the ring business, is immediately and hastily tangled, but this becomes only a mild jest to help sustain the festivities of the last movement (Act V). These are its main business as they are in masques and in *A Midsummer Night's Dream* and a few comedies besides, and as a result of so much time spent on them, the joy they celebrate is examined with unusual care and defined with unusual precision. It is the joy associated with Belmont, toward which the characters have been moving throughout the play, the experience of life as it actually is in contrast to the nightmare suggested by the trial scene.

The duet of Jessica and Lorenzo, the messengers' reports, the music, and the dialogue of Portia and Nerissa form a prologue which gradually modulates into the action. In a performance without intermissions, its opening duet and the messengers' reports give the other characters time "to get to" Belmont from Venice. The controlled delight of the lovers, laced with amusement, establishes the tone of the movement. The casual, unhurried tempo of the whole prologue effectively brakes the pace and paragraphs the action. The music and the great verbal magic swiftly build, what must be built, a solid reality of joy and of beauty.

They are earthly joy and beauty. Lorenzo and Jessica speak singingly; they are in love, but they are not dizzy with their rapture; they smile at themselves. So with the music and the moonlight which the words create. Both are part of the scene's beauty and its powerful enchantment, but both are carefully established as imperfect shadows of a greater beauty. Music as Lorenzo describes it is a beneficent moral and psychological force, calming the hot passions of animals and temporarily changing the nature of anything however "stockish, hard, and full of rage." It is also cause, metaphor, and touchstone of the good in human character:

> The man that hath no music in himself,
> Nor is not mov'd with concord of sweet sounds,
> Is fit for treasons, stratagems, and spoils;
>
> (5.1.83–85)

Yet above this music there is the music of the spheres, a metaphor of the divinely ordered harmony inaudible to human ears:

> There's not the smallest orb which thou behold'st
> But in his motion like an angel sings,
> Still quiring to the young-ey'd cherubins;
> Such harmony is in immortal souls;
> But whilst this muddy vesture of decay
> Doth grossly close it in, we cannot hear it.
>
> (5.5.60–65)

What the muddy vesture of decay can hear, then, is limited to a coarser, earthly harmony; yet this is still beautiful and morally good.

Moonlight has a similar significance. Presumably, at least in the afternoon performances at the public theaters, it was purely verbal, yet, no less than the music, it provides the indispensable ambience which separates the action from the workaday world and places it in half-ideal, dreamlike loveliness. But it is only half-ideal. In their duet the lovers associate it with passionate love betrayed or deceived—Troilus, Thisbe, Dido, Medea—but also, smilingly, with both their own frailty and their own unshakeable fidelity. It also provides the setting, as Lorenzo's lines create it,

> How sweet the moonlight sleeps upon this bank!
> Here will we sit and let the sounds of music
> Creep in our ears,
>
> (5.1.54–56)

for the audible concert and for his lecture on the harmony of perfection, blocked from human hearing by the flesh. In the mixed theatrical metaphors that the stage presents, it is the half-light in which human beings perceive the lovely earthly harmony, which is the imperfect image of the harmony of perfection, blocked from their hearing by the flesh.

Similarly Portia and Nerissa, when they enter a moment later, moralize upon the whole hierarchy of light:

> *Por.* That light we see is burning in my hall.
>   How far that little candle throws his beams!
>   So shines a good deed in a naughty world.
> *Ner.* When the moon shone, we did not see the candle.
> *Por.* So doth the greater glory dim the less.
>
> (5.1.89–93)

And Portia concludes, as Bassanio enters, with the comment,

> This night methinks is but the daylight sick;
> It looks a little paler. 'Tis a day
> Such as the day is when the sun is hid.
>
> (5.1.124–26)

This gradation runs from candle to moonlight to full daylight. Always the greater glory dims the less, the candle dimmed by moonlight and that in turn becoming "the daylight sick." In the analogous hierarchy of values, beginning with the good deed in the naughty world like the candle shining in darkness, the moonlit world before us is clearly halfway up the scale to the full blaze of sunlit perfection. Even so the night's music gives rise to Portia's comment,

> Nothing is good, I see, without respect.
> Methinks it sounds much sweeter than by day.
>
> (5.1.99–100)

and to Nerissa's explanation,

> Silence bestows that virtue on it, madam.
>
> (5.1.101)

233

Both music and moonlight, in short, serve to define the setting as a limited, earthly good, a beautiful half-light or earthly concord, equally distant from darkness or discord and sunlight or the music of the spheres. This use of music and scenery—or its verbal equivalent—to define the setting as a state of being is not quite novel, but it is less crude and obvious here than in earlier plays. The use of setting or place, sometimes identified by scenery, as a state of being is a feature of the earliest moralities—the scaffolds of the World, Flesh, Devil, and Covetousness in *The Castle of Perseverance*, for instance or the castle itself. It is less common in the extant Elizabethan moralities with their social emphasis and simpler staging, but the house of Lady Lucre or of the Ladies Love and Conscience in *The Three Ladies of London*, the house of Fortune in *Liberality and Prodigality*, the wilderness in which old Fortunatus has lost his moral and financial way at the beginning of Dekker's play, and the Fountain of Self-love in *Cynthia's Revels* all indicate that such a practice was not foreign to late Elizabethan dramatic thinking.

This function of music is less easy to document although the theatrical use of mournful music, noise, and discord to indicate Hell or the infernal and joyful song to indicate Heaven or the heavenly seems to date from the liturgical drama. There is also such musical symbolism as that indicated for the dances of the three ballets of sin in *Mind, Will, and Understanding* or for the amorous warfare staged in the Elizabethan *Fortress of Perfect Beauty*, where the music represents the sweet psychomachia of desire. The music that accompanies the dumb shows which serve as prologues to the five acts of *Gorboduc* seems to use an instrumental symbolism. The violins of the first dumb show, for instance, apparently symbolize the fraternal and political harmony which is later broken. Drums and flutes, on the other hand, accompany the fifth dumb show, in which armed men march about the stage and fire their pieces, signifying the "tumults, rebellions, arms, and civil wars to follow." One suspects a similar kind of musical symbolism in other Inns of Court plays, like *The Misfortunes of Arthur*, in the various royal entertainments, and in some of Lyly's plays, but stage directions are lacking or too vague to be of help.

The printed Jacobean court masques, however, provide abundant evidence of precisely this use of both scenery and music, albeit in a much more elaborate and more highly stylized form. Jonson's *Hymenaea*, already cited, is an especially good case in point since, like *The Merchant*, it ends in a celebration of marriage, and treats marriage as an earthly shadow of divine harmony —though it stresses the resemblance rather than the difference. There the elaborate scenery and lighting, actually visible, combine with music and patterned dances to symbolize the joy and concord in terms which, though more elaborate and esoteric, belong to the same iconographical and philosophic traditions as Shakespeare's casual symbolism. Except for its abstruseness *Hymenaea's* use of theatrical effects is not untypical of the masque and is largely derivative from the earlier tradition of festive entertainment and pageantry of the court, the Inns of Court, and the city. Shakespeare seems clearly to have been working within this tradition.

As production time runs, this "prologue" actually occupies about half the last movement. It is itself action in the sense that a masque is action, quite as much as the short scene that follows. Indeed, if we think of this little masque as primary, the ring scenes, both before and after, serve chiefly to provide a dramatic pretext for its existence. Chiefly but not entirely. The ring business does provide a convenient way for Portia to reveal her disguise and for sorting out the lovers; it keeps the joy of their meeting from having too bland a flavor, it restates the final theme, and it is fun.

It presents the joy of the journey's end in lovers' meeting for which the audience has been waiting and exemplifies it not as a ride into the sunset or as joy unconfined, but much as the prologue had symbolized it, as something bounded by an amused awareness of human limitations.

For Antonio, Lorenzo, Jessica, Portia, and Nerissa, the scene merely ratifies the happiness on earth which they have been virtually assured of. For Bassanio however, it is the recognition scene. As Portia goads him, he must face his own guilt, even though it was incurred through obligatory gratitude, and, like Shylock and Antonio he learns that he must rely on mercy: "Portia, forgive me this enforced wrong" (5.1.240). This is something, but he must also face the apparent fact that he is betrayed and a cuckold, and then that he is merely harmlessly deceived, merely a fool. He has been shown as Perceptive Man; he has seen through gold, lead and silver; he has soliloquized wisely on the deceptiveness of appearance; in the great central choice of existence he has chosen substance over shadow, using reason rather than fancy. But he is still human, guilty, deceived by appearance, a fool. The revelation comes as happy news, but the happiness involves a smile at his own deception. "Were you the doctor, and I knew you not?" (5.1.280), he asks Portia, and then as he embraces her he adds,

> Sweet Doctor, you shall be my bedfellow.
> When I am absent, then lie with my wife.
>
> (5.1.284–85)

This is joy but not the dizziness of rapture. It is intelligent and amused. He has progressed to that knowledge of his own weakness which Portia started out with. That in itself is insufficient for happiness but necessary, and in attaining it, Bassanio has completed his escape from Venice to that good attainable on earth which is represented by Belmont.

Gratiano is a fleshly parody of Bassanio in this scene as in the play. A muddier vesture of decay encloses him, and the Belmont he has escaped to seems to be a sensualist's heaven. Such at least is a plausible interpretation; it is consistent with playing him, in the trial scene, as a passionately vindictive worldling, and it provides the tableau of graded and contrasting *summae bonae* which Lyly used to end *Campaspe, Endymion,* and *Love's Metamorphosis,* and which Shakespeare himself uses obviously and emphatically to end *Twelfth Night, As You Like It,* and *Measure for Measure.*

But again, it is also possible, here as in the trial scene, to play Gratiano as more Prince Hal than Falstaff. Taking guidance from his early line, "let me *play* the fool," the actor may play Gratiano as rather the man conscious of his role, acting the role of the worldling and sensualist but, though feeling the worldling's passions, not their slave. This interpretation also seems plausible, and it has the virtue, by making him less repulsive in the trial scene (not really vindictive), of making his happiness in the finale more acceptable. In this interpretation he is like Portia in that he begins with a realization of his own folly that Bassanio only finally achieves.

Either interpretation offers a comic experience of great range and fullness. Above all, it includes, what any comic experience must include if it is to be taken seriously as the felt reality of life, its opposite experience: life felt as tragedy. Life is not always comedy, either of the joyful sort or the amusing, and one does not avoid the tragedy by simply denying it. Somehow life as tragedy must be acknowledged. It is the triumph of this play, therefore, that it grants the tragic experience its validity and momentarily realizes the full thrust of tragic agony. In presenting life as comedy the play shows it not as without tragedy but, like Dante's *Commedia*, as tragedy passed through, an escape from tragedy. And it is an escape, not into utopian bliss, but into the limited joy and wisdom that are actually possible on earth—joy and amusement at the human condition seen with all its foibles—that Socratic wisdom which is the awareness of one's own folly.

Notes to Introduction (pps. 1–17).

1. *Validity in Interpretation* (New Haven, Conn.: Yale University Press, 1967), p. 4.
2. Ibid., p. 24.
3. See below, p. 16. I have no quarrel, however, with Hirsch's selection of the author's intention as a norm for interpretation.
4. Eleanor Prosser, *Hamlet and Revenge* (Stanford, Cal.: Stanford University Press, 1967), chap. 1.
5. Church of England, Homilies, *Certaine Sermons or Homilies, Appointed to be Read in Churches in the Time of Queen Elizabeth I, 1547–1571,* 2 vols. in 1 (London, 1623; reprint, Gainesville, Fla.: Scholars' Facsimilies & Reprints, 1968), 1:78.
6. The argument is conveniently and persuasively summarized by Stanley Wells in *Literature and Drama, with Special Reference to Shakespeare and his Contemporaries,* Concepts of Literature Series (London, 1970), *passim.*
7. The point has become a truism in the last twenty-five years, but it bears repeating. It was first applied systematically (and powerfully) to Elizabethan drama by Alan Downer in "The Life of Our Design: The Function of Imagery in the Poetic Drama," *The Hudson Review* 2 (1949): 242–263.
8. Jocelyn Powell, "Marlowe's Spectacle," *Tulane Drama Review* 8 (1964): 195–210.
9. Ibid., p. 195.
10. Hirsch, *Validity in Interpretation,* pp. 164–198.

Notes to Chapter I (pps. 21–55).

1. Madeleine Doran, *Endeavors of Art* (Madison, Wis., University of Wisconsin Press, 1954), p. 296.
2. *Ludus Coventriae or The Plaie Called Corpus Christi,* ed. K. S. Block, Early English Text Society, Extra Series, 120 (1922).
3. E. K. Chambers, *The Elizabethan Stage* (Oxford, 1923), 4:224.
4. Ibid., p. 187.
5. Robert Dodsley, *A Select Collection of Old English Plays,* 4th edition by W. C. Hazlitt (London, 1874–1876), 3:295.
6. Ibid., p. 299.
7. Bernard Spivack, *Shakespeare and the Allegory of Evil* (New York, 1958), pp. 332–333.
8. Thomas Dekker, *The Dramatic Works,* ed. Fredson Bowers (Cambridge, 1953–61), vol. I.
9. "The Life of Milton," *Lives of the English Poets,* ed. G. Birkbeck Hill (Oxford, 1905), 1:185.
10. Spivack, *Allegory of Evil,* p. 127.
11. Ibid., pp. 297–298. The same criticism, although Spivack does not make the point explicitly, would seem to apply to Iago, whom he sees as a simi-

larly divided dramatic character.

12. "Historical Criticism and the Interpretation of Shakespeare," *Shakespeare Quarterly* 10 (1959), p. 7.
13. *The Macro Plays*, ed. F. J. Furnivall and A. W. Pollard, E.E.T.S., Extra Series, 91 (1904).
14. Ibid.
15. *Quellen des Weltlichen Dramas in England vor Shakespeare*, ed. Alois Brandl, in *Quellen und Forschungen zur Sprach- und Cultur-geschichte* 80 (1898).
16. *On Christian Doctrine*, trans. D. W. Robertson Jr. (Indianapolis and New York: the Library of Liberal Arts 1958), 3:14 (10).
17. Ibid. 3:23 (15).
18. Boccaccio, *Boccaccio on Poetry*, ed. and trans. Charles G. Osgood (New York, 1956), p. 62.
19. B. F. Huppé, *Doctrine and Poetry: Augustine's Influence on Old English Poetry* (Albany: State University of New York Press, 1959), chap. 2.
20. H. -I. Marrou, *Saint Augustin et la fin de la culture antique* (Paris, 1938), p. 486, cited by Huppé, p. 73.
21. John Scotus Erigena, "Expositiones," *Patrologia Latina*, ed. Migne, 72.146, quoted from Huppé, pp. 54–56. Cf. D. W. Robertson, Jr., *A Preface to Chaucer* (Princeton, N.J.: Princeton University Press, 1962), p. 60: "It is not difficult to cite evidence to show that during the Middle Ages and, indeed, well into the Renaissance, figurative expression in both literary and visual art was designed to lead the mind through exercise to a spiritual understanding."
22. *Le Sponsus*, ed. L. P. Thomas (Paris, 1952), p. 47.
23. Thomas, *Le Sponsus*, pp. 34–35; see also Bede, *PL* 92.107; Jerome, *PL* 26.191.
24. An incisive review of this critical position is offered by Eleanor Prosser, *Drama and Religion in the English Mystery Plays* (Stanford, Cal.: Stanford University Press, 1961), pp. 3–13.
25. Rosemary Woolf, "The Effect of Typology on the English Medieval Plays of Abraham and Isaac." *Speculum* 32 (1957): 805–825; V. A. Kolve, *The Play Called Corpus Christi* (Stanford, Cal.: Stanford University Press, 1966), pp. 57–100. See also D. M. Anderson, *Drama and Imagery in English Medieval Churches* (Cambridge: Cambridge University Press, 1963), pp. 22–26.
26. Kolve, *The Play Called Corpus Christi*, p. 2.
27. Woolf, "The Effect of Typology," p. 810; Rosamund Tuve, *Allegorical Imagery* (Princeton, N.J.: Princeton University Press, 1966).
28. Kolve, *The Play called Corpus Christi*, p. 4.
29. *The Chester Plays*, Part I, ed. Hermann Deimling, E.E.T.S., Extra Series, 62 (1893).
30. Karl Young, *The Drama of the Medieval Church* (Oxford: The Clarendon Press, 1933), 2:258–64.
31. Woolf, "The Effect of Typology," p. 812.
32. *Complete Works*, ed. C. H. Herford, Percy and Evelyn Simpson (Oxford,

1925–52), 7:91.

33. Ibid., p. 213.
34. Ibid., p. 313 and note.
35. Ibid., p. 209.
36. Ibid., pp. 209–10.
37. *Shakespeare and the Popular Dramatic Tradition* (London and New York: Staples Press, 1944), p. 28.
38. *The Townely Plays*, ed. George England and A. W. Pollard, E.E.T.S., Extra Series, 71 (1897).
39. See below, ch. II, pp. 67–69.
40. Erasmus, *The Praise of Folie*, trans. Sir Thomas Chaloner, ed. Clarence H. Miller, E.E.T.S., Original Series, 257 (1965), p. 37. The symbolism of the Sileni was given wide currency as the subject of one of the longest of the articles in Erasmus's *Adagia* (Chil. III, Centur. III, Prov. I) where it was developed into a satire on social and ecclesiastical corruption. The article was also published separately in several languages.

Notes to Chapter II (pp. 56–75).

1. Alfred Harbage, *Annals of English Drama, 975–1700*, revised by Samuel Schoenbaum (Philadelphia and London: The University of Pennsylvania Press, 1964).
2. David M. Bevington, *From Mankind to Marlowe* (Cambridge, Mass.: Harvard University Press, 1962), chaps. 4, 12, and 13.
3. Chambers, *Elizabethan Stage*, 4:214.
4. Ibid., p. 217.
5. Ibid., p. 227.
6. Ibid., pp. 227–28.
7. Ibid., p. 232.
8. Ibid., p. 239.
9. Ibid., p. 241.
10. *The Book of Sir Thomas More*, ed. W. W. Greg, Malone Society Reprints (Oxford: Oxford University Press, 1911), lines 919–22.
11. John Marston, *The Plays*, ed. H. Harvey Wood (Edinburgh and London: Oliver and Boyd, 1934–39), 2:259, 263.
12. Jonson, *Works*, 4:19.
13. Chambers, *Elizabethan Stage*, 2:144.
14. Schoenbaum, in his revision of Harbage's *Annals*, lists eighteen moralities or partial moralities between 1600 and 1642. Eleven were probably or certainly produced under academic auspices. Their authors, short titles, and approximate dates (taken from Schoenbaum's first column) follow: Anon., *Liberality and Prodigality* (Revival of *Prodigality*, 1567?) (1601); Anon., '*Locus, Corpus, Motus*', (1605); Thomas Tomkis, *Lingua* (1607); Anon., *Time's Complaint* (Part of *The Christmas Prince*) (1608); John Fletcher (with Beaumont? Field?), *Four Plays, or Moral Representations*,

in One (1612); Anon., *Microcosmus* (1612); Anon., *Heteroclitanomalo-nomia* (1613); Anon., *Pathomachia* (1617); Barten Holiday, *Technogamia* (1618); Anon., *The Part of Poor* (title assigned from actor's part), (1618); Anon., *Stoicus Vapulans* (1618); Thomas Dekker and John Ford, *The Sun's Darling* (moral masque) (1624); James Shirley, *The Contention for Honour and Riches* (1631); Richard Zouche, *The Sophister* (1631); Francis Bristowe, *King Free-Will* (trans. Bassano's *Tragedia del libero arbitrio*) (1635); Robert Davenport, *A Dialogue between Policy and Piety* (1635); William Strode, *The Floating Island* (1636); Thomas Nabbes, *Microcosmus* (moral masque) (1637); Mildmay Fane, *Time's Trick upon the Cards* (1642).

15. G. K. Hunter, *John Lyly* (Cambridge, Mass.: Harvard University Press, 1962), chap. 3.

16. *The Tudor Interlude* (Leicester: University Press, 1958), pp. 93–99.

17. George Wapull, *The Tide Tarrieth No Man* (1576), in *English Morality Plays and Moral Interludes*, ed. Edgar T. Schell and J. D. Shucter (New York: Holt, Rinehart, and Winston, 1969), pp. 311–69, lines 1666–67.

18. Desiderius Erasmus, *A Book Called in Latin Enchiridion*, trans. anon., Methuen reprint (London: Methuen, 1909), p. 83.

19. Wapull, ll. 189–90.

20. *The Trial of Treasure* in Robert Dodsley, ed., *A Select Collection of Old English Plays*, 4th edition by W. C. Hazlitt (1874–76), 3:285.

21. *The Alchemist* 1.1, in *Works*, vol. 5.

22. *A Preaty Interlude Called, Nice Wanton*, in *Specimens of the Pre-Shakespearean Drama*, ed. John Matthews Manly (Boston, 1897), vol. 1.

23. Thomas Norton and Thomas Sackville, *Gorboduc* (1570), in *Chief Pre-Shakespearean Dramas*, ed. Joseph Quincy Adams (Boston: Houghton Mifflin, 1924), p. 505.

24. Ibid., p. 512.

25. John Nichols, ed. *The Progresses and Public Processions of Queen Elizabeth* (London, 1823), 2:310.

26. *Gallathea* 4.2.21–60 in John Lyly, *The Complete Works*, ed. R. Warwick Bond (Oxford: Clarendon Press, 1902), 3 vols. All references to Lyly are to this edition. In this and in all quotations from texts printed after 1540, abbreviations have been expanded and the usage of *u, v,* and *i, j* modernized.

27. Fredson Bowers, ed. *The Dramatic Works of Thomas Dekker* (Cambridge: The University Press, 1953–61), 2:107.

Notes to Chapter III (pp. 76–97).

1. See J. Dover Wilson, *The Fortunes of Falstaff* (Cambridge: Cambridge University Press, 1943), pp. 18–21. Wilson points out the resemblances of Falstaff to the Vice as misleader of Youth in early sixteenth-century moral interludes and illustrates the point by reference to Riot in *Youth* (c. 1520). Cf. also M. M. Reese, *The Cease of Majesty* (London: E. Arnold, 1961),

pp. 68–69. Both Wilson and Reese emphasize the morality as a dramatic pattern of the Shakespearean history play.

2. Raphael Holinshed, *The Last Volume of the Chronicles of England, Scotland and Ireland* (London, 1577), 4:1789.

3. Ibid., p. 1790.

4. Ibid.

5. *The Magnificent Entertainment Given to King James . . . upon the day of his Majesties Triumphant Passage . . . through . . . London.* in *Dramatic Works*, ed. Fredson Bowers, 2:298.

6. Jonson, *Works*, 7:213.

7. Ibid., p. 221 (my translation). "Ergo cum ex summo Deo mens, ex mente anima sit; anima vero & condat, & vita compleat omnia quae sequuntur, cunctaque hic unus fulgor illuminet, & in universis appareat, ut in multis speculis, per ordinem positis, vultus unus; Cumque omnia continuis successionibus se sequuntur, degenerantia per ordinem ad imum meandi: invenietur pressius intuenti a summo Deo usque ad ultimam rerum faecem una mutuis se vinculis religans, & nusquam interrupta connexio."

8. "Hymenaei: Ben Jonson's Masque of Union." *Journal of the Warburg and Courtauld Institutes*, 8 (1945): 107–45.

9. On the identification and definition of Magnificence, see William O. Harris, *Skelton's Magnificence and the Cardinal Virtue Tradition* (Chapel Hill: University of North Carolina Press, 1965), chaps. 3, 4.

10. W. Wager, *The Longer Thou Livest and Enough is as Good as a Feast.* ed. R. M. Benbow, Regents Renaissance Drama Series (Lincoln, Neb.: University of Nebraska Press, 1967), p. 72.

11. *From Mankind to Marlowe*, p. 164.

12. *The Tide Tarrieth No Man*, lines 61–62. The lines also define Courage's dramatic character (as deceiver) and establish it as a metaphor of the moral ambiguity of his "quality."

13. Patrick McGrath, *Papists and Puritans under Elizabeth I* (London: Blandford Press, 1967), pp. 150–53.

14. *The Three Ladies of London. . . . by R. W.* (London, 1584) in Dodsley, *Old English Plays*, vol. 6. The ascription to Wilson is plausible but not certain. He was probably an actor as well as a playwright, associated with the Queen's Men of the eighties and early nineties and later with Strange's Men and the Admiral's Men. All references are to the edition in Dodsley.

Notes to Chapter IV (pp. 101–135).

1. *Respublica*, ed. W. W. Greg, E.E.T.S., Original Series, 226 (1952).

2. "The Basis of Shakespearean Comedy." *Essays and Studies, 1950*, New Series, vol. 3 (London, 1950), p. 4.

3. *The Macro Plays.*

4. *A Play of Love*, The Tudor Facsimile Texts (New York: AMS Press, 1970), sig. E iv.

5. The three plays are Redford's *Wit and Science* (c. 1539), which Bevington (*From Mankind to Marlowe*, p. 22) shows to have been written for
a boys' company, perhaps Paul's; the anonymous *Marriage of Wit and
Science* (c. 1568), also probably written for a boys' company and acted at
court, and Francis Merbury's *Marriage between Wit and Wisdom* (1570
or 1579), written for a popular company (Bevington, pp. 23–25). All three
are close variations on the same theme.

6. Nicholas Udall, *Roister Doister*, in *Chief Pre-Shakespearean Dramas*, ed.
Adams.

7. Ludovico Ariosto, *The Supposes*, trans. George Gascoigne, in *Chief Pre-
Shakespearean Dramas*, ed. Adams.

8. Robert M. Durling, *The Figure of the Poet in Renaissance Epic* (Cambridge, Mass.: Harvard University Press, 1965), pp. 123–29.

9. "Italian Comedy and The Comedy of Errors," *Comparative Literature* 19
(1967): 250.

10. Una M. Ellis-Fermor, *The Jacobean Drama* (London: Methuen, 1936), pp.
204–5.

11. Peter Saccio in his *The Court Comedies of John Lyly* (Princeton: Princeton University Press, 1969) notes this feature as paratactic dramatic structure and relates it to the similar parataxis of much of the dialogue in the
play (pp. 29–40). The point is well made, but a paratactic structure is by
no means peculiar to Lyly's plays; it is a common feature of moralities
early and late, e.g., *Mind, Will, and Understanding, Nature, Magnificence,
Respublica, The Tide Tarrieth No Man, The Longer Thou Livest*, and
The Three Ladies of London. It seems related, as noted above, to a strong
emphasis upon thematic unity.

12. Saccio, pp. 26–94.

13. Ibid., pp. 92–93.

14. With the exceptions noted below, my disagreements with Saccio's well-
argued interpretation are irrelevant to my own argument. Lest I seem to
distort his thesis, however, for an appearance of agreement, I note that he
seems to find the problem of personal identity in the play more important
than, I think, most Elizabethans would (pp. 61–62, 80, 88); he "plays" the
comedy for less satire and humor than I am urging, and he finds the imagery of the "scratched face" more important than I think it would be in
production.

15. Saccio finds Apelles' appreciation of Campaspe's beauty ("O beautiful
countenance, the express image of *Venus*, but somewhat fresher: the only
pattern of that eternitie which *Jupiter* dreaming of asleep, could not con-
ceive again waking" 3.5.40–43) a more solemnly exalted Neoplatonic rapture than I would play it as or expect educated Elizabethans to see it as.
To praise a woman's face, the visible flesh, as the Platonic form is nonsensical confusion by Neoplatonic—or commonsensical—standards. It is
also the kind of amiable folly which serves the ends of comedy.

16. See above, Chapter I, p. 55. On Ixion, see e.g., Abraham Fraunce, *The*

Third Part of the Countesse of Pembrokes Iuychurch, Entituled, Amintas Dale (London, 1592), p. 16.

17. Saccio, p. 153.
18. Saccio, pp. 118–19.
19. Saccio, p. 146. B. F. Huppé, Review of Peter Saccio's *The Court Comedies of John Lyly* in *Renaissance Quarterly* 23 (1970): 478.
20. See Thomas W. Baldwin, *William Shakespeare's Small Latine & Lesse Greek* (Urbana: University of Illinois Press, 1944), vol. 2.
21. See Chubb, "Italian Comedy and The Comedy of Errors," pp. 240–51. Although Chubb does not consider *Mother Bombie* related to the *commedia grave*, the present analysis suggests the possibility of a fairly strong influence of the latter on Lyly.
22. B. F. Huppé, "Allegory of Love in Lyly's Court Comedies," *ELH* 14 (1947): 105.
23. Saccio, p. 164.
24. Ibid., pp. 164–65.

Notes to Chapter V (pp. 135–153).

1. Robert Greene, *The Plays and Poems*, ed. J. Churton Collins (Oxford, 1905), vol. 2. All references are to this edition.
2. This dramatic metaphor was first analyzed by William Empson in *Some Versions of Pastoral* (London, 1935), pp. 32–33.
3. *On Christian Doctrine*, I. 35 (39).
4. *The Institution of Christian Religion*, tr. Thomas Norton (London, 1561), Y 2^{r-v}.
5. "An Homilie Against Excesse of Apparrell," in *Certaine Sermons or Homilies, Appointed to be Read in Churches in the Time of Queen Elizabeth I, 1547–1571*, 2 vols. in 1 (London, 1623; reprint, Gainesville, Fla.: Scholars' Facsimilies & Reprints, 1968), 2: 102–3.
6. Alulfus, in *Patrologia Latina* 79.1318.
7. *Commentarii in Scripturam Sacram* (Louvain and Paris, 1875), 4:264.
8. *A Commentarie upon S. Paules Epistles to the Corinthians*, trans. Thomas Timme (London, 1577).
9. The conclusion of the play does this, at least for the loyal and patriotic Elizabethan spectators, almost literally. Friar Bacon utters a joyful prophecy of the glory of Elizabeth and her reign; and King Henry, inviting everyone to the wedding feast, adds,

> Only your hearts be frolicke: for the time
> Craves that we taste of nought but jouysance,
> Thus glories *England* over all the West.
>
> (2100–2102)

Notes to Chapter VI (pp. 154–168).

1. Shakespeare, *The Complete Works*, ed. George Lyman Kittredge (Boston and New York: Ginn and Co., 1936). All citations from Shakespeare in my text are to this edition.

2. *A Record of Ancient Histories entituled in Latin Gesta Romanorum . . . Now newly perused and correct, with some thing added, by R.R[obinson]* (London, 1609), H 1ᵛ. The *commedia grave* discussed by Louise Chubb in her article cited above is probably more to the point as a shaping influence on Shakespeare, though perhaps less so as a shaping influence on his audiences. Miss Chubb does not suggest a specific Italian "source" for the *Comedy of Errors* and is sceptical of the possibility that there was one. R. Warwick Bond, however, in a little-noticed essay ("The Framework of *The Comedy of Errors*," *Studia Otiosa* [London: Constable, 1938], pp. 43–50) made the plausible suggestion that Shakespeare borrowed several features of his plot from Giovanni Cecchi's *L'Ammalata*, published at Florence in 1555. I have not read Cecchi's play, but to judge from Bond's analysis of it, it might well have implied the kind of significance characteristic of the *commedia grave*.

3. Cf. Pierre de La Primaudaye, *The French Academie*, tr. T. Bowes (London, 1618), Part II, chap. 43: "Will beeing corrupted of it selfe through sinne, letteth loose the bridle against the judgement of reason, and so suffereth her selfe to bee carried headlong by her evill affections in following some false shewe of good." cited by Hankins, *Shakespeare's Derived Imagery*, p. 79. Mr. Hankins gives an illuminating discussion of some of the imagery by which Shakespeare alludes to the subject, on pp. 57–64, and 76–83.

4. "*The Comedy of Errors*, 'Old Adam new apparell'd'," *Shakespeare Quarterly* 7 (1956): 453–56.

5. The ninth of the Thirty Nine Articles makes the same point more solemnly: "Original sin . . . is the fault and corruption of the Nature of every man . . . whereby man is very far gone from original righteousness, and is of his own nature inclined to evil, so that the flesh lusteth always contrary to the spirit: and therefore in every person born into this world, it deserveth God's wrath and damnation. And this infection of nature doth remain, yea in them that are regenerated . . . although there is no condemnation for them that believe and are baptized. . . ."

Notes to Chapter VII (169–190).

1. For a partial history of the theatrical metaphor, see E. R. Curtius, *European Literature and the Latin Middle Ages*, trans. Willard R. Trask (London: Routledge, 1953), pp. 138–44. Anne Righter's interesting study, *Shakespeare and the Idea of the Play* (New York: Chatto and Windus, 1962), discusses Shakespeare's use of the metaphor in detail. Although her discussion touches some of the same points as the present study, her approach and aim differ.

See also Jackson I. Cope, *The Theater and the Dream: From Metaphor to Form in Renaissance Drama* (Baltimore and London: The Johns Hopkins University Press, 1973). Cope's admirable and exhaustive study was published too late for consideration in this study.

2. Heuterus, *De Rebus Burgundicis* (1584) in Richard W. Bond, ed., *The Taming of the Shrew*, Arden Shakespeare, 2d ed. (London, 1904), Introduction, pp. xlvi–xlvii.

3. Simon Goulart, *Admirable and Memorable Histories*, in *Shakespeare's Library*, ed. W. C. Hazlitt, 2d ed. (London, 1875), 4: 403, 405.

4. Barckley, *Felicitie of Man*, C 5ᵛ.

5. "The Waking Man's Dream," *Shakespeare's Library*, ed. W. C. Hazlitt (2d ed., London, 1875), Pt 1, Vol. 4:407–8.

6. *A Very Excellent and Learned Discourse, Touching the Tranquillitie and Contentation of the Minde*, trans. Ed. Smyth (Cambridge, 1592), B 1–B 1ᵛ. See also Roland Mushat Frye, *Shakespeare and Christian Doctrine* (Princeton: Princeton University Press, 1963), pp. 130–32.

7. *The French Academie*, ¶ 6.

8. Jean de Serres, *A Godlie and Learned Commentarie upon . . . Ecclesiastes*. trans. John Stockwood (London, 1585), sig. ¶ 6ᵛ–7.

9. Robert Parsons, *A Booke of Christian Exercise . . . by R. P., Perused . . . by Edmund Bunny* (London, 1585), M 6ᵛ–M 7. I cite Bunny's Anglican revision as the more popular and influential of the two versions, but the passage quoted is substantially identical with Parsons's original Catholic version.

10. De Serres, C 5.

11. *The Woman's Prize, or The Tamer Tamed* (c. 1611); the exposition of the opening scene makes it clear that Katherine has died, that Petruchio is known as a terrible wife tamer, and that his new bride intends, to the incredulous amazement of her friends, to tame him.

12. Pierre Boaistuau, *Theatrum Mundi*, trans. J. Alday, Revised Edition (London, 1581), A 4ᵛ–A 5.

13. Desiderius Erasmus, *The Praise of Folie*, trans. Sir Thomas Chaloner, ed. Clarence H. Miller, e.e.t.s., Original Series, 257 (1965), pp. 37–38.

14. *Utopia and a Dialogue of Comfort*, ed. John Warrington, Everyman's Library, rev. ed. (London and New York: Dutton, 1951), pp. 47–48.

15. Ibid., pp. 48–49.

Notes to Chapter VIII (pp. 191–206).

1. C. L. Barber, *Shakespeare's Festive Comedy* (Princeton: Princeton University Press, 1959), pp. 119–20.

2. Paul A. Olson, "A Midsummer Night's Dream and the Meaning of Court Marriage," *ELH* 24 (1957):101–3. Olson's entire article deserves close reading. The present study, which was written independently of Olson's brilliant essay, though it differs from the latter in approach, emphasis, and

in several details, arrives at a closely similar interpretation.

3. Barber, p. 123.
4. Philip Stubbes, *The Anatomy of Abuses* (1583), quoted from Barber, p. 21.
5. Barber, p. 119.

Notes to Chapter IX (pp. 207–237).

1. See Toby Lelyveld, *Shylock on the Stage* (Cleveland: Press of Western Reserve University, 1960); also John Russell Brown, "The Realization of Shylock," *Early Shakespeare*, Stratford-Upon-Avon Studies 3 (London and New York, 1961), pp. 187–210.
2. See Romans 7: 513.
3. The remark was considered to apply to Jews living after Christ's advent who had not embraced Christianity.
4. Introduction to *The Merchant of Venice*, Arden Edition, 7th ed. (Cambridge, Mass.: Harvard University Press, 1955), p. xl. Brown quotes J. Palmer's remark from *Comic Characters of Shakespeare* (London, 1946), p. 79.
5. Coghill, "The Basis of Shakespearean Comedy," pp. 18–23.
6. *The Merchant of Venice*, ed. John Stevens (Toronto: Festival Editions of Canada, 1970), pp. 5, 7–10, 144. The production was that of the Stratford (Ontario) Festival in the summer of 1970.
7. A version of the casket story appears in the late sixteenth-century English translation of the *Gesta Romanorum*. Like all stories in the collection, it is heavily allegorized. Concerning the superscription, "who chooseth me shall finde that his nature desireth," the maiden who must choose one of the three caskets remarks, "if I choose this vessell, what is within I know not, but well I wot there shall I finde that nature desireth, and my nature desireth the lust of the flesh, and therefore this vessell will I not choose."—*A Record of Ancient Histories entitled in Latin Gesta Romanorum*, trans. R. R[obinson] (London, n.d. [1595]), H 1ᵛ.
8. See, e.g., Johanne de Virgilio, *Allegorie Librorum Ovidii Metamorphoseos*, ed. Fausto Ghisalberti, *Il Giornale Dantesco*, vol. 34, New Series, no. 4 (1933), pp. 43–107, sub *Andromeda;* also George Sandys, *Ovid's Metamorphoses Englished, Mythologized, and Represented in Figures*, ed. Karl K. Hulley and Stanley T. Vandersall (Lincoln, Neb.: University of Nebraska Press, 1970), pp. 219–220. The symbolic equivalence of Hercules and Christ is one of the oldest mythographic traditions, and Milton can still make use of it in "On the Morning of Christ's Nativity." Cf. Sir Walter Ralegh, *History of the World* (London, 1829), 2:167 and D.C. Allen, *Mysteriously Meant* (Baltimore, 1971), sub Hercules.
9. See Gal. 3:5–14.
10. See, e.g., Andrew Willet, *Hexapla in Genesin* (Cambridge, 1605), pp. 288–91: "Gregorie compareth the Jewes to Esau, which sought by their own workes to please God: the Gentiles to Jacob, that found a more compendi-

ous way by faith. . . . I will let passe the allegories hereupon framed: as how Ambrose understandeth by these cloathes put upon Jacob, the scriptures taken from the Jewes, and given to the Gentiles. . . . Augustine excuseth Jacobs speach by the mystical sense: where he saith I am Esau, he saith, if it be referred to Jacobs person it is a lie: if to Jacobs bodie that is the Church, it is true."

Index.

249

Two thousand copies of this book
were published by State University of New York Press
Albany, New York, in July 1975.

Design by Freeman Craw.

Most of the display letters for the title page, Parts I and II headings,
and chapter numerals are from the seventeenth-century Fell
types which were bequeathed in 1697
to the University of Oxford by Dr. John Fell.
Some of the swash and italic letters have been redrawn in character with
the original cutting and with other printing of the period.
The punches and matrices for the Fell types are the oldest punches and
matrices surviving in England today.

The text and chapter headings were set
by Vail-Ballou Press, Inc., Binghamton, New York,
in Janson, a type originally cut in Holland as were the Fell
and other fonts used in England during the
seventeenth century.

Printed by letterpress on Mohawk Cortlea Text.
Binding in Columbia Linen
with lining papers of French Gray
Cortlea Cover.